Praise for *Death Rights and Rites*

"Filled with personal stories and written with a compassionate heart, this book is a must-have guide for navigating the tragic terrain of a loved one's passing. In one volume, it covers not only the spiritual aspects of this passage, but the practical and legal issues as well. A wonderful book for a difficult subject, guiding you before, during, and after death comes near your door. Should be in everyone's library."

—Anodea Judith, author of *Anodea Judith's Chakra Yoga*

"This is a significant and timely book, full of heartwarming stories to inspire you and ease your fears. I learned many things that I will definitely put into practice as I prepare for my own death and those of my loved ones. In our modern culture we have lost touch with the beauty and sacredness of death, and the need for meaningful rituals that are aligned with human needs and the ways of the natural world. This book shares ways we can re-gain and re-claim our rightful ease and natural way with death."

—Susan Campbell, author of *Getting Real*
and *Saying What's Real*

"Judith Fenley has created a weaving of practical, spiritual, political, ritual, and always compassionate wisdom for approaching the process of death. Bringing a sense of the organic and natural unfolding of the conclusion of life in a body, she tells stories, provides resources, encourages reflection, and always emphasizes the importance of honoring the individual needs and desires of the loved and loving ones finding their way through death. May this book be a guide and companion to those seeking support in choosing and following the appropriate path for themselves, their loved ones, or for their own journey assisting others as a death guide."

—Selene Vega, author, dancer, psychotherapist,
and owner of spiritmoving.com

D1242044

DEATH
RIGHTS
and
RITES

About the Author and Contributor

Rev. Judith Karen Fenley is an ordained metaphysical minister, a Pagan priestess, a certified home funeral guide and death midwife, a health practitioner, a gardener and garden consultant, a mother, a grandmother, a peasant woman reincarnated, and a wild dancer. She has a professional background in nursing, although she left professional employment in favor of maintaining a natural health consultant practice for over thirty-five years. Her love of the soil, its care, and its interrelatedness to everything, particularly living sustainably, underlines her work and energy. As a ceremonial facilitator, she weaves an understanding of the chakra system, sound healing, and Earth-centered traditions into a fabric of self-expression and life practice.

Creating life passage ceremonies with participants—from birth to coming of age, marriage, and death—is her joy in a shared experience of transformation. She offers Labyrinth Quest events in a seven-circuit garden labyrinth (cocreated with women friends on her fifty-ninth birth celebration). It is an offering of Earth-wisdom as an experience of walking a labyrinth in meditative practice and as a metaphor for life.

The practice of honoring death's passage, with respect for all traditions and perspectives, is an integral part of her work. Assisting families and friends in caring for their beloved when they are passing or have passed on into the Mystery is one of the deepest and most profound experiences in her life.

For over fifteen years, she has worked as a student and a guide and in the capacity of her private practice, Harmonizing Healing Choices & Sacred Paths. In the capacity of a chaplain and death midwife, she assists people with bereavement and grief, also facilitating Memorial Remembering services. She trained for this work with Jerrigrace Lyons, the founder and director of Final Passages Institute of Conscious Dying, Home Funeral and Green Burial Education. She is part of the Final Passages Core Council.

Although she has written articles and poetry for her own and friends' pleasure, this is her first book.

Rev. Oberon Zell was a significant inspiration for this book and paved the way for its publication. He holds a bachelor's degree in psychology, sociology, and anthropology from Westminster College in Fulton, Missouri, and went on to graduate studies at Washington University in St. Louis. His seminal work on the Gaea Thesis in the early seventies has helped foster a growing awareness of Earth as living Mother.

A founding father of modern Paganism, Oberon has pursued a broad spectrum of interests over half a century, ranging from mysticism and philosophy to art and writing. He is one of the most highly regarded figures in the new movement of "green religion" that emerged in the latter half of the twentieth century, and his influence has spread far beyond that movement, helping to bridge the gap between spirituality and science.

Oberon is a lecturer, author, philosopher, ecologist, shaman, and artist. Initiated in several mystical traditions, he is an ordained priest of the Earth Mother, Gaea, and cofounder of the Church of All Worlds, incorporated in 1968.

Oberon's literary accomplishments are similarly wide-ranging. He founded the groundbreaking journal *Green Egg* and served as its publisher for four decades. His book titles include *Grimoire for the Apprentice Wizard, Companion for the Apprentice Wizard, Green Egg Omelette,* and *A Wizard's Bestiary.* With his wife, Morning Glory, he cowrote *Creating Circles & Ceremonies: Rites & Rituals for All Seasons and Reasons* as well as their life story, *The Wizard and the Witch.*

An award-winning artist, Oberon has illustrated countless magazines and books since the 1960s. But he is best known for his magickal jewelry and figurines of gods, goddesses, and mythical creatures. His most famous work is his revelatory sculpture of "The Millennial Gaia."

Oberon is also the founder and headmaster of the online Grey School of Wizardry, which offers more than five hundred classes in sixteen departments for students aged eleven and older. In addition, Oberon regularly presents workshops and seminars and has officiated at spiritual ceremonies involving as many as four thousand participants.

A Practical Guide to a Meaningful Death

DEATH
RIGHTS
and
RITES

Reverend Judith Karen Fenley
with Oberon Zell

Llewellyn Publications
Woodbury, Minnesota

First Edition
First Printing, 2020

Cover design by Kevin R. Brown
Cover illustration by Charles Joseph Slucher
Editing by Samantha Lu Sherratt

Llewellyn Publications is a registered trademark of Llewellyn Worldwide Ltd.

Library of Congress Cataloging-in-Publication Data
Names: Fenley, Judith Karen, author. | Zell-Ravenheart, Oberon, author.
Title: Death rights and rites : a practical guide to a meaningful death /
Judith Karen Fenley with Oberon Zell.
Description: First edition. | Woodbury, Minnesota : Llewellyn Publications,
[2020] | Includes bibliographical references and index.
Identifiers: LCCN 2020038054 (print) | LCCN 2020038055 (ebook) | ISBN
9780738748818 (paperback) | ISBN 9780738755397 (ebook)
Subjects: LCSH: Death—United States—Handbooks, manuals, etc. | Natural
burial—United States. | Funeral rites and ceremonies—United States. |
Paganism—United States—Rituals.
Classification: LCC GT3203 .F46 2020 (print) | LCC GT3203 (ebook) | DDC
306.90973—dc23
LC record available at https://lccn.loc.gov/2020038054
LC ebook record available at https://lccn.loc.gov/2020038055

Llewellyn Worldwide Ltd. does not participate in, endorse, or have any authority or responsibility concerning private business transactions between our authors and the public.
All mail addressed to the author is forwarded but the publisher cannot, unless specifically instructed by the author, give out an address or phone number.
Any internet references contained in this work are current at publication time, but the publisher cannot guarantee that a specific location will continue to be maintained. Please refer to the publisher's website for links to authors' websites and other sources.

Llewellyn Publications
A Division of Llewellyn Worldwide Ltd.
2143 Wooddale Drive
Woodbury, MN 55125-2989
www.llewellyn.com

Printed in the United States of America

Dedication

Though words cannot express
What words cannot express…

… We feel in our hearts
The sorrow of your loss.
Surely death and loneliness
Are the cruelest gifts of lifelong love.

Yet we who choose such love must
Drink deeply from the bitter cup
Believing in the end that it will leave
Behind a taste of lingering sweetness.

May She be with you
In Her dark-winged form.
Blessed Be.

Morning Glory Zell
(May 27, 1948–May 13, 2014)

In Memoriam

...

MORNING GLORY ZELL

May 27, 1948–May 13, 2014

She lived a Priestess;
She died a Queen;
She rose a Goddess!

(Susa Black)

And

IRIS MAY EVANS FENLEY

July 15, 1919–July 17, 2001

She remains our "Wild Iris Mama"
I feel your absence and your presence daily!

Disclaimer

This book is about personal experiences in relation to death and death care. It also references known and/or researched information.

This book in no way advocates breaking any laws or state statutes regarding death care or laws protecting the public from essential sanitation issues.

Consult local laws, your personal physician, and/or the deceased family member or friend's physician for any immediate concerns regarding appropriate care of the deceased.

It is vital to consult the laws of your state and local county protocol regarding care of deceased persons before handling, assisting, or counseling the death care of a person in your family or in your care.

This book is not a course in home funerals and natural death care. It is a narrative of experience and presents possibilities. If you are interested in pursuing greater knowledge and wish to serve others regarding natural death care, do your due diligence to find out what you need to know.

Pseudonyms are used for all persons in the narrative stories shared, except for family members whose actual names are used. They gave permission to use their personal names.

Contents

FOREWORD

It is encouraging that so many fine books on death, the death experience, per-spectives about death, the afterlife, and near-death experiences are appearing in bookstores and even on the bestseller lists. For one to show up that exam-ines and proposes a look at death and death care—from what is broadly called a natural death care perspective—is even more exciting. It is a delight that this book is authored by one of Final Passages Institute's own graduates.

Judith Fenley initially contacted me in 1998 when a friend asked for her sup-port through the sad approach of her son's death. Participating in his home funeral cemented Judith's commitment to enroll in the initial levels of Final Passages Institute's training. It also significantly affected the way she and her siblings orchestrated their mother's passage and home funeral a few years later. It was an honor to be the guide for the Fenley family through their mom's home funeral service.

Judith began her formal studies with Final Passages in 2004. Her prior ini-tiation occurred in her early years as a proponent for a more natural view and understanding of death. This view had been stimulated by early childhood and young adult experiences with death. This awareness merged with her interest and profession in natural health care advocacy.

As a student, Judith dove deeply into the process. It was apparent that the niche it opened for her was a natural extension of who she is. She has been a staff leader for many of our Level 3 trainings, and she continues to be a vital support to our nonprofit educational initiative and mission as an advocate for home funerals and a member of our Core Council. She is a very capable home funeral guide and death midwife.

In this book, Judith shares her personal story of growth and wisdom in a warm, readable, artful, practical, and supportive way. Even as a strong advocate voice for home funerals and green burial alternatives, she repeatedly identifies choices for the reader, asking them to consider their own desires and encouraging awareness of their choices in their personal death care options.

There is an examination of how as a culture we find ourselves with a prevalent for-hire death care system and a legally protected industry. What this means regarding our personal loss and gain is also explored. There is a fresh look at the historical events that gradually, and not so gradually, generated today's death care assumptions in our modern culture.

She asks the relevant question, "What do *you* want?" Examples are offered of how to proceed and connect with your own inner guidance. Questions to consider are given in the spirit of diversity and respect.

Advocating and training related to home funerals are what I am most familiar with. This book adds another significant factor. Indigenous Earth-based spirituality and conceptions of ancient Pagan and modern Neopagan beliefs are often overlooked and dismissed. Yet an Earth-based seasonal liturgy and a primary axiom to "do no harm" match with humanitarian and natural perspectives and are acknowledged in this work. It is refreshing to read that Pagan views of death coincide with and support a natural Earth-honoring view of life and death akin to the teachings of our Indigenous relations. A familiarity with various religious practices and with death as a respected Pagan priestess brings a helpful understanding to what is occurring today in the Neopagan-organized churches in this country.

What is offered here is enriching in countless ways. I believe readers will appreciate the ideas shared in this work and value the resources provided in the text. There is value here for everyone.

As a person who has been committed to natural death care—specifically, the home funeral movement—following my own initiation into this work over twenty-five years ago, I applaud what Judith Fenley offers with contemporary views of death as the miracle of life. Oberon Zell's requiem in honor of his wife and lifemate, Morning Glory, is a beautiful tribute. It will stand for all time.

We all are invited to see death as part of life as we allow ourselves to entertain this idea and prepare ourselves in new and old ways that support our choices. The invitation to explore your journey with the support of those who choose to reclaim an intimacy with hands-on death care and home funerals—carried out in the home and directed by family and friends—*is essential for our time.*

I wholeheartedly encourage readership of this valuable book. It can assist you in becoming aware of your core beliefs and discovering your personal quest for how you wish to pursue your own decisions regarding death care. There is much to consider when faced with these issues.

As the founder-director of Final Passages, I am honored to be included in this book in various instances as well as listed as a resource. I personally welcome anyone interested in exploring their own journey related to death to join us in whatever ways engage their body and spirit. *It is time we speak of death!*

—Jerrigrace Lyons, May 1, 2018

———

Jerrigrace Lyons is the founder-director of Final Passages Institute of Conscious Dying, Home Funeral and Green Burial Education. She is also a consultant, minister, death midwife, and guide in her private practice, Home and Family Funerals.

PREFACE:
ABOUT THIS BOOK

Profound personal experiences provided the impetus that inspired the writing of this book. This writing began to take form in the wake of the home funeral for Morning Glory Zell. Oberon Zell, Morning Glory's lifemate of over forty years, was a major influence and contributor to the idea of this writing as we shared the tender experiences of her death-passage into the Mystery and a home funeral in a community-oriented setting.

An intimate community surrounded Morning Glory, enduring her long convalescence and eventual passage. Together in community, we orchestrated her loving vigil, home funeral, and graveside green burial in the Church of All Worlds cemetery. This complied with a mandate from Morning Glory and evolved as a *vision and an assignment*. It became an extremely important and meaningful process for all involved. The impetus to share how beneficial it is to embrace and deal with death naturally—contrasted to what often transpires— moved and motivated this writing.

My task, as a friend and home funeral guide, was to companion and guide the process along. My focus was to facilitate the community to carry out their legal rights and rites. Processing grief and preparing for one's eventual passage is incredibly important. Communicating ways to assist others who wish to care for loved ones as they pass in a way that is artful, sacred, and supportive, both practically and legally, is dear to my heart.

In the grieving aftermath, with Oberon's encouragement and offering of ideas and connections, a project that spanned some tumultuous years began. We were both processing grief, dealing with life's challenges, and maneuvering obstacles. In this book, I invite you to explore the ways I have learned to mitigate death's presence in a sustainable manner that is respectful of the Earth.

I find my experience with death gives me a meaningful vantage point from which to share with you.

Book Intention

The intention of this book is to present practical and conceptual guidance that supports viewing death as a natural process managed by the family and community of the deceased in a framework of seeing and accepting what is, exploring ways grief is expressed, and honoring the passage of loved ones. It is a narrative of experiences and an exploration of the quest for meaning in the face of death that confronts us all.

Some of the issues addressed in this book include the following:

• in-home care for a dying person;

• in-home aftercare for the person who has died;

• legal concerns, such as durable Power of Attorney, death certificates, permits for transportation and burial, and other relevant legal issues;

• options for final disposition of the body (with particular emphasis on green burials and other natural options);

• sacred rites and rituals that celebrate death, such as last rites, cleansing and preparation of the body, wakes, funerals, and memorial services;

• historical perspectives and exploration of how we, as a culture, became conditioned to relinquish the death care process to the "professionals";

• examinations of why many now choose to reclaim the sacred act of caring for their dead; and

• a discussion of the green burial movement as a natural choice in the context of ecological and sustainable options.

Right relationship with the Earth underlines ecological concerns to "do no harm." Rather than allowing corporations designed to profit from the loss that follows death and dictate the way either cremation or burial is handled, many hearken back to ancient traditional practices—practices that naturalist, Indigenous, Western Pagan, Orthodox Jewish, Buddhist, and Muslim peoples choose to follow. In this context, the green burial movement is explored as a more natural choice.

For many, cremation is an unsavory choice, yet cremation often seems the only option other than the extremely expensive and distasteful mortuary practices of embalming, burial in a fancy coffin, and being set in a concrete vault in the earth. In recent years, there has been a realization that cremation also creates a high carbon footprint. This awareness underlines the grave ecological issues of our time.

A natural earth affinity is seen in the idea of a loved one's body being interred without preservation, allowing the body-temple to return to the elements in the bosom of Mother Earth. One cherished tradition is to plant a fruit tree on the grave above the heart of the one interred. This is still seen in some ancient sites, preserving a unique and beautiful ancient heritage.

As our collective mindset shifts and different types of burial grounds are acquired by those who support and desire an ecological approach, the essential need for natural alternatives to final death care will be more prevalent. I hope and anticipate, along with the notable recent growth in a worldwide community of more Earth-centered spiritual practices and religious ceremonies, that this shift will be fostered.

Death Is before Us All

It is a journey we all *get* to make. It is not the morbid reality we have been taught to think it is. It is our life's work, in a sense. Someone confronts death every day on this planet. Today or another day, it is someone you know.

Taking responsibility for conscious living, right livelihood, and conscious dying are among relevant hot topics and concerns. Death Cafés, death preparation talks, and trainings for death midwives are happening at local coffee shops, seminars, and conferences. Visionary leaders are contributing to new ways of viewing death and turning attention to the ultimate final journey of a lifetime. Exploring how to embrace death naturally as has been done for millennia is today's quest.

A consensus among caring professionals, counselors, health-care workers, priests, priestesses, and lawyers is that a document, such as the Advanced Care Directive, should be promoted and is essential to have on file. (The Advanced Care Directive is California's legal document. California also distributes a document called Five Wishes, which may be used in lieu of or in addition to the

Advanced Care Directive. Either of these documents establishes your wishes for medical care, intervention, life-support choices, and more.)

A Path to Here

Oberon's path converged ultimately with the death of his beloved lifemate, Morning Glory. Their journey together for more than four decades leaves such a great void in his heart and soul. The experience he gained from her home funeral fostered a desire for that information to be shared.

The path that I have been privileged to traverse is enriched by the intimate experience of assisting others to take care of their own beloved ones in the environs of home and family. I was deeply affected by the passage of my beloved "Wild Iris Mama," whom I continue to feel tangibly each day. Honoring my friend Morning Glory was another significant, deepening experience.

For these reasons and more, my training and following the practice of other trailblazers with whom I studied propel me to work as an advocate for natural death care and to assist and educate families for their home funerals and green burials.

The Question Is

What do you want regarding your death? How do you wish to be cared for if you are ailing or suddenly stricken with a life-threatening disease or an accident? How do you wish to pass from this life? What would you want if you were in a position to choose your death experience? How do you wish for your body to be cared for once you no longer inhabit it? How do you wish to be honored when you pass on?

In this book, these questions and more are examined. Explorations of possible, specific, and multiple answers and options for you are considered. DIY (do-it-yourself) possibilities and reclaiming natural concepts prevalent today are particularly addressed. This book is dedicated to education related to home funerals and the limited use of the funeral industry. Ways to mitigate the legal system and how to take on the task of caring for a loved one without the controlling interception of the funeral industry are described.

A family may hire a funeral director as needed rather than be managed by one. Religious, spiritual, and cultural practices and how they may relate to or support the quest are considered. Questions about the afterlife and the Mystery of what is are acknowledged. Developing your own rites and rituals is encouraged and supported. Personal stories illustrate concepts and are intended to inspire creativity in your own process.

This book presents timely considerations that address these questions and concerns. It is time to have a profound and essential conversation—with yourself, your spouse, your parents, your loved ones, and your community.

This book is your companion. It may open your mind and heart to what death means to you. It may inspire you if you are called to be with a dying friend or family member. It may encourage you to pursue decisions about your own ultimate journey.

It is anticipated that this book will be a welcome addition to the many periodicals and books on death, the afterlife, and how to approach one's inevitable, ultimate journey. I am glad to be in conversation with you and welcome your comments and shared experiences.

Respectfully and with deep affection,

Judith Fenley

SECTION ONE
GROUNDING EXPLORATION

CHAPTER I

CURIOSITY & COMMON GROUND

Death is a mirror in which the entire meaning of life is reflected.
—*Sogyal Rinpoche*

What is death? Do we live to die? Why are we here? Is there a place, a space, beyond this one where consciousness abides? Is death, in a sense, a birthright? We do not ask these questions every day. However, they, along with many others, linger in our peripheral awareness and affect how we live day by day.

———

As a young girl, I ran to my mother one day carrying a dead robin. "Mama, may I bury this poor bird in our yard?" Supportive of my curiosity and love of nature, she gathered scraps of fabric and a shoebox for me. I added flowers, laid the little bird to rest in the shade of an old apple tree, and knew Robin would never be again.

I recall sitting quietly beside Robin's grave and feeling a sense of awe. I was affected by death's presence. Yet did I acquire an understanding of death, its depth of sorrow or finality? As I reflect on this memory, I feel a rekindled sense of spirit presence that I could not conceptualize in words at that time. It remains so in my memory, nonetheless.

This was my first gentle brush with the Mysteries of death and the grave.

———

Death was not always this easy or gentle. On a spring day in April of 1958, my mother and I were creating a rock garden in the front of our new home in San Diego, California. She had gone to the backyard when an official dark green car pulled up in front of the house. A man and a woman got out and asked for my mother. I went to the backyard, only a short distance away, to fetch her. It took forever to reach Mother. It felt like I was walking on a slow-moving treadmill. (In retrospect, I now understand this experience as a "time-warp" phenomenon of being between the worlds where time awareness and knowing-ness are different from our ordinary reality. In future times, I would experience this repeatedly in the presence of birth and death.) Some other details are vague, yet I clearly recall her reply when the couple suggested that they speak with her privately: "This is my eldest daughter, and anything you have to say to me, she can hear."

My father, a naval officer, had drowned at sea. The impact was phenomenal. A deep silence fell upon my mother and me. A letter I'd just received from him reminded me I was "Daddy's big girl and Mama's little helper." Nearly fourteen years old, I rose to meet the challenge and became my mother's partner, caring for our home and my three younger siblings.

Even though I accepted the task as "Mama's helper," my sorrow bubbled up. Alone one day in my bedroom, gazing at a framed picture of my Daddy Al, I pounded my fist on the dresser. "You get back here! Get back here *right now!*" My father had left the month before with hugs and promises to return before Christmas. Visions of a peaceful and beautiful afterlife were not in my mind as I yelled. My heart ached; denial crept in. He was *not* dead! *I could feel him.* I even heard him remind me to be "Mama's helper." I obeyed and expected him to come home as he had promised.

At his memorial, I wore a specially chosen feminine "sailor-style" outfit. I sat in the front row with my mother and sister, Linda (age ten). The open casket allowed a "viewing" for others who walked by directly in front of where we stood. However, as "Mama's little helper," I stayed in place, setting an example for my younger sister, as Mother asked me to do. She felt it was best if my sister did not see our father's dead body, and apparently that went for me as well. When I extended my neck just a little, however, a bit of his face was barely visible to me. It was a very strange and surreal experience. Regretfully, our younger siblings, Gini (age six) and Paul (age four), were left in the care of neighbors since mother's thinking was that they were too young to be in attendance.

Typical of the 1950s, family therapy was not the norm. We dealt with the grief, each in our own way. Mother felt she had to be strong for her children; friends and neighbors commended her resilience.

In recent years, I've come to realize grief is experienced and dealt with in various ways, affecting development and resulting in different perceptions about life and death. Grief interacts uniquely with the experience of death and bereavement. I have learned that grief—minimally acknowledged, relegated to recesses of the mind—has affected my worldview, as well as those of my sisters and brother, in different ways.

As a high school student and active youth leader in the Presbyterian Church, I became interested in world religions. Life and death perspectives, particularly related to various beliefs, doctrines, and cosmologies, fascinated me. I set my sights on becoming a postgraduate student at the San Francisco Theological Seminary in San Anselmo, California. Although I did not follow that plan and later went on to nursing school, I remained fascinated with what happens after death and perspectives canonized by various religions regarding death.

Years later as a student nurse on a medical ward, I attended a patient who died. It was strange to see a gurney wheel in empty and roll out with a covered body. I was left with an empty bed and room to clean. I felt a void inside. What was *natural* about how that death occurred? Was there a better and more respectful way to deal with death that felt more "right?"

There were others close to me whose deaths made their mark. A few experiences follow that were peak moments for me, followed by one that provided a turning point epiphany.

Sometimes death is unconsciously foretold. Grandmother Anna remarked that this was her "best Christmas ever!" She recalled definitively many "best ever" times only six months before her death in July of 1976.

My beloved mother was still very active when she spoke of "Daddy remodeling another house for us" as a premonition of her time. Even so, she immediately stated she was yet to be around much longer to "pester" us. An aneurysm occurred four months later that eventually led to her death.

Other times, deaths startle us. This was so with the unexpected death of my vibrant Aunt Lilli and my father's sudden drowning.

A turning point occurred for me with my friend Derrick's death. It opened a yet deeper awareness to something beyond death. I was struck with an understanding of an ongoing spirit-life experience with the tangible perception of Derrick's ongoing consciousness.

———

Derrick was a talented musician and beloved friend. He rented a room in a sister's house where I, too, stayed for a while. As he practiced his upright bass late at night, I'd drift off to sleep with the soothing rhythm, the feeling of the entire house vibrating and the pulsing sound reverberating through my body. I was enchanted.

Later, my husband, Michael, and I lived nearby, and Derrick would come to visit. He always had at least one instrument with him—most often his violin or guitar. We loved to listen to whatever he would play from his extensive inner playlist. Sometimes he'd ask us to name a country. Then he would extemporaneously play its music. What a joy!

We'd known Derrick for a number of years when his childhood cancer returned. His lighthearted energy persisted as his health waxed and waned. Eventually, as his health deteriorated, I'd often stop by to visit and simply be with him.

"Judith, everything is God!" he told me one day in his soft, incredulous voice. "Really, I mean *everything* is God! Like, you are God; I am God; that wall is God … the chair is God … it's amazing! Everything is God. I mean every *thing* I see *is God …*"

His voice would tire and trail off. After a while, he would remark again how miraculous and amazing it was, *that all was God.*

Derrick moved to a room at a friend's house on our street. He figured he would die in that room. Michael and I visited him more frequently. We marveled at his courage, even as his body deteriorated. One day, I went to visit, and he was not there. He'd been taken to the hospital.

I went to the hospital and, as always, he was glad to see me. Part of my work was massage therapy, and Derrick appreciated my touch. He said that reaching under his back and running my hands up his spine relieved his pain. It helped him stretch out morphine doses by hours.

Derrick asked again for that touch. His friend Barron and I were the only ones in the room. For a long time, we shared silence, only occasionally speaking quietly. I stood at the head of the bed, running my hands along Derrick's spine.

"Dear brother and sister," Derrick began, "it is time for me to leave …" I felt something that is hard to describe, except to say it was like levitation. His back was still against my hands, yet something was lifting off. It was an amazing sensation.

Another person walked into his room, a woman I did not know. She hadn't seen Derrick in a while and was cheery and glad to see him. Strangely, as she walked in, I felt another peculiar sensation. I can only describe it as a plunk. It was not a heavy plunk; it was like energy had settled back into Derrick's body. Moments before, it felt as if Derrick was leaving his body; now, it felt like he was back.

He conversed quietly with the woman and assured her that he was not in extraordinary pain. After a brief time, he thanked her for coming and let her know he needed to rest. She left.

Almost immediately I felt the lightening sensation of levitation again. He started to say the same words. I believe he only said, "Dear sister and brother …" As his voice trailed off, I felt a lightening of his weight and a lifting off of his energy—an incredible sensation. Simultaneously, I became aware that his breath had quietly stopped. I knew viscerally that Derrick had found his way through the veil and beyond.

My hands stayed under Derrick's back a moment longer. I could feel a tingling sensation around my shoulders and a soft vibration touching me all over. The air around me felt very light and fluffy. I almost felt like I was floating and even a little dizzy.

Everything felt wordless. I looked across the room at Barron, who was sitting quietly in a chair. Perhaps he was dozing. Softly, I projected my voice across the room. "I'm going home. Please call me soon."

I would have stayed; however, I knew Barron wanted his own time with Derrick.

As I walked into my house, the phone rang. "That's Barron calling to say that Derrick has passed," I told my husband, who handed the phone to me. I listened while Barron explained that shortly after I left, a doctor came in and pronounced Derrick dead. I thanked Barron for calling. I hung up.

I sat down. Michael sat quietly beside me, understanding intuitively what was transpiring. Eventually, I told him of the experience. This profound experience some forty years ago changed my life. My understanding of death, a certainty of spirit presence, and an *ongoing-ness* of life were embedded in every cell of my body and every auric layer of my spirit body that day. It has never left my awareness. Of Life Eternal, I am certain.

————

In this book, I will engage in a conversation and exploration of the natural ways I've discovered to manage death. I've learned so much being a home funeral guide and death midwife. I'll share with you various ways to navigate this territory while assisting you to ask your own questions, explore and come to your own decisions regarding your death, and find ways to communicate your wishes to your loved ones. *This conversation is for anyone!*

I don't *want* to die; I want to be conscious of making healthy choices about *how* I die. My intention is to find acceptance when the time comes and be present for my death. I laughed out loud when a friend read this gem quoted from an autobiography by the actor-comedian Steve Martin: *"I'm so depressed. I just realized this death thing applies to me!"*[1]

————

Religious and spiritual practices attempt to explain life after death in countless ways. Some claim to be the one and only truth. I believe *if* there is only "one way" (as friends of fundamental persuasions insist), the one way is the way within, and there are as many versions of the one way as there are spiritual seekers. They all have a "right-ness." Each expresses the *one way* as it is understood from that person's vantage. The value is individual. Respect for the other and the other's view is part of the path.

I am reminded of a Little River Band song that says it well. (I paraphrase here.) They sing of the many apparent paths evident to climb a mountain and yet remind us that no one knows the many pathways that exist, and when reaching the top, one finds that the shared view is the same view for all who are there.

---

1. Martin, *Born Standing Up*, 193.

This metaphoric mountain climb can foster a sense of common experience, even on differing paths, where our questions, opinions, precepts, and beliefs in regard to life and death converge. In death and dying, we are united in a common reality. On this common ground, we are offered natural ways to explore with *curiosity* and adjust and/or embrace our beliefs. Like the natural curiosity of children, we can learn from life and death. Curiosity provokes and propels us to learn from life itself day by day. *Curiosity may be our greatest teacher.*

Ancient and Indigenous perspectives that express an intimate and irrevocable connection with the Earth make ultimate sense to me. Death is part of our nature, a sacred ritual of passage that we all *get* to go through. The inevitability of death is a certainty in all our lives; it grabs our attention in unique and immediate ways. *We all get to die.* It is natural; it is inevitable. Yet, we have been conditioned to fear death and to do everything in our conceived power to avert and deny it.

How is it something so certain, something that awaits us all, is often fearfully denied, avoided, and significantly unplanned for? Considering its inevitability, it's surprising there aren't more conversations about death. We will ultimately face death whether we plan for it or not. Conversations about death are helpful and liberating.

Facing death's presence consciously may help diffuse inherited and harbored fears and discomfort. Diffusing and releasing fears may enrich life, offering greater presence of mind, peace, joy, and vitality. I invite us to explore and speak from the heart of curiosity. *It is time to talk about death.*

The following questions may help:

- How do you wish to experience *your* death?
- What preparations might make your daily life easier and less fettered?
- How does the way you live affect what you will eventually experience when death comes?
- Can experiencing the death of a loved one create deeper understanding?
- How may you help someone be more at ease about death, especially when it is imminent?
- Can the quality of last days be improved and more peaceful with acceptance and preparation?

• Can we be fully alive today and ready to accept death when it comes our way?

It is appropriate to review and reconsider these questions periodically. It is an ongoing process of self-discovery that evolves and changes. Updating documents regarding our life and death choices also requires periodic review.

————

In Mexico, the road to the cemetery is often named the *camino de la igualdad*—the path of equality. Everyone, rich or poor, eventually goes down that road. Whether our view is from a road, a mountaintop, a deathbed, a valley floor, an ivory tower, a sterile hospital room, or our own precious home, *in death's passage, we are on common ground.*

Similarly, death has been called "the great equalizer," uniting us in ways unlike any other life experience. It unites us with others as we grieve a felt loss of a loved one. It unites us with the task of attending to and honoring the body remains. It unites us in an age-old process of anticipation—be it fear and trembling or acceptance, ease, and curiosity. Yet we, especially in so-called developed countries, are mostly taught that death is a final, sad event, and that someone else—for hire—will take care of the details for us. We do not need to handle it—or even necessarily face it ourselves.

————

Recently, I spent considerable time with Annie, one of my closest friends, in what became her last days. She said she was "done with life," yet she still had more time to wait. She asked that I be with her at the end to hold her hand. She was quiet most of the day. In the wee hours before dawn, however, she'd frequently call out and wish to talk. I would lie beside her as she voiced her questions and concerns about the unknown that lay before her. The interweave of her various beliefs and those of others would arise. It was ludicrous, even humorous to her, that many seemed to require belief in an exact and structured cosmology. The idea of an "eternal sleep" sounded rather comforting to her, yet she chose to remain curious. She wanted to hear what I felt or believed. We imagined it differently, yet we agreed it was a Mystery and, therefore, a great curiosity.

In the early days of a new year, Annie passed over the threshold. After a brief agitation, she gave in to her last task. Her hand, gently resting in mine, occasionally shifted along with her deliberate breath. Her final breath sounded like an accomplished sigh: "There, I've done it!" I could hear an inaudible determination from her once energetic voice.

A sense of peace and pervasive quiet followed. It was cascading all around us. Sitting quietly with the intensity of the moment, the deep silence, and my heightened awareness, I was suspended in the midst of what had just occurred. Once again, time stood still. I felt cloaked in a pervasive, protective, "no-thing-ness."

It was reminiscent of my girlhood experience with Robin and of a sluggish, surreal walk on a treadmill to find my mother.

———

What will we get to experience when our turn comes? How much do we get to create our experience? In my privileged, albeit limited, experience, I believe we find and affect our own way by how we live.

I've witnessed death's diversity dance: quiet, uneventful "slipping away" deaths; resisted, agonizing deaths; gentle, conscious deaths; and beatific, remarkable deaths. Some deaths are prolonged and others are swift. Some people wait for loved ones to be present; others wait for everyone to leave the room. Everybody gets their own "last word."

I am curious. I desire to experience whatever and however death plays out for me. I want to be healthy enough to recognize when it is time to let go and healthy enough to watch the show.

A Threshold Choir song, extrapolated from a traditional Navajo prayer, comes to mind:

When you were born you cried
And the world rejoiced
Live your life so that when you die
The world cries and you rejoice …

Kate Munger founded the Threshold Choir following an experience in which she sang to quell her uneasiness as she sat with a dying friend. Its official inception was on the equinox of March 2000. Now there are over one hundred chapters worldwide where volunteers sing to people who are facing grief, suffering, or death. Many songs originate spontaneously as members are touched in the moment. I am privileged for the few times I have sung with Threshold Choir and anticipate doing so more in the future.

———

An encouraging universal and ecumenical movement exists that embraces a sentiment of inclusiveness and respect for all traditions. One of my favorite bumper stickers includes symbols of various religions displayed on dark blue with white letters that proclaim "Coexist," a reminder that in life and in death we do, in truth, coexist on common ground.

The concept of inclusion rather than exclusion supports the metaphor of the many paths to climb a mountain—more in alignment with the "Golden Rule," a universal truth that shows up with different words in every religion. Perhaps this is akin to what Jung called the "collective unconscious."

Fervently held doctrines and "one-way-ism" exhibit *contractive energy* and lead to inner and outer antagonism. Curiosity and wonder are *expansive energy* attitudes and lead to deeper acceptance and appreciation for each other in our common journey. Paying attention to our body's energy, whether in contraction or expansion, is a way to self-understanding.

Everyone is welcome in this exploration—in heaven, in the Summerlands, in Valhalla, in Nirvana, pushing up daisies, over the hill, beyond the sunset, into the Great Beyond, kicking the bucket, over the rainbow, into the Mystery—all expressions and euphemisms make sense.

Ritual gatherings and passages of all sorts—baptism, coming of age, marriage, handfasting (a Pagan term for a ritual union in lieu of or along with a marriage ceremony, which may occur concurrently or at another time), death, and memorials—are times when family, friends, and community come together. Such times bring varied and unique beliefs to a mix of people who care for each other despite different frames of reference.

Gatherings in the context of honoring death are likely to include persons of diverse philosophical and religious perspectives. Accepting and finding ways of common ground is essential in order to support communication about how to connect, merge, include, and uphold varied perspectives and thereby achieve creative ways of honoring the passage of our beloved dead with rituals that include all who are present.

———

Death is an incredibly unique time in our lives, however it presents itself. An axiom I learned long ago from a dear friend who was a hospice volunteer is that each of us gets to "live and die in character." Years later, her husband passed after a protracted experience with cancer; during the moment of his gentle passage, a beacon of light ignited. With his family surrounding him, he joined them in singing "Amazing Grace." He went in and out of apnea states, occasionally opening his eyes and uttering, "Splendid, splendid!" His profound presence fostered curiosity, imagining what his experience was in those quiet moments.

I received a similar message from my "Wild Iris Mama." (My mother, Iris May, was named after the wild iris that bloomed in May on her parents' Oregon homestead. I frequently referred to her this way.)

One beautiful, warm summer day a year after her passing, I was visiting with a friend in my garden. We waxed eloquent about consciousness and its ongoing-ness. Suddenly, I heard my mother's voice *drop* into my awareness. *"If you only knew,"* her voice declared. A few stunned seconds later, I heard her voice again: *"It's more than you can even imagine!"*

These words did not come in the form of a thought, deduction, or even a conscious reflection. The words dropped in from beyond my realm of awareness. Now, on the best authority, I know wherever *it* is, and however *it* is—*it* is *something else (!)* and beyond my capacity to *"even imagine."*

———

"The world is holy. Nature is holy. The body is holy. Sexuality is holy. The imagination is holy. Divinity is immanent in nature; it is within you as well as without. *Most spiritual paths ultimately lead people to the understanding of their own connection to the divine ... The energy you put out into the world comes back."* [2] (Italics are mine.)

---

2. Adler, *Drawing Down the Moon*, 2–3.

Margot Adler, an admired Pagan author, writes that diversity is one of the most prevalent characteristics found among Pagans. Recognizing some of the most commonly held beliefs, she reminds us that this diversity enhances us all. A primary directive adopted from ancient Wiccan lore is to *do no harm*. Inadvertently, it supports and encourages diversity in the garden of life.

———

All phases of life are holy. Death is holy. Death is a sacred passageway to the eternal Mystery beyond.

Here is what I come to: death is part of our nature, a sacred rite of passage that we all *get* to go through. The inevitability of death is a certainty in all our lives, no matter our age, health, religious affiliation, political position, gender identification or orientation, and even our assumed infallibility. Death insists on our attention in a unique and often immediate way. *We all get to die.*

Belief systems of major religions express doctrines of a death and an afterlife that reflect the concept of the Hermetic axiom: *"as above, so below."* Some people of humanitarian bent might merely declare that "death just is what it is," or, as expressed by the Latin phrase *res ipsa loquitur,* "It is as it seems." We will revisit this phrase later. What death is exactly seems beyond our precise knowing, which is why the bards of old and today sing of the *Mystery*.

I believe our purpose in life and our approach to death is fulfilled as we extend our curiosity about the Great Mystery. This book explores what it means to prepare for and face our own death and the passing of those we love. It is a sacred time filled with a full range of feelings from loss and grief to release and renewal. It is essential to find common ways of working together to honor the being, the body-temple, the spirit, and the desires of our dearly departed loved ones.

———

A man whom I consider one of the great metaphysical and esoteric writers of our time is the late Manly P. Hall. In *Words to the Wise*, he writes,

Nature is the divine criterion of all merit and demerit. By the mysterious process of Nature we come into being; by equally mysterious process we are preserved and

perpetuated for a certain time; and in the end, by these same mysterious processes we depart from this theater of physical action.[3]

Greater intentionality in our awareness of death along with healthy curiosity will foster greater acceptance of this mutual ground. It is akin to arriving on the mountain precipice where the common view we share invites our expanded exploration.

I bring my curiosity to this explorative conversation with you. The spirit of grace and curiosity welcomes us all. By living fully, we are invited to find acceptance in the natural presence of death in our lives. Blessed be.

---

3. Hall, *Words to the Wise*, 32–33.

CHAPTER 2

GROUND OF INNATE
RIGHTS & RITES

When the heart weeps for what it has lost,
the soul laughs for what it has found.
—*Sufi Aphorism*

It is important to recognize, speak of, and claim our rights and our rites. They are our *naturally ordained belongings*. To begin, I'd like to establish how I see this essential ground. I believe that our innate and inherent relationship to death is natural and obvious. Yet, as a culture, we have hidden that truth. It is time for us to see again and reclaim what is rightfully and personally ours.

Below is a quote I submitted for consideration in a code of ethics document, which at the time Jerrigrace of Final Passages and I were collaborating on:

Throughout humanity's existence, care of the dead occurred in the context of family and community. It is an innate right of people to care for those deceased from this life. Most states in the USA support, in various ways, the rights of families in this regard.

At the graveside green burial of his beloved lifemate, Morning Glory, Oberon Zell declared, "We now participate in what is likely the oldest ritual of our kind—casting flowers upon the grave, as the beloved's body is returned to the earth."

Earlier, a community member had dug a grave on a slope above a large gathering site. He also fashioned a beautiful, simple coffin made of unfinished rough-cut wood with bark exposed on one side, slated sides, and an opening at the top. On the day of the memorial, six pallbearers carried the coffin with their beloved priestess shrouded in iridescent cloth and surrounded by rosemary and lavender boughs over a bridge to a large open meadow. Memories and tributes were shared in Circle as a horn of Irish whiskey passed to each speaker in turn. The pallbearers then carried the coffin to the uphill gravesite. There, the coffin, attached by ropes, gently swung above the grave before it was placed ceremoniously in the awaiting earth.

As if on cue, children present responded to Oberon's declaration. Spontaneously, they began the sacred ritual with the flowers; adults followed suit. A thick floral array covered the shrouded body of the priestess like a soft blanket of color and protection. When her body was completely covered with flowers, bare handfuls of earth were then cast in the grave.

This continued until the flowers were no longer visible. Only then, shovels and rakes layered soil upon the grave. A slow and spontaneous ritual ensued, culminating with an artful mound outlined with stones, dirt clods, and a heart-shaped rock. An apple tree planted over the priestess's heart, along with other natural treasures, completed the ritual. The group quietly admired the artful offering.

Only a loving and dedicated family and community could have enacted this sacred, cocreated rite.

No script or prearranged ritual could have been more appropriate or beautiful. As the ritual ended, a communal outbreath sigh was uttered. A feeling of awe drifted through the gathering as we slowly meandered and quietly wandered down the hill.

―――

We learn by doing, through "exposure education." Hands-on experience opens up different perspectives; we can conceive newly presented options. With the experience of creating our own death rituals, we allow a new, natural understanding of sustainable living and dying to unfold. We may remember who we are in a different way. We may discover another way to orchestrate and reclaim our personal and collective rituals.

―――

From my protestant, liberal family upbringing and identity, to 1960s social activism, hippie back-to-the-land living, and an ecological perspective—all a haven for my earthy nature, I eventually found an organic identity as a naturalist and Pagan. This was an internal and external process that led to a deep belief and understanding that life goes on and on in one eternal flow of change and transformation.

Personal history disclosures and relevant reflections related to what I have come to consider credentials seem important to share. My husband, Michael, was an ordained minister, initially in the United Church of Christ (UCC; formerly Congregational Church). I began solitary Pagan studies in the late sixties and seventies, where I found an affirmation of my worldviews. As back-to-the-landers, we left it all in the dried dust. There we raised our family and ourselves. Michael was later reordained in the Church of Divine Man, a metaphysical denomination. At the time, we considered it a mutual ordination. As cocelebrants, we officiated at many weddings, funerals, and other ceremonies. He frequently introduced and honored me as his "Pagan wife." Often, spontaneously channeled inspiration and innovations evolved into our ceremonies. After our separation in 1992, I enrolled in a correspondence ministry program and was ordained though the University of Metaphysics. From there, I further integrated a Pagan orientation and performed a solitary, self-identified priestess ordination on a solo camping trip. An integral part of my spiritual growth and orientation is sitting in Circle. A Circle is a nonhierarchical orientation mode for speaking and listening. I have been a member of a Sacred Sisters Circle group for over twenty years, since its inception.

A significant teacher in regard to my spiritual training was and continues to be the compost. One day as a young back-to-the-lander, I was about to turn the compost when I was profoundly struck with the vitality and fecund nature of this mass of garden and kitchen waste. While previously seeming dead, it now smelled alive—crumbly and full of earthworms and other critters! Transfixed, I was aware of transformation occurring before my expanded vision and understanding. The compost was life-giving and in continual transformation. The cycle of life and death was evident. I realized I, too, was a part of this process.

"This is reincarnation in progress!" I uttered. "Nothing is ever lost. I am not lost. I am here and will one day become part of this warm, vital, earthy compost heap." My compost epiphany imparted a revelation that offered a more grounded understanding of the cycle of life, death, and rebirth. We are living soil, not dust. The vitality of decaying matter is renewed in the process of decomposition.

Now, over fifty years later, I've been teased, tested, and fondly called a "Compost Queen," an "Organic Ogress," and an "Earth Mama." I am a humbled student of the Earth, grateful for the many valuable lessons that continue as "way-showers" along the way. We are living legacies and expressions of the cycle of birth, life, death, transformation, and rebirth.

This transformative cycle is exemplified in the elemental returning process of death's aftermath. Bodies are buried in the *earth* with only natural protection; burned by *fire* upon an altar; wafted into the ethers of *air*, lifted by birds of carnage; and dropped into *water* in the deep abyss of the sea. This is a mystical, biochemical, organic process that is enacted literally and symbolically in the realm of the elements returning to nature.

Nature, also called the Great Mother or Gaea, draws to her the miraculous return to the *All* that is. Gaea spirit keepers of air, fire, water, and earth are the great recyclers of what is. Transformation occurs. It becomes what *is* only to change again and again. New forms of life infused mysteriously by the breath of vitality or spirit (or however one calls the nameless One) are enlisted in this cyclical process of *re-turning to the great cycle of birth, life, death, and rebirth.*

Our bodies are vessels for spirit in an organic, transformative, material journey. A marriage of matter and spirit occurs, and no separation of the body, mind, and spirit is possible until that magical, terrible, and exuberant moment we call death. Death has no finality; it is a point on the ongoing cyclical nature of Being.

A revelation of spirit nature emerged when assisting with a friend's home funeral. Three able-bodied people (two men and I) were about to lift a dead woman's body and carry her down a hall. Either of the two strong men alone could have easily carried her when she was alive, yet now we prepared for the inevitable "dead weight" of her body.

It was all the three of us could do to make the short trek down a hall with her lifeless body. As we laid her out, her husband reflected aloud, "Now, I understand what spirit brings into the body. It brings the light. It brings lightness. It is the light in us that is our vitality. When the vitality and light of spirit leaves the body, the condensed weight of the elements is what remains." In silence, we gazed at her and looked into each other's eyes, feeling her spirit all around us, yet her body-temple of heavy, condensed elements lay before us, as she was lying-in-grace and beauty. The truth we shared became a tangible, mutually felt "shiver" running through our bodies. We sensed her spirit smile through our faces. The spirit that inhabits the body is of the light.

A full 360-degree turn, and we re-turn to the elements of earth, fire, water, and air as a part of the great cycle of re-turning—even as spirit or vitality also return to the vast Mystery.

——

We may desire to live and die naturally, yet we hardly know what that means. We have relinquished essential responsibilities in a postindustrial society to an economically oriented "corporatocracy" and are left feeling impotent and bankrupt. For example, we have left farming to agribusiness, governance to corruption and manipulation, and our dead to a corporate funeral industry. Each business protects primarily the "bottom line," even though they may express another stated purpose. *(Corporatocracy* I originally thought was a friend's made-up word. I found it was accepted into dictionaries in late 2011 and refers to a collective, conspiratorial, subversive, controlling phenomenon or mindset, supported financially and philosophically, which primarily occurs behind closed doors by corporate concerns and is followed by lobbying pressure, the result of which affects the populace and replaces democracy.)

The result is that we do not know what it is to live a "natural life." In contrast, we live "normal lives" devoid of essential links to our own nature and to nature itself. Within this normalcy, we continue to reenact the artificialities of today's modern death care. (I think the word *normal* is often used when a more appropriate word could be *natural*. Normal is not necessarily natural. Normal is a statistical term that refers to a mathematical position on a graph and is a comparative measurement of something.)

We find ourselves at a curious threshold, one where many of us share a mutual desire to reclaim a way to live and die naturally and sustainably with the Earth. We seek to find common ground with each other, ourselves, and with the unknown as we seek to declare our humanity and our curiosity about life and death. We are maneuvering this terrain and exploration where much has been lost, or perhaps only misplaced.

This is not to propose foregoing the benefits of technology and science. Rather, it is with regard to *how* they are used, in the context of responsibility. The issue is the consequences that result from science and technology's implementation without the constraint of morals and values that support sustainable and harmonizing life.

Many of us are part of what is now recognized and fondly referred to as the Reclaiming Movement. We are reclaiming home and natural birth (lay and registered nurse midwifes, gentle birthing rooms). We are reclaiming our right as caretakers and stewards of the Earth (Earth Day, 1970; Earth First!, 1970s). We are reclaiming our collective right to shelter and nourishment (The Hunger Project, "We Are the World"). We are reclaiming our right to clean air and real food (the organic movement, sustainable living advocates, establishment of the EPA—December, 1970). We are reclaiming natural egalitarian concepts of relationships and collective governance (Think Globally—Act Locally, grassroots activism). *And, we are reclaiming the right to care for our dead, in the context of family-directed home funerals.*

Starhawk is a founder of the Reclaiming Collective (1979–80) and a conceptual movement that blends aspects of spirit, politics, and awakening eco-consciousness as part of the living Earth. The movement is associated with goddess and Earth spirituality, the ancient Wicca tradition, and Neopaganism. Starhawk has written many books, including *The Spiral Dance*, an early classic that invited many people to be part of an emerging movement. Together, we danced the Spiral Dance. Together, in morphic, resonating ways, we initiated reclaiming many traditional rites of passage, such as birth, coming of age, moon cycles, marriage, and, most especially, right relationship to the Earth in health, farming, activism, and even governance.

Due to this context, my purpose in life and with this writing is aligned with the home funeral and green burial movements and dedicated to the sensibility of these ideas radiating to ordinary consciousness.

If the local funeral parlor is not going to take care of a grandmother, the neighbor, or a friend killed in an automobile crash, who is? Whose work is it to choose options that are right for *our* circumstances? It seems to me that it is *our* work, *our* task, *our* chore, to care for our own people (or pets) in death as in life. That is the focus of natural, personal death care, which is reemerging again today.

It is our *innate right and, ultimately, inherent response-ability* to attend to this sacred act of assisting in the cycle of returning. In doing this, we face and realize an important aspect of our personal path and can discover a spiritual and natural understanding of our life and death, however we decide to handle death's presence.

We bandage our wounds, soften our callouses, handle our grief, deal with our loss, and grapple with our understanding of what has transpired, expired, and transformed before our eyes. We weep, we enact, we reclaim what is ours.

When this work is relinquished or taken from us, we miss an essential part of our very lives. *This is our natural work to do.* It is our *innate and essential right* to care for our loved ones in life and in death.

CHAPTER 3

INHERENT VALUE

The Nature of Life includes the Eventual Miracle of Death.
—Final Passages Brochure

"Isn't it weird to touch a dead person?" my brother, Paul, asked when our family discussed the inevitable approach of our mother's death.

"Not really," I replied. I knew of our mother's wish to simply have her family be the ones to care for her in a hands-on manner without involving a mortuary. Our mother became acquainted with Jerrigrace Lyons of Final Passages when we called on her assistance for a friend. Our mother had declared, "That's how I want it to be for me."

When Mother Iris passed, my brother, our two sisters, and I reverently washed and dressed our mother and transformed her room. The room of a dying woman became a living altar to her—living because the room was filled with her presence even as her now-lifeless body was "lying-in-honor" in a room filled with light and love and warmth and color. Rose petals from the garden just outside the window created a rainbow of color and a delightful scent around her body. Soft music played continuously. A look of peace and ease was upon her face. One of her doggies insisted on staying as a sentinel in the room.

Family and many close friends ventured quietly into the room. Some of them were timid at first, yet they came away feeling a sense of peace after viewing her anointed and honored body lying with a peaceful countenance.

My brother pulled me aside shortly after our family ritual and said, "Thank you. That wasn't for anyone else to do but us."

Transformation

Paul's transformation was a joy to me, even in the grief of my mother's absence. The reality of this transformative energy is eloquently relayed in a quote on the Final Passages brochure and website: "The Nature of Life includes the Eventual Miracle of Death."

Brother Paul's two offspring—Mom's youngest grandson, Aaron, of eight years and granddaughter, Marissa, of ten years—were among those who were quite timid at first. They held tightly to their daddy's hand, hesitatingly venturing in to view their grandmother. After that first cautious time, they entered countless times on their own. They hung pictures in the window, creating a stained-glass effect. They got up close to Grammy's face and whispered to her. They even kissed her cheek. It became their mission to assist others who came by to enter the room. They shared their confidence and let people know how valuable it was to be there. "Grammy Iris is really glad you came to see her and send her on her journey," they wisely told a few uneasy adults.

My own transformative moment occurred as well. Crying moments after Mother's passage, I uttered, "I just can't believe you are gone, that you are not here."

I heard my mother's voice distinctly drop into my head. "I'm here. I'm everywhere." Vibrational chills shuddered through me, and I was instantly aware that I could feel her in a tangible way—in me, all around me; in every breath, I breathed her in. Yes, she was everywhere!

Over the years of being involved in this work, I have seen many versions of this transformation. Timid or even openly disgruntled people slowly, quietly, or suddenly show up with light in their eyes and express their amazement and gratitude that they themselves cared for their family member or friend.

An example of a gentle transformation occurred while assisting with a home funeral of a man who had just died. The sister of the man's wife was present and visibly uncomfortable. Repeatedly, she voiced her discomfort with seeing her brother-in-law and kept apologizing, saying she was sorry she could not be more helpful as it was just strange and weird to see death so closely. Later, after the wife and I had washed her husband and adjusted his garments, I asked the wife's sister if she could help pick out fabrics to adorn the place where he lay to make it into an altar. She picked through fabrics and chose the right ones from my collection. She helped drape them around the bed. At one point,

I looked up to see her face glowing with radiance. She smiled. "Why, this is just wonderful, isn't it? It is really beautiful. I am so glad I'm here."

———

These stories are a reminder about how natural death care may be an essential piece in our own process of understanding. As noted in the previous chapter, when this piece of our journey is relinquished or taken from us, we miss out—*we suffer*. Realizing why and how this is so is part of a mutual exploration with you, our readers.

Caring for our own dead is a means to understand the natural place death has in our lives. It assists us in understanding that someone we love has really passed on. It helps us accept what has occurred and may ease our grief in whatever way might be right for us at the time. Perhaps it makes grief more real, tangible, and important. It gives permission for us to grieve as we wash and dress and anoint our loved one. It gives us permission to speak to that person in a way that we may not have done before when they were alive. It helps us find closure along the way. It does not remove or cancel grief, yet it allows grief—its natural place in the moment and beyond.

Many people remark that they can feel the energy, even presence, of their loved one, although to touch the flesh of their departed is to notice that they are not there. They are no longer contained within their flesh. Their body—where they have resided all their many or few years—is to be honored. Yet the knowledge that they are no longer using that body is a tangible feeling. I recall a young woman saying that touching her friend's deceased body helped her accept her death. She could feel her energy all around her. The peaceful presence allowed her to feel that her friend was truly all right. She realized then that she, too, was okay. She would miss seeing her and calling her on the phone, yet she knew she could connect with her spirit.

The Ritual Bath

The washing of a loved one's body is a natural process. The sacred act of a ritual bath is personal and intimate. It is an honoring of the person who lived in that body. No stainless-steel sterile table and unfamiliar hands attend this process. It is an intimate personal ritual.

The ritual bath often provides opportunity for transformation. I recall an incident when the daughter of an elderly woman who died directed emphatically that she wanted us (the home funeral guides) to take care of the washing of her mother. She planned on leaving the room. Yet she lingered. After I prepared the warm water and was about to begin, I sensed the right moment to gently offer her a washcloth. I suggested she might like to just wash her mother's face. She took the cloth and from that moment on was fully engaged. Merely holding the cloth was enough for her to find her natural place in the process. She went on to help with the dressing and the makeup. Only she knew how her mother would want it done, she said. I've often noticed that if the deceased person wore makeup or styled their hair, a daughter or a close friend will know how to most naturally do their makeup and their hairdo.

Dressing the Body

Sometimes a person chooses what clothing they wish to wear at their own funeral. One might confer among friends, "What shall I wear for my grand finale?" When the dying person is aware and preparing for their death, the consideration of what to wear takes deliberate care. Choosing what a loved one will wear often provides a family with a pause that relieves their anguish for a moment. I've been privy to long conversations as people deliberate over this question with serious, humorous, tender, and, finally, practical and/or elegant decisions.

One mother knew that although her son was very theatrical, he also loved the idea of formality. The result was two different attires. One initial dressing had a thespian flare. It was a personal view for his mother and attending family who appreciated his look in a flowing gown and turban. Later dressed more formally, he took on a very distinguished look in his three-piece suit, befitting his final viewing among friends.

Remember my friend Annie? She studied law and chose a T-shirt that read *res ipsa loquitur* (Latin for "it is as it seems," mentioned in the previous chapter). A long-standing joke we'd shared was about the idea that we could tell what "it" was when perhaps even professionals were perplexed and, from our view, did not have a clue. That shirt over a gray-striped turtleneck, jeans, and a gray scarf was her perfect outfit as she was lying-in-grace on a simple off-white raw silk undercloth with a red and gold pillow cover beneath her head. In her own way, she was exquisitely "as it seems."

When a person is being washed and dressed, there are opportunities to speak to the beloved and say things that help complete something needed in the relationship. I've often been privy to overhearing what was an obviously two-sided conversation. The one side that I could hear with my outer ears often would astound me with its candidly spoken nature, its depth and essential feeling. It suggested an interaction I could only imagine. Later, the person might confide how significant that moment was, and how deeply it helped them accept their friend or family member's death when they *got* what they heard from the other side.

Creating Space

When my friend's son of thirty-three years died, she called me in the middle of the night. I drove right over, as promised. As we washed his body, we cried, and we each spoke to him. I felt him hearing me in a way that had never happened before. I heard my own candid declarations and confessions to him that completed for me a deep forgiveness and acceptance of who he was in my life.

By dawn, his mother was sitting with him. I was doing housekeeping in her living area. Before his death, she had said that she did *not* want a dead body in the house after he passed. She asked that we find another place for his body until we carried him away for cremation. She called out to me from the room where she sat with her son: "Does Richard need to leave now?"

"No," I replied, "He does not need to go anywhere until you are ready."

"Oh, good," she said, "because Rich doesn't want to leave here at all, and I don't want my son to go either!" A transformation had just occurred. Although we had arranged for another place for his body, she now felt differently. She felt communication with her son had occurred, and she was now comfortable with him being there. She said something to the effect of, "His spirit is *here*, and does not want to be separated from his body yet."

The room had been very dark and dreary. We opened up the curtains, letting morning light flood into the room. Guitars he played and other personal artifacts were arranged around him. The room transformed into a celebration of Richard and who he was. His sister and various friends commented on how peaceful he now looked. They felt an acceptance of his need to go.

Artifacts from a loved one's life are an important part of creating personalized energy in the room around their body. If they rode a surfboard or a motorcycle or were a dancer, an artist, or a musician, artifacts from their life journey placed around their body create a sacred space that expresses their essence in a way that no mortuary place could ever replicate.

Lit candles, special music, pictures of them throughout their life, family photos, and pictures of people special to them add to a sense of a person's uniqueness. Lying-in-honor this way creates a sacred space, a living altar, to honor their life expression. What was perhaps a sickroom becomes an altar full of light, reflecting aspects of a life lived. Added touches such as these also may make it more comfortable for visitors and spark recollections of their friend.

Coffin Considerations

Choosing to build or decorate a coffin is yet another opportunity for completion and healing. Many people find that building or decorating a burial container offers an outlet for feelings and grief to be expressed. It allows the artist in them to emerge. A friend of a deceased woman made a beautiful shroud from fabric covered with dragonflies. Her husband remarked that his wife's spirit was being carried off on the wings of dancing dragonflies.

Brother Paul insisted that a cardboard coffin, which the rest of us felt content with and even looked forward to decorating, was not sufficient in his eyes for his mother. He was an extremely busy carpenter and yet found time to express his grief and his art in one of the most exquisite and personal coffins I've ever seen. The bottom was an elongated heart; the container was an angled, long rectangle; the top was in the shape of a *flutterby* (original word for butterfly); and the spine of the flutterby was a long, raised redwood piece culled from wood that Mom's brother, Howard, had timbered long ago. Paul traced, carved, and burnished into the redwood the image of an iris flower our artist mother had drawn. It was a unique tribute to our mother, Iris May.

People find various innovative ways to create a container for a loved one's body or cremains. There are companies that supply biodegradable containers, shrouds, and exotic containers for cremains. Yet many find that engaging in their own container-making process is therapeutic.

As people share in this activity, they have an opportunity to integrate feelings, sense a spiritual connection with the deceased, and bond with each other. Quiet conversation or even laughter and bantering may occur while people are building and/or decorating a body container. This is providing another gift of healing for participants. It gives a family more ways they can participate in their home funeral. Friends who wish to help may also join them. Some who are more timid about hands-on care of a dead person have a comfortable place of involvement. A place of healing is generated in the process.

Children often lead the way in such an artistic endeavor. One such child-dominated occurrence seemed at the time very disjointed and an uncoordinated jumble of crazy art. The twin great grandsons of a woman of ninety-four years enlivened the event. I smile at my memory of this humorous time. The boys ran about between their own and others' artistic designs. They used a lot of black paint to outline the art. I felt the outlines might be too dark and cover up the artwork. Yet the result was amazing! It resembled an oriental tapestry. It was beautiful and reflected the life of a woman who loved to travel and had a particular appreciation for ancient Chinese art.

The artistic expression of coffin art results in a priceless container that nothing manufactured with expensive materials could ever match. The shared time enriches the moment and provides another level of acceptance. Like Tibetan monks who, in meditation, create a sacred sand mandala they later brush aside, mourners paint remarkable art that shortly will be cremated or buried along with a loved one. The art becomes a therapeutic outlet. Many coffins are uniquely beautiful treasures, photographed as keepsakes. They add to snapshots of other special moments throughout the home funeral and are kept for later remembrances and reminders of an inner process as well.

Grieving and Its Value

The process of caring for the beloved in the context of a home funeral is as varied as the family who orchestrates it and the life that they honor. A home funeral gets to be however it is. It reflects the values and personality of the person who has passed as well as the perspective and personalities of family and friends who participate in their varied ways. It is a family-directed event.

Moments of grief shared and healing energy are an integral part of what is or may be facilitated.

This does not circumvent the grief or the inner turmoil and reflection that the days to follow may bring. Yet all these examples of the process and whatever occurs in the home funeral may be a testament to the resilience of the human spirit and an important avenue for grief's healing path. It doesn't supplant the support from others such as friends, pastors, priestesses, priests, and grief counselors. Yet, it does provide a framework for understanding the life-and-death reality in the moment. The energy and support of friends and family will likely be essential in days that follow and at later times as well. The grief of bereavement is especially significant as loss of an intimate family member also incorporates one's own history.

Grief has its own unique way with us. Each person experiences grief differently. It involves multiple ways to process, accept, deal with, and move through the often murky waters of sorrow and grief. Recovery of natural joy in living takes time. Yet it is the providence of living with awareness that allows transcendence from painful, acute grief to recovery and balance. In 1992, I was privileged to attend a seminar on grief facilitated by Stephen and Ondrea Levine. In the midst of many people sharing deeply their sorrow and pain in personal life tragedies, Stephen said, "It is a wonder that any of us chose to continue to live on in the face of so much pain, yet the presence of magic makes it possible to choose and find a way to live in joy." (Paraphrased from my memory.)

I've suggested ways that these natural homemade rituals may bring lasting value to those living. Yet there is another unknown value about which we might speculate. What is transpiring for the one who has just died? Is their spirit still hovering nearby, watching the care of their body-temple and listening to what is being shared among their loved ones? Some suggest that perhaps even the spirit of the loved one gets to further process their life and feel how loved and seen they are. Many religions and cultures speak of a "life review" that each person experiences after they pass on. There are many ideas about what is occurring for one deceased from this physical life. These ideas and philosophies open another conversation worth sharing regarding current religious philosophies and ancient religious cultures, beliefs, and rites. For now, it is a comforting thought to imagine that, from their mysterious vantage place, a loved one who has passed on from this life can appreciate our personal care and love.

Each home funeral is unique and reflects the family and the deceased person as their own unique energy and values are expressed and enacted. There is no cookie-cutter scenario or exact protocol. The home funeral may be short and simple or long and elaborate. It may be ceremonial and filled with planned or spontaneous ritual or without ceremony and fanfare at all. It may be as simple as intimates holding hands around their beloved and honoring their journey onward. A spontaneous prayer may be offered, releasing a loved one to Divine Spirit (however named). It is an unfolding sacred ceremonial occurrence, whatever unfolds. Many people may attend, or the event may involve only a very few intimate members.

The miracle of death has been honored in life. An innate rite is enacted; inherent value is felt.

SECTION TWO
LEGAL GROUND
& BREAKING GROUND RULES

CHAPTER 4

RELINQUISHING RIGHTS— LOSS & GAIN

I am sorry for your loss. We'll take care of all your concerns.
Let us serve you in this hour of need.
—*A commonly heard phrase from funeral industry professionals*

Taken at face value, the above words seem benevolent and well-meaning. When someone we love dies, we are likely encompassed by sorrow and adrift in our grief. At this delicate and precarious time, the many practical and legal tasks required in the aftermath of a death are unwanted interruptions. Having someone show up with the experience and knowledge to help handle essential matters would fill a great need. In "days of old," traditionally, what frequently occurred was a gathering of family and close friends in the home of the deceased or a family member. A priest, prominent community member, or close family friend may have joined to help them navigate such a tumultuous time, console them, and handle the necessary care of the deceased's body.

Today, a legal industry outshines the family in these matters. While stating sorrow for your loss, they simultaneously issue a price list and feed their coffers. Where is the personal connection and hands-on assistance that we genuinely need in this situation?

The question is this: Does this experienced assistance need to come in the form of a legalized industry that must, by its nature as a business, attend foremost to its bottom line?

As a culture, we have invented a new kind of modern death care. While the funeral industry takes the "problem" of dealing with our loved one's remains out of our hands, it has also evolved into a legally protected, lucrative, and, sadly, occasionally unethical business. Our cultural mindset has deferred to what can be seen as an exploitive industry. This is somewhat understandable as we experience the pain of loss and our *perceived inability* to handle necessary, practical steps that follow a beloved's passing.

I believe we've lost touch with a natural inclination. We've essentially given away a valuable and time-honored process that can help us to face and release our fears. In doing so, we've lost personal hands-on experience that affirms our natural ability, our common task, and our full rights in regard to natural death care.

Many observe a need for regaining the capacity to sort out our options, see the bigger picture, and make personal, sustainable choices. Are we acting according to our true beliefs, or does the established funeral industry's overriding presence influence us enough to dismiss a natural tendency to take care of our loved ones personally in death as well as we do in life?

———

In previous chapters, we considered our *innate right* to care for our dead and confirmed its meaning and value. With that being true, how then did this natural and common process, for centuries handled in the context of family and community, become a "commodity," removed and remote from our common experience?

Many people today don't even question the funeral home business model. When I mention that I educate and assist families who wish to care for their own dead at home, a most common response is, *"Really? Is that legal?"*

Yes, it is legal. Nearly all states in this country give legal recognition and provision for caring for a loved one's death at home in the context of family. *Why*, then, do so many people not know this? Ironically, the processes of cultural change, abetted by the funeral industry maneuvering legal loopholes and public opinion, has now made choosing the more personal option unnecessarily labor-intensive and circuitous. Furthermore, many people are unaware a choice even exists.

While there are kind and concerned people who run funeral homes, the overriding *funeral industry* embraces bottom-line tactics that have been used successfully on grieving customers for many years. There is the implication, either overt or covert, that the amount of money spent on a funeral indicates the degree of love a family has for their deceased. I find this to be a preposterous equation. Grieving people may be pressured or guided into the purchase of a "package deal," which might include items or processes they don't need or want. Yet they are not able to remove those items from the "highly discounted" death package.

Embalming is a prime example of a "feature" foisted upon people by funeral directors who imply or openly state that it is required by law. To this day, many people believe that embalming is necessary and/or required. Yet here's the truth: *federal law does not require embalming.* Some states require it in specific situations. Interstate transport usually requires it, although there is a way around this requirement with a special Ziegler travel box for the body.

The official position that embalming is beneficial and essential to sanitize and preserve the body is still invoked as a sales tool, however. Mortuary personnel are not likely to mention that embalming involves very toxic chemicals that are inherently harmful to the Earth as well as to the health of people who work with embalming fluids.

What is true and can be confirmed is that the claim that embalming is necessary for sanitation and preservation safety has been shown to be completely false. Embalming is extremely toxic to the Earth. Leakage of embalming fluids into the soil and groundwater is an extremely undesirable outcome.

For a humorous exposé about embalming, watch "Is Embalming Dangerous?" by Caitlin Doughty, a mortician who speaks about the dangers of embalming. Doughty is an advocate for funeral practice reform and accepting death.[4]

———

Expensive caskets featured in fancy showrooms are another perceived necessity. Bereaved persons may be routed to the expensive models with the implication that plain or inexpensive caskets are inferior, undesirable, or even disrespectful to the departed. Inflated charges for services have been a routine manipulation. This is especially true with those associated with major conglomerates. A no-exception protocol for packaged services has been their *modus operandi.* They may invoke either specious legality or prey on the feelings

---

4. Doughty, "Ask a Mortician—Is Embalming Dangerous?" https://www.youtube.com /watch?v=p3rlc1qS258&t=10s.

of bereaved persons, indicating that something is "right," "normally done," or "legal." The bereaved might not have the energy to argue.

At the time of death, funeral home "customers" are likely more focused on their grief than evaluating whether what they're being sold is a necessary expense. The pressure applied on a grieving family can be immense, and they may interpret this pressure as being about their loss, not their purse—until later, when the cost hits them.

———

It is valuable to access references confirming grievous protocols by the funeral industry. A most exceptional resource is the book *Final Rights: Reclaiming the American Way of Death*, coauthored by Lisa Carlson and Joshua Slocum. *Final Rights* discusses the history of the funeral industry from the perspective of questionable mortuary practices (like sales of services and items), embalming claims and status, historical framework, political and corporate interactions, and consumer protective organizations and includes state-by-state chapters outlining each state's statutes, mandates, and general protocol. The mutual efforts of these coauthors in *Final Rights* make it an essential standard and quintessential resource for anyone interested in the subject and for natural death advocates. It is concise and readable.

Both Carlson and Slocum continue as advocates and activists working for more transparency in the funeral industry. Carlson is the executive director of the Funeral Ethics Organization. Joshua Slocum is the executive director of the Funeral Consumer Alliance (FCA). Together, they call out consumer abuses when they occur, provide research, and are a boon to protecting our rights. The FCA is an organization that, in addition to being a longtime leading-edge consumer watch organization, maintains an excellent website that regularly updates legislative changes and provides resources for reporting industry abuses.[5] The website presents an opportunity to join online and support the work of public education, local consumer alliances, and those presenting options for death care today.

———

5. Funeral Consumers Alliance, https://funerals.org/.

Recently, I was away from home when the husband of a special and long-time neighbor died. Returning home, it took a while to realize I didn't see Rosa and Miguel out walking together. I finally approached Rosa and learned Miguel had passed peacefully at home with his family. She was immensely grateful for that. However, the funeral home cost of transport, embalming, church viewing, paperwork, and whatever else was done was over ten thousand dollars. It was an expense that she could ill afford. She had no idea of her *actual choices*. My sadness at the death of a dear neighbor was underlined by my sadness at not having been available to Rosa to at least present her with other options.

———

No one disputes that a business, by its very nature, must take care of itself. To maintain itself, it generally looks to extend its reach of services and become seen as an indispensable societal necessity. However, the funeral home business model is *not* an indispensable societal need. While funeral homes may be an *option*, they are just one of an array of choices.

Few people realize that what is now called a "traditional" American funeral service is actually a construct of the modern funeral industry. You may hear: "I just want a simple, traditional service; the mortuary will pick up the body, and we will have a brief service at the funeral chapel." Yet this choice bears scant resemblance to what was originally authentic, traditional death care and to what ensues behind the secret curtain of a funeral home. Besides, various ethnic groups and religions also have their own way of handling the body of a loved one and creating a commemorative ceremony.

If we were to look behind the scenes of a modern funeral home, what we would actually see is not a simple or traditional process at all. The involvement and payment of transporter, cosmetician, hairstylist, dresser, embalmer, viewing costs, deep-grave-digging equipment operators, grave liners or vaults, lowering-mechanism operations, grave closure costs, endowment (maintenance costs), paperwork and filing costs, and other "incidentals" all add up to an expensive affair that is anything but simple. Is it any wonder that cremation has nearly supplanted burial in this country? American death care today is often referred to as a "cremation nation."

In her groundbreaking books *The American Way of Death* and *The American Way of Death: Revisited,* Jessica Mitford took on the funeral industry with meticulous research and a dogged persistence in uncovering evidence of hidden industry practices.

It was in the late 1950s that Mitford—prodded by her lawyer-husband who had uncovered the common funeral home practice of setting prices for services according to the amount of insurance benefits available to the family of the deceased—set herself to write a detailed exposé of the organized tactics of funeral directors and funeral industry associations.

I recall that her investigation and subsequent bestselling books resulted in articles in the *San Francisco Chronicle, Saturday Evening Post,* and other prominent publications. Public interest grew, and consumer funeral societies were formed. The media attention precipitated a huge crisis within the funeral industry.

Industry association insiders reacted like spoiled brats who had had their special toys taken away. Even before publication of Mitford's book, the industry got wind of her investigation and went on the attack through its trade publications, even going so far as to attempt to block publication by threatening publishers. Some in the industry assumed the book would never sell and felt little concern. Yet its first printing sold out, igniting a firestorm of public discussion and high praise from reviewers. In return, the funeral trade journals launched a counteroffensive to combat what they called the "Mitford syndrome."[6]

One thing that shook them up was Mitford's exposé of the practice of embalming—something she called the "ultimate fate of almost all Americans." She pointed out that its prevalence was merely "an aid of providing economic stability to the industry." The book also detailed impeccably the lobbying, maneuvering, abusive tactics, and irregular influences the funeral industry used to gain legal protection for its established lucrative practices. As a result of these shenanigans, Mitford wrote that an effective, legal, and near-monopoly for the handling of the "corpse" emerged as an "American tradition." She pointed to the utter fabrication of such a "tradition" and became a considerable irritation to the funeral trade.

Mitford suggested in her foreword that even "ethical undertakers" are questionable—perhaps even more significantly than their "shadier colleagues" whom she labeled "crooks." She explained the "ethical" reference refers to the

---

6. Mitford, *The American Way of Death: Revisited,* xvii.

adherence to an "industry-created code of ethics," devised to cover the business practices that sustain and market an emotional advantage over the consumers who buy their products.[7]

Mitford's books, albeit long and detailed, are as full of adventure and intrigue as detective thrillers. They are highly readable and entertaining. She tears to shreds the funeral industry's defense of, "We're just giving the public what it wants." She illustrates how public opinion was swayed by the industry's "lies and half-truths." While an industry attempts to throw blame or responsibility on public sentiment and claim that it's only acceding to popular request, a read of her work lays out a convincingly different scenario.

The value of Mitford's revelations of what happens behind the scenes is indisputable. However, I see a loss along with the gain. As a result of her exposé, the actual so-called disposition of the body resulted in a shift away from burial to cremation. Dare I say that with this shift to a no-fuss-no-frills direct cremation, we may have abandoned the sacred task of attending to the *body-temple* with honor and respect and the need of some for a ritual or ceremony. Suddenly, there was only the absence, the grief, and perhaps a perplexing void. Our exploration of other choices may provide a renewal of deeper meaning.

Laderman writes there was *not* as much bad press toward the funeral industry in the 1980–90s compared to in the wake of Mitford's exposés. He claims that the attention she garnered about the industry's monopolization actually fostered nostalgia for "traditional values of trustworthiness, candor, humor, and familiarity."[8] As an industry defender, he supports the funeral industry as a legitimate business and indicates the values mentioned above *are* associated with family-owned funeral homes. Another view discussed is that the funeral industry is the culprit responsible for victimization of innocent grieving people. From my perspective, his position is one of a modern apologist for the funeral industry, even as his books relay an excellent overview of the history.

The point is that the simple act of placing a recently deceased-person in a box and burying the body, once a private prerogative, somehow became a major industry. Points listed below illustrate this further:

---

7. Mitford, *The American Way of Death: Revisited*, xi.

8. Laderman, *Rest in Peace*, 193.

- The practice of embalming required a skill and chemicals not found in a family kitchen. The maneuvering and cornering of the market was amped up. The industry defense was that this practice was essential because it was sanitary and protected the public (seriously!). To this day, many people in the funeral business maintain this argument, although it has been thoroughly debunked.[9]

- The concept of "memorialization" created a need for a lifelike "object" to view, implying that the natural occurrence of death was something abhorrent and to be feared.

- The entrepreneurial concept that the amount of money spent corresponded to the love of family and friends for the deceased evolved. Naturally (and statistically), this worked well in the industry's favor.

- Funeral directors, embalmers, morticians and undertakers elevated from simple caretakers of the deceased to "high priests" by the self-awarding of specious titles like "death specialist" or even "grief counselor."

- Market-corner stronghold and status was maintained, even with a slowly occurring shift to a more popular cremation option and away from the usual burial.

- Funeral trade conglomerates emerged as monopolies of the funeral trade. Mitford reports that many in the funeral trade are "pleased to call them leaders in the 'death care' industry, in their 'drive to upgrade and up-price funerals.'"[10] The conglomerates are SCI, or Service Corporation International (Houston, Texas corporation, founded in 1962 and the largest conglomerate), with brands such as Dignity Memorial, Dignity Planning, National Cremation Society, Advantage, Funeraria Del Angel, and the Neptune Society; the Loewen Group (the second-largest conglomerate and a Canadian group); and Stewart Enterprises. They have purchased the largest percentage of funeral homes, cemeteries, and crematories in the US to the tune of huge profits. They are able to hide behind a profitable curtain in the name of public safety.

- The problem of funeral home abuses was compounded and spurred on by the existence of these mortuary conglomerates, known as the "Big Three."

9. Slocum and Carlson, *Final Rights,* 57, 62, 63.

10. Mitford, *The American Way of Life—Revisited,* 188.

For years, they systematically bought up small, family-operated funeral homes. Their ploy was to keep family members on as staff and retain the family name, yet conduct a corporately owned and operated business, with emphasis on increasing consumer cost, profit margins, and products to sell. They represent countless funeral homes in the US and forty-nine other countries.

Many professions form trade associations to support their field of work, interrelations, and collegiality, and assure the public of their ethical standards— all noble motives. However, funeral industry associations at the local, state, and national level are historically less benign. The National Funeral Directors Association (NFDA)[11] is one of the largest and most influential trade associations of the funeral industry. Their lobbying efforts have fostered legal protection and strengthened the industry stronghold.

If you have seen the TV series *Six Feet Under,* you may recall the episode where the owners of a small funeral business resisted the pressure to sell to a large corporation. They were threatened and eventually suffered a mishap perpetuated by agents of the funeral conglomerate. This scenario was allegedly based on real-life events suggestive of the kind of pressure exerted on such small businesses.

Tactics such as this, as well as the accumulated history of many consumer tragedies from the late 1950s to early 1970s, brought funeral consumer advocates to the point where they felt compelled to take a stand. Slocum and Carlson's book substantiates and details further the actions of particular consumer advocates who spoke up and called into question what was occurring in the funeral trade.[12]

One would think that the ruckus Mitford and others stirred up and the public outcry that resulted would have engaged local, state, and federal representatives to dig deeper into the concerns of their constituents. In fact, remarkably little regulatory action ensued.

Early in the 1970s, prodded by public outcry, one member of the Federal Trade Commission (FTC), an agency mandated to protect consumers, was concerned enough to initiate an investigation and subsequently propose some

---

11. www.nfda.org.

12. Slocum and Carlson, *Final Rights,* 117–127.

consumer support. An FTC "Funeral Rule" was proposed in 1974, approved in 1982, and finally implemented in 1986. The purpose of the FTC rule was to regulate the manner in which services and goods of funeral homes were presented to customers and to protect and give specific rights to consumers.[13] See page 214 for a specific outline of the FTC Rule.

This sounds encouraging; however, a look at subsequent FTC involvement sadly shows they have ignored their own mandate and capitulated to funeral industry pressure. Rather than acting as a consumer watchdog, the FTC rolled over to become a covert protector of funeral association practices acquiring legal status, thanks to the funeral industry's effective lobbying and its alliances with government officials.[14]

It seems the "American way of death" is also an American success story. Funeral homes, supported by industry ingenuity, inventiveness, and so-called scientific research, have whisked the act of caring for the dead out of the family home and into a choreographed funeral home milieu. They perceive their customers as attached to their dead yet neither willing nor capable of dealing with a dead body. And so the industry steps in and expands, anticipating the seductiveness of their campaign and its effectiveness.

The industry offers, on our behalf, an infinite variety of services—for which they are financially compensated. They handle the distress of the moment, have scientific equipment, and produce a pleasing last view and "memory picture." They declare they are saving you from dealing with the trauma of loss in such a sad time. In effect, they are making money off your loved one's corpse.

What could possibly alter this well-established and protected situation? Is there a way to relate to an out-of-control industry and find a balance that serves the entire population?

Presenting alternative and different perspectives from what is promoted by the funeral industry is one of my primary aims in this book, enabling you with a broader range of choices that can include, though not exclude, more than just what the industry offers.

Historically, family-owned funeral homes have been part of their local communities. Many genuinely and caringly served neighbor families. Their

---

13. Slocum and Carlson, *Final Rights*, 98, 99.

14. Ibid.

contribution is noteworthy. As neighbors, they rose to the occasion and helped when help was needed. Many such proprietors lived in their place of business, offering services while providing a modest living for their families. Their place of business actually was a funeral *home*.

As a home funeral guide with many acquaintances in the funeral industry, I've learned that there are funeral directors and cemetery owners who enter the trade as proponents of natural death care. A few have trained as home funeral guides. A few are even members of the National Funeral Alliance.[15] One cemetery owner who allows green burials at his site confided that he is "very frustrated and challenged by many of the industry mandates."

For instance, I owe a debt of gratitude to the owner/director of a funeral home who reminded me that church cemeteries in California are not subject to cemetery law. He chose to assist rather than impede our natural process. His reminder supported the legal filing of the disposition permit, and I was able to assist the family and group of friends with a green burial on the designated cemetery of a Pagan Church property. They, the family and friends, members of a Pagan Church, were honoring a mandate to commit their recently deceased priestess to the earth. The exquisite event was in large part the seed and impetus for writing this book.

It is of paramount importance to educate ourselves, each other, the public, and medical professionals—who are in touch with the dying—of the greater range of options beyond just handing over death care to a funeral home. We deserve to be aware of hands-on death care as one viable option. I've found that when hospice workers and/or hospital personnel get to experience a home funeral with more hands-on death care by a family, their preconceived notions and committed opinions often shift. Some officials in agencies dealing with death are unaware of the legal statutes of family death care and may act in good faith to curtail a family's rights.

A prime example of this was when my ex-husband, Kenneth, was dying in a hospital. The hospital was informed by Kenneth's family that they had previously made special arrangements with a mortuary and planned to transport the body to the mortuary in their own vehicle.

---

15. www.homefuneralalliance.org.

A well-meaning hospital staff member informed the local coroner of their plans, and a young, newly hired deputy coroner arrived to tell the family that the hospital morgue staff—not *the family*—*must* handle the body. Although I was still en route to the hospital with other family members, I was able to coach Kenneth's wife's friends over the phone, providing the California statute that supported their plan. A short time later, with his family surrounding him, Kenneth—beloved husband and father—died. Fortunately, the deputy coroner, after further checking, confirmed that the family's plan was supported legally.

There is a silver lining in this encounter. The deputy coroner, in tears as she hugged Ken's wife, told her that she was grateful to have learned something important. She shared how deeply touching the experience was for her and relayed her hope that more families would learn of their rights, experience death in a more natural way, and discover an amazing opportunity to be aware of death differently.

Another fortunate result was my and Kenneth's son Todd was able to carry his father in his arms and transport him to the mortuary. This affected him deeply. He was the one to greet his brother Greg and take him to be with their father, providing a connection that his brother sorely needed.

We have no way of knowing how the decisions, choices, and actions we carry out may make an impression and affect others. A ripple effect may alter another person's view, initiate an inner dialogue, and open someone up to participating in a new experience.

———

Domination by the funeral industry only seems to have ended hands-on death care, supplanting it with the sanctioned funeral home "viewing" of a manicured and "lifelike" facsimile of our loved one, arranged by societally approved and certified "handlers of death." While this may be an unexamined reality for some people, others call into question its validity.

We are indebted to trailblazers who have stepped out of the cultural comfort zone to question, expose, and ponder the status quo, as well as find and support natural ways of viewing and caring for the deceased. Another chapter will discuss a few of these remarkable people and indicate their achievements in reclaiming choices for natural death care availability.

To some readers, the ideas presented here may still seem foreign and foster feelings of uneasiness. This is understandable. The systematic, intentional, and manipulative process that has arisen to assure an industry of its legal position has had an effect of turning our culture away from what was seen as a natural process for countless centuries. You or others you know may still wonder why anyone would choose to participate in a direct hands-on process in the care of the dead. You are not required to jump on this bandwagon. There isn't just one way for us to relate to the care of our beloved ones who pass before us.

As I finished editing this chapter, a text arrived from my son Todd, telling me that another of our family-tribe had passed. We had two weeks earlier to the day celebrated the eightieth birthday of this strong and determined woman. She frequently declared she did not believe in getting sick. So when she heard a diagnosis of fourth-stage cancer, she said she knew it was her time. She wanted no "life-saving" medical intervention. She would celebrate her planned birthday party, enjoy her friends, and be on her way. She did just that as she entertained friends and family in her spirited style all afternoon and into the evening. Apparently her spiritual bags were packed. Her party was, in effect, her own designed "last rites." With her close family around her, she peacefully left this realm. I salute this dear friend of over fifty years and honor her as an Ancestor Wise Woman who exemplified doing "it" her way.

The point is that a circle of family and friends has a right to decide how to honor and memorialize the one they love. There is no cookie-cutter template! It is your choice. Your way is open to options you may not have known about until now. And your quest and your reward is your personal discovery. You are invited to become part of reclaiming your choice in a movement honoring death's passage.

CHAPTER 5

AN AMERICAN WAY OF DEATH

Thinking and talking about death need not be morbid;
they may be quite the opposite.
Ignorance and fear of death overshadow life,
while knowing and accepting death erases this shadow.
—*Lily Pincus*

In the previous chapter, we observed that the practices and pervasiveness of the funeral industry have become ingrained in our culture, relying on a business model to take care of the very personal matter of death. Today, this transaction is seen as inevitable and indispensable. Yet how did we get here?

The following quote from John Muir targets our civilized concepts of death and suggests that children, which I take to mean the child in all of us, will find in nature a "divine harmony" that can remove death's sting.

On no subject are our ideas more warped and pitiable than on death ... Let children walk with nature let them see the beautiful blendings (sic) and communions of death and life, their joyous inseparable unity, as taught in woods and meadows, plains and mountains and streams of our blessed star, and they will learn that death is stingless indeed, and as beautiful as life, and that the grave has no victory, for it never fights. All is divine harmony.[16]

Since its inception, the mortuary industry has ensured its own legal protection in the name of protecting us from the realities of death. When and how did this transition take place? Why are the industry's presence and practices

---

16. Muir, *A Thousand-Mile Walk to the Gulf,* 50–51.

seen as inevitable and indispensable? How did people in earlier times traditionally take care of their dead? How did care of the departed become a profitable business?

The concept of avoiding the face of death is not new. Grief over the loss of a loved one is perhaps as ancient as our existence. Yet it's only been a few generations since American culture began to accept the idea that death should be taken out of our hands almost entirely.

The familiar "frog in hot water" metaphor applies. If a frog were tossed into a boiling pot of water, it would jump out right away. However, if placed in water that is gradually heated up, that same frog would be unaware of impending doom until it is too late.

Gary Laderman's books, *The Sacred Remains* and *Rest in Peace*, cover in detail how the business of death care from the antebellum period to the modern day developed and how changing perspectives and events shaped and altered the landscape of this emerging industry. I found the books both fascinating and disturbing. Historically and culturally, they are interesting, yet it's disturbing to realize how the funeral industry emerged and surreptitiously orchestrated and maneuvered legal protection for the so-called "common good." Laderman believes that people do not wish to deal with death. He makes death sound so untouchable that it requires trained professionals to do the job correctly. He holds staunchly to his idea of the correct handling of the "corpse" (his word) and indicates this is a job for trained industry professionals. He sees that the safe and sanitary care of the corpse is necessary and that the industry provides that need.

To many of us, it seems almost unthinkable: a fabricated industry arises, supplants natural death care, acquires a tenacious grasp, and legally protects itself, and this transformation slips by our personal and social awareness. Many people today consider it distasteful, "yucky," or morbid to deal with death. Death is considered to be the responsibility of the undertaker, the funeral home, the law, the coroner—but certainly not ours. *Why would anyone want or choose to deal with a dead person?*

Well, once upon a time . . .

Being laid out in the family parlor was an American tradition. It continued to be common practice in rural America well into the twentieth century. At some point, however, burial practices began to shift. From our country's earliest years and into the mid-nineteenth century, an emerging death industry began laying groundwork for today's modern burial practices and maneuvering for legal support.

Earlier in this country, death most often occurred in the home. The family cared for and sat vigil with an ailing family member. A loved one was tended until the very end. A person who died elsewhere might be carried home on a makeshift stretcher by neighbors, friends, or witnesses to the death.

To our pioneer forbearers, death was family centered and family directed. It was a simple, earthy event. A family member might fashion a plain pine box or engage a local cabinetmaker to build one for them. A collective of family and friends, likely organized by women, would gather to wash and dress the body, which was then laid out in a cool, unheated room, such as the parlor, where relatives, family, and friends could pay their respects and offer comfort to the living.

A formal or informal funeral service was often held in the home or nearby church. Family and neighbors (pallbearers) might carry the coffin on their shoulders to the final resting place, often walking through town to a churchyard or private family cemetery. A gathering of mourners might follow, creating a funeral procession through streets or open meadow.

The family men, friends, or a parish groundkeeper would likely have already dug a waiting grave. Variations on this scenario were determined by many factors, such as wealth, locale, religion, ethnicity, and resources. Vigils, wakes, wailings, church and home services, ceremonies, and rituals were part of the communal support system, bonding participating family and friends. Survivors certainly felt the impact of loss, yet death was an integrated aspect of community and family life.

This common practice, with variations according to local customs, changed over time. Yet it still lingered on for many years in our country. This practice could actually be characterized as the authentic and traditional "American way of death."

The growth of capital enterprise and an industrial impetus in American colonial life were significant factors in the initial and gradual change of funeral practices. An ever-expanding and aspiring middle class began to imitate the courtly, genteel conduct of those members of the British upper-middle class who had immigrated to the New World.

High-society customs and even manuals spelled out details of polite behavior, from table manners and daily business protocol to the proper display of good taste at funerals. Especially among the wealthy, coffins were handsomely made of fine hardwood and adorned with fancy hardware; a coffin should be an expensive and beautiful work of art, reflecting status and good taste.[17]

Coincidentally, by the mid-1850s, the advent of industrial mass production made the trappings of a "tasteful funeral" more affordable. The process used in the manufacturing of metal cookstoves provided another radical change that altered the simple coffin. The biodegradable pine box was no longer sufficient; a more expensive metal coffin was now deemed necessary. The six-sided coffin was trimmed and aligned into a rectangular box less suggestive of a dead body. The word *coffin*, considered déclassé, was replaced by *casket*, suggesting a precious object certainly more worthy of finer goods and services.[18]

The local carpenter-turned-casket-builder began evolving into a full-time professional undertaker. Over time, undertaking grew to include servicing a family with full-service funeral underpinnings—body care, carriage, hearse, grave digging, and coffin. The coffin might even be outsourced and produced by someone else, such as a metal fabricator or fine furniture maker. The undertaker and his full-service business was becoming a welcome convenience, one that was evolving into a sought commodity.

———

The catastrophic event of the Civil War played a role in transforming the aspiring undertaker into an indispensable "professional." By military tradition, the dead on both sides were buried where they fell, their bodies often covered only by their blanket or uniform. As the conflict took place mostly on Southern battlefields, the grief was compounded for Northern Union families, since distance made the fashionable "traditional" funeral impossible. Many Northerners were appalled by the thought of burial on "foreign soil." Relatives, friends, or even undertakers were sent to locate remains and ship them home. Laderman tells of bereft family members searching, often in vain, through piles of bodies, hardly identifiable, to find their loved ones.

---

17. Laderman, *The Sacred Remains*, 43, 45.
18. Ibid., 46.

Countless problems arose in transporting putrefying corpses. Even expensive caskets blew up from the gas buildup of decay inside airtight containers. Consequently, Northerners began to explore an ancient strategy of preserving bodies known as embalming. Up to this point, only anatomists had utilized this procedure on medical cadavers. Enterprising "Embalming Undertakers" learned the technique from the anatomists and set up morgue operations near battlefields.

In the later part of the war, thousands of slain soldiers were preserved with a liquid solution of arsenic, mercury, and other toxic chemicals for the purpose of giving them a decent funeral. A well-preserved, "natural-looking" body could impress family and onlookers. Newspapers and magazines were fascinated that undertakers added this newly created technology to their art. However, for many years, most Americans opposed the idea of embalming. Christians were particularly offended by what they considered a "Pagan" or "Egyptian" practice. Some even called for "Christian decency" to be returned to traditional funeral practice.[19]

It is noteworthy that ancient practices of body preservation and mummification utilized dehydration or blood draining and natural essential oils, minerals, and herbs—a natural process is markedly different from the toxic chemical soup of Civil War days or the even more toxic concoction used today.

In the nineteenth century, embalming was touted as being sanitary, scientific, and protective of public health. It became a feather in the cap of the new breed of undertakers who advertised that it could "restore the bloom of youth,"[20] adding a stature and an endorsement to the emerging trade. Even today this stance is touted as truth, although it has long been proven false (as we noted in the previous chapter) and, not to mention, abusive of the Earth.

The funeral of President Abraham Lincoln visibly brought the practice of embalming into the mainstream. Lincoln's embalmed body, laid out in a wooden coffin, was viewed by a million mourners in the White House, followed by thousands more on a funeral train to Illinois. His peaceful, "natural-looking" expression impressed viewers and demonstrated that viewing could occur long after a death occurred. Lincoln's pleasing countenance softened popular resis-

---

19. Laderman, *Rest in Peace,* 61–62.

20. Ibid., 28.

tance, and embalming thus secured itself a permanent place in American death customs.[21]

Laderman discusses other high-profile deaths in both of these books. He writes that public opinion and a fascination with the "corpse" was an indication of a loss of personal touch with death. He relates public preoccupation with the deaths of certain celebrities and prominent figures—such as Errol Flynn (millions filed past his elaborately displayed corpse and even vandalized his personal effects) and the tasteful (yet embalmed) state funeral of President John F. Kennedy. Although Kennedy's body was embalmed, it is notable that the president's brother Robert Kennedy had read Jessica Mitford's book and spoke of the importance of its influence.[22]

Not only did the Civil War sanction embalming, it also elevated the importance of the local undertaker, now "Undertaker" with a capital U. Obviously, a family could not embalm and preserve their loved one; it was now a surgical procedure requiring knowledge and skill that only the embalmer-undertaker possessed, along with the patented embalming fluids.

A third party was now required if a family wanted their loved one prepared for a "viewing." The undertaker was usurping the family as the primary agent related to death care and the full-time funeral "director" was born.

Initially, that undertaker would prepare the corpse in the family home or even in his own house. By the early twentieth century, the funeral "parlor"—a cozy replica of a family home—appeared, and death moved more permanently away from the family circle. The family sitting room, once referred to as the parlor, became the "living room," possibly making a distinction from a room associated with dying and a funeral *home*.

—

As we entered the current era of "modern" medicine, death happened less and less at home and more often in a hospital, becoming a medical procedure rather than a natural process. A higher prevalence of degenerative disease, along with violent causes of death like accidents and suicides, contributed to the necessity for medical and hospital intervention.

21. Laderman, *The Sacred Remains*, 157–63.

22. Ibid., 158–63.

Today, we have what could be referred to as "industrial dying." Hospital control and monitoring of the process of death has become commonplace. Pharmaceutical companies and hospitals control the dying process with modern surgical last-ditch efforts and ICU-cloistered rooms for the dying, and hospital morgues have all contributed to the process of erasing death from the home and from view, producing experiences like the one I had as a young nurse when I witnessed a patient being whisked quickly out of sight.

Another feature promoted by the death industry today is an emphasis on "pre-need" purchase of death plans and products. This practice has many complications and those considering it should be fully aware of traps they could unwittingly fall into. All too often, small-print loopholes conceal higher costs. For example, relatives of the deceased are not likely allowed to change plans or will pay extensively if they do, no reimbursement is possible if a family moves or changes the way they want to handle death care, and so on.

I wish to sway any inclination to consider so called "pre-need" contracts. Pre-need sales have too many hitches in them. Carefully crafted clauses cover the industry and not persons whose circumstances may change due to a physical move out of state or the area, a different emotional perspective, or any variety of changes. Pre-need purchasers are likely to be locked into arrangements of the pre-need contract that do not allow for any change or release from the contract. It can be a devastating situation. It is valuable to discuss and plan ahead, though not to pay ahead! *"Pre-need Sales—It's not 'all taken care of.'"* And, *"It Always Pays to Plan Ahead; It Rarely Pays to Pay Ahead."*[23]

―――――

Death has become effectively separated from ordinary everyday life, while the idea that life should be sustained and extended no matter what is prevalent. Dying is seen as a defeat instead of the natural culmination and eventuality of life. These ideas contrast a healthful, natural view toward increasing longevity.

Today, I hear of more families who are calling into question the practice of "disappearing" their loved ones. They are asking for time to *be* with the process. Some, with the blessing of sympathetic hospital staff, are creating rituals and celebrations of life right there in the hospital room. Some even carry their loved

―――――――――――――――――――――

23. Slocum and Carlson, *Final Rights*, 80–112.

ones home to create a home funeral. Hospice programs, sponsored by hospitals, are also gaining acclaim and becoming more easily available to family homes.

As noted in chapter 4, education about the process is the key to a healthier relationship with death and its aftermath. Often an exposure to natural death care concepts and experiences expands understanding, and people are grateful for a new perspective. Like in the deputy coroner who allowed the body of my sons' father to be handled by the family, reorientation and transformation is occurring.

As part of a "Reclaiming Movement," today's baby boomers, hippie minimalists, politically astute activists, young yuppies, and even many of the upwardly mobile population are becoming more aware, informed, and interested in a DIY approach to death. This underlines the importance of education, fostering a more natural approach and declaring the rights of people to care for their own dead in the context of community.

——

Today, whether your participation is as simple as rethinking what personal path you choose, being involved in life-sustaining choices with others, being on an industry "watch" to call into question inappropriate legislation, becoming more educated and assisting in public education, doing your own home funeral for a family member, informing your family of your wishes in regard to your death, or becoming a home funeral educator or guide—*you have a part to play.*

Find and connect with supportive constituents—counselors, hospice workers, hospital chaplains, close friends, and neighbors. Share your views, entertain conversation and debate, organize Death Cafés, form a study group, assist an existing organization that distributes copies of Advanced Care Directives and the Five Wishes, attend an introductory lecture of one of the organizations advocating death awareness, or take a course from one of the home funeral training programs available. The documents referenced are the names of California's legal documents. If you reside in another state, find out what laws apply to death care and what documents are called for in your state.

Discover your path; tune in to your heart as you explore your inner and outer worlds. Our collective experience, orientation, and activism can call us as a society to create new ways from old experiences or ways of thinking. Remember, history is not static. Public opinion is always shifting. We are active players in the unfolding story—of loss, gain, renewal, and reclaiming.

I believe there is room for many ways to support and protect all constituents. There is room for funeral homes that provide sustainable options for families who desire support in the care of their deceased family member. There is room for home funerals that are carried out by family and friends. And there is room for the home funeral guides who are able to educate, support, and assist families to do what they are allowed to do legally, helping them find ease in carrying out the process.

It is about returning to our own core values, rather than reacting to or succumbing to a corporate money-focused mindset. It is essential that we allow the corporate death industry its own natural death. It does not need to be our primary focus of resistance. *We are called to attention as we reclaim our innate right and heritage in new ways that are born out of our commitment to living naturally and sustainably on this Earth.*

Paradoxically, nothing is ever lost. Awareness is shifting away from corporate handling of our lives. The corporate mentality has attracted many watchdogs. There are many people organizing efforts to reclaim hands-on expression in their lives from birthing practices, growing food, educating our children, caring for elders, and directing the customs and actions surrounding death.

Sustainable, Earth-centered spiritual practices and interests are fostering this trend. We are part of a living history—a story of a people who are evolving and maturing. We can move toward the implementation of sustainability. We are the living legacy of our ancestors as we provide for the health of future generations. Thus, as we find ways that allow us to see how we got here, expand our awareness, and relate to life's challenges and death's connection, we will, as a culture, nurture and support more sustainable death care options as they evolve.

CHAPTER 6
INNATE VERSUS THE LEGISLATED

*We are questioning the validity of the most basic
assumptions that underpin the contemporary funeral business:
the notion that money spent equals love shown.*
—*Josh Slocum, Preface to Final Rights*

As already discussed, the turning point in how we relate to death culturally has changed over time. To capsulize thus far: An industry took shape and grew as a response to significant events such as the industrialization of our society and the tactical engineering of a budding industry. It developed in the context of an emerging cultural shift toward legalization and homogenization. This occurred in the absence of an attentive consciousness of people and a society that overlooked the larger picture. Perhaps it was veiled by convenience, genuine need, laziness and/or good intentions. Various factors such as the industry's intention to take control of the funeral business or society's blindness to what was being lost had consequences that weren't necessarily beneficial for society as a whole. An unaware populace can be seen as a connecting thread in the takeover that runs unstopped alongside an industry where the bottom line is a primary guiding force, absent of a moral obligation. Is there another way?

If meaningful dialogue and conversation are to take place, we must establish and support mutual respect and not create battlegrounds of conflicting partisans. A valid reclamation of energy, grounded in respect, can assist and motivate us to create and establish more natural modes of dealing with death in sustainable ways as we navigate the territory and build coalitions to interact with the legislative process.

We are all cocreators of the way we, in this country, approach death and accept the industry's hold on death care, even as we are seekers for a more natural and sustainable way of relating with death. As we live respectfully and recognize the intrinsic value in our diversity, we are benefited by our melting-pot populace that enriches our collective experience of death and death care with a breadth of cultural variations.

An innate or inherent right versus a legislated right is a legitimate point of debate. Has an attempt to deny natural rights occurred, resulting in obliterating ancient truths? What is our most cooperative stance?

Our collective mindset with a confluent mixture of belief and tradition has resulted in a watered-down approach to many ethnic and religious traditions. We wholeheartedly embrace scientific achievements, yet often without regard to values and morals. Businesses have taken advantage of this fluid context and commandeered a corner in the death industry. Over time, business models have taken precedence over older traditions and natural ecological considerations. The ground of this conflict is the funeral industry itself and our own psyches. It has become a moral issue of our time, requiring both an external and internal process.

The funeral industry does not meet the desires of a growing number of people who prefer to choose more natural and sustainable modes of handling death care. Finding acceptable ways to coexist alongside the funeral industry— which represents only one option—is a significant point of departure in an ongoing conversation.

As someone who proposes natural death care, I believe we facilitate the process by focusing on caring for our own dead, thereby affecting a change in consciousness that radiates out from our actions. The "hundredth monkey theory" reminds us that we are moving toward that edge. There are indications of authentic changes being made among people who own and run independent funeral businesses. They offer fair services. They accommodate home funerals with reduced pricing and are open to liaison relationships with people who help families.

It is essential to examine where the internal issues, questions, and conflicts reside in us. How have we incorporated the idea that death is to be feared, denied, and avoided? If we are to be effective agents of personal, social, and cultural change, self-examination is critical before confronting a corporate mentality in an industry that is protected by legislative mandate. We are *the face in the mirror.*

Seeing how death care and the funeral industry mindset affect society is not an issue only for health educators, sociologists, ministers, home funeral guides, activists, and ecologists. We all are needed as watchful observers and activists. A valuable place to explore inquiry is in public talks, seminars, and trainings. Out of an informed, knowledgeable, and experienced base, effective changes and legislative action can emerge.

———

Who legislates? Is it the actual legislators who are sworn to protect and represent their constituents and advocate for their concerns? Or is it the industry and its lobbyists who manipulate, threaten, coerce, and pressure legislators with financial support to acquire their goals? Big conglomerates wield tremendous pressure and prestige to manipulate and maintain legal protection. Understanding history, current practices, and existing legislation is helpful to put issues in context and perspective.

In our society, businesses must attend to their bottom line in order to succeed. The funeral industry is no exception. Yet a bottom-line mentality can easily become the primary guiding principal at the expense of the environment and individual choice, elevating stabilizing economic interests above other concerns. Mission statements may promote and appeal to higher values yet hide more dominating actions. A conflict shows up when corporate industry sees its position as indispensable and exerts efforts to position legal protection and eliminate other options. A rose garden façade (metaphorically and literally, as actual rose gardens frequently grace entrances to funeral homes) distracts the intent and quells fears that result in acquiescing to what is mistakenly seen as the only legal choice available.

I am not here to berate wonderful people I know and respect who own funeral businesses. There are many who, like medical doctors, entered the profession out of caring and interest in people and pursue right livelihood. Criticisms are directed at an amorphous corporate entity concept that overtakes and dominates the legitimate place of local funeral homes that *are there* to assist families who *choose* to utilize their services. (This is a pointed reference to the constitutional amendment known as Citizens United that gave corporations the same right to free speech rights as citizens, essentially establishing personhood for corporations. Refer to the MoveOn movement, which seeks to overturn that constitutional law.)

Questions arise in regard to right grassroots activism. It is incumbent to explore creative and healing ways to face and deal with the overall issue. After all, it is our own historical and current processes that are the challenge. How shall *we* deal with death care, the industry, and the legislative process and issues? How do *we* delineate and frame the issues in such a way that real discussion can occur both in intimate groups and in public discourse?

True, our inherent and innate right to care for our own dead is unfairly obscured by a protected funeral industry. Yet, also significant is that just as an innate right exists, *there is also appropriate action to take in order to maintain that right.* Our task is to traverse this ground without malice to discover where conflict is present before reasonably challenging the industry and legislation. Meanwhile, it is incumbent to act in accordance with the laws and mandates of our state to care for our dead. We lose our rights if we lose sight of what we can do.

Restoring Families' Right to Choose is an excellent booklet published by the Funeral Consumers Alliance (FCA) and the National Home Funeral Alliance (NHFA). In keeping with what I propose, this booklet emphasizes how important choice of death care options is for any family and the essential need for legislative change. It is available for a nominal cost and can be ordered from the NHFA website.[24]

Reflect on your feelings and desires in regard to your death, educate yourself as to what you can do in your state, fill out legal documents that establish and define your wishes, and share your views with your family, friends, and community. If you have an inclination to be a conduit for change, get training as a home funeral guide, join with others to form a legislative watch, and decide how you wish to relate to others in your local community as an active home funeral guide, an activist, a speaker, or a lobbyist. *The world is our oyster. Our pearl is in reclaiming the truth of what is an innate, inherent right, and in speaking out on behalf of that awareness.*

---

24. https://www.homefuneralalliance.org/home-funeral-books.html.

It is up to us to see conflicts in a creative way at local, individual, and community venues. This work is intended to support understanding of what is, to align our efforts with the inroads we can make, and to support personal and collective choices. I suggest that that is our mission.

What follows are two working lists of ideas and concepts: food for thought. Some notations reiterate concepts previously discussed. The first list below focuses on truths we have touched upon that support natural death care.

We Hold These Truths

- *It is okay—not "yucky"—to care for our own dead.* Granted, we have much to overcome. Some cultures, especially those with a distinct caste system, see those who care for the dead as lacking dignity, lowly, despicable, and unclean. It is time to clean up our own concepts.

- *It is valuable and supportive to take care of a loved one after their passage.* Remember the scene in the movie *Gandhi* where Gandhi admonishes his wife for complaining that it's beneath her dignity to clean the latrines? Gandhi delivers a message: there is no unclean task. In contrast, many of us who align with reclaiming energy find and feel it is a privilege and an honor to participate in natural death care.

- *One can find acceptance in the process of grief's healing.* The Japanese film *Departures*, directed by Yōjirō Takita, expresses a transformative capacity in a unique and exquisitely detailed telling of a man who at first feels ashamed of his profession and then finds healing, recognition, and acceptance in the beauty of caring for the dead.

- *It is not too difficult or cumbersome for a family to accomplish caring for the dead.* See the PBS film *A Family Undertaking*, directed by Elizabeth Westrate, to see a few examples of families who undertook the process, and reflect on the ideas presented. It is easier and more natural than one might imagine!

- *Some knowledge and assistance is helpful.* This is especially true given how much we, as a society, have forgotten. It is essential to know your state laws and local protocols. Learn the availability of local and national support and education. To lessen the oppositional stance, learn how to accomplish a home funeral by availing yourself of training and reading.

Know what you want and/or what a loved one wants. Become familiar with the necessary documents.

- *There are available references and home funeral guides to bridge the gap in your knowledge and ability to manage caring for a deceased family member.* Such references are given throughout this work and on the websites of Final Passages, FCA, and the NHFA.

- *Written resource guides are available that describe how to do a home funeral.* When a death is anticipated and planned for, available resources facilitate a family successfully doing it all on their own. This is the primary cornerstone of this book. The Bibliography is also helpful.

This second list focuses on actions to consider if you are interested in pursuing natural death care. They are offered as summaries and support our discussions thus far:

Possible Actions

- *Take advantage of all local support*: medical, hospice, home funeral guides, and local record departments. If an unexpected or unplanned death occurs, the presence of supportive people—trained, familiar, and comfortable with the process of natural death care in the home—can help a family create a worthwhile and beneficial experience.

- *Seek home funeral guides.* Persons familiar with local laws who know how to deal with the required documentation and how to assist families with natural death care can help a family with home funerals if they are allowed in the state of residence. Find a guide to help. Home funeral guides are grounded in a heartfelt intention and tradition. (Please note that home funeral guides and death midwives are not funeral directors. They are educators and offer hands-on educational and technical support for a family to orchestrate their own home funeral. They generally work on a donation basis or may charge a nominal fee to cover expenses and time spent.) Home funeral guides support utilizing a funeral home, cemetery, or crematorium as needed. They are familiar with services that a funeral home, cemetery, or crematorium offer and know which ones are willing to work with families who choose a home funeral. The point is that the family is on *their time* rather than *mortuary time*.

- *Establish a legislative watch with other concerned persons.* If you wish to take on an active social-political stance, there are areas of concern where participation is needed. A legislative watch's discovery could be significant if a funeral business or an association is lobbying for legislation to limit legal family participation in natural death care. Refer to *Final Rights* for examples of other issues and problems to watch for in your state.

- *Take advantage of local trainings.* Support local and national education in death care choices and support organizations that offer such programs.

- *Be a member of and support the Funeral Consumer's Alliance*, a nonprofit organization dedicated to protecting funeral consumers' rights nationwide through education and advocacy. They support avoiding cultural and commercial pressures to conform to a "new normal" with the funeral industry in a transaction that many are hard-pressed to afford.

- *Be a member of and support the National Home Funeral Alliance.* This is a coalition of home funeral guides, organizations that educate others about natural death, and anyone interested in natural death care. *Restoring Families' Right to Choose*, a booklet available on their website, includes a section called "What to Do When Families' Rights are Challenged" with more ideas of actions to take.

- *Write articles, speak out, fill out your Advanced Care Directive and/or the Five Wishes document, and plan your own home funeral!* Let your family and friends know your wishes! The names of your state documents may be different from these California documents. Find out from your local vital records department what your state documents, statutes, and requirements are.

- *See the film* A Family Undertaking *and start a support group.*

- *Create a discussion group, Death Café, or study group.* Develop a list of perspectives about death, questions and concerns about death, and ways to explore feelings about death together (e.g., books to read, speakers to engage, and debates to arrange).

- *Start a death book club.* Read and discuss books on death and death experiences.

- *Call your county Office of Vital Records.* Introduce yourself and ask how they assist or work with families who choose to take care of their own dead.

Let them know you are interested in their services with regard to your own family.

———

We are a fledgling movement, community, and consciousness, coming of age as we build skills, resources, and alliances to meet the need for home funeral education and service.

We are awakening. We call ourselves and each other to question, read, study, and act. We are reclaiming our relationship to death. We are renewing the ancient and timeless tradition of caring for our dead. We will learn what we need to know and help each other along the way. Our movement is a rediscovery and reclaiming of what has been our right all along.

Legislation may have obscured and undermined the truth, yet truth remains. Appropriate legislation and regulation can and will follow our acts of courage and love. We will speak out and discover how to work within existing laws and how to effect changes needed to reclaim our innate and inherent rights. We will continue to be deeply affected by the deaths of our loved ones as we deal with our grief. This is an authentic and genuine stance for which there is no apology.

Finally, it is not a contest between innate rights and legislative ones related to death and death care (or any issue for that matter). Innate rights are *a priori*. Knowing the truth personally and collectively is important. It is essential for the truth of innate rights to be acknowledged and supported with appropriate legal endorsement. This is the goal of reclaiming and calls for our voice and action in a reeducating process that will benefit all beings.

CHAPTER 7
TRAILBLAZERS & FOLLOWERS

She who binds herself to a joy, Doth the winged life destroy;
But she who kisses the joy as it flies, Lives in eternity's sunrise.
—*William Blake*

The way death is handled in this culture leaves many feeling mystified and disoriented. It seems to accentuate and prolong grief's hold rather than allow death's natural and essential place in our life process. Often this handling of death leaves a person feeling empty and perplexed at the lack of meaning and floundering for relief. If you find this is true for you as well, I assure you, you are not alone!

Perhaps you are among those who have observed death handled in ways you deem bizarre, dehumanizing, strangely fabricated, sterile, and unfeeling. You may have felt hopeless about finding more comfortable and natural ways of handling death. A strong intuitive sense may echo within that *there is another way*. Still, you wonder where to find support and direction.

Where do we turn for help?

———

Imagine that you are a trailblazer, cutting through tangled brush, not knowing how to reach a destination, cut by brambles as you struggle your way along. You know you must get through this entanglement. You keep going, even as tears flow down your face and spontaneous cries utter forth from deep in your gut. Bleeding and scarred, you finally emerge in a clearing. The sky opens up. The elation you feel is tempered by the difficult experience of grief you still carry. Yet you are empowered and know that you have successfully traversed and blazed a path through. You have an invaluable story to tell. You know that others can also follow this trail as their own, even as it may need continual blazing and maintenance.

———

Fortunately, there are death-awareness trailblazers from whom we can benefit. Their hard-won success did not happen easily. They blazed inroads that we all may benefit from—in their writings, films, art, and more. Herein are stories of just a few of our modern trailblazers who have altered the current resurgence and confront the corporate death care mindset. Their trailblazing created paths with new choices, broader knowledge, greater proficiency, more support, and better understanding to help us reclaim our natural innate cultural diversity and freedom in the care of our dead.

Flagship efforts of these modern trailblazers supported those who wished to act independently of the funeral industry. Subsequent years led some to combine efforts with others to promote hands-on death care and funeral experiences in the home. Organizations developed educational programs and trainings. The enhanced awareness and knowledge spurred on those who had a more gentle death experience to help others with natural death care. People became more aware of what was possible. The number of those caring for our dead in sensible, sustainable, Earth-loving ways that honor people and the process of natural death care keeps growing.

These trailblazers disseminate information and educate about natural death care rights. They take a stand in their communities. They provide trainings, presentations, books, and films. Today, numerous people have studied with these trailblazers. Their journey is an extension of paths previously blazed, and inroads to support natural death care continue to develop. The path widens, becomes more visible, attracts more followers and trailblazers, and gains attention, even in the face of some in the death industry who may wish we were not around.

———

Jerrigrace Lyons is one of the early trailblazers and my personal mentor. Her journey began when a dear friend died, leaving clear instructions that her friends, rather than a mortuary, would handle her body. At that time, her friends had no idea something like that could be done. Neither did they imagine being bold enough to do what their friend wanted. Yet that is the beginning of Jerrigrace's story. Now, Jerrigrace's story has been told countless times and can be found in newspaper and magazine articles and in broadcast interview archives. It is told most intimately in her trainings that now span more than twenty-five years. Her experience came to fruition—from her early hesitation and wondering, to action, and finally to accepting the work of helping others along the path of natural death care. Initially, her work went by the name of The Natural Death Care Project. Now, it is widely known and acclaimed in the organization she founded, which is officially known as Final Passages Institute of Conscious Dying, Home Funeral and Green Burial Education. Final Passages is established as a nonprofit educational organization.

Supported by a board of directors and numerous volunteers, Final Passages offers many avenues to learn about natural death care. Three levels of training are offered throughout the year. These trainings primarily take place in Sonoma County, California. Yet Jerrigrace and her husband, Mark, travel the world to bring trainings to supportive communities. Locally there are community events, one-day seminars, speaking engagements, and movie nights that celebrate the "miracle of death," as is stated on the Final Passages brochure.

The Final Passages trainings offer directions to help a family handle all the legal aspects—including the paperwork for death certificates and disposition permits—of hands-on death care. This full range of legal education offers a family the option for a thorough sense of autonomy. It allows them to be more in charge of their entire home funeral. It results in families being able to make their choice for the final committal and arrange for a burial site or cremation as they so determine (and on their time rather than on mortuary time). Arrangements are made when they are ready. It is empowering and rewarding, as a family is fully independent of a corporate business. A home funeral guide who develops this skilled proficiency is able to assist client-families with the paperwork. The legalities of death care are vital to learn and teach, enabling a family to navigate the entire process if they so choose. I concur with how empowering and worthwhile it is to assist a family with this part, even though it is tedious, exacting, and initially intimidating.

Home and Family Funerals is the private practice of Jerrigrace Lyons through which she is available as a home funeral guide. In that capacity, she has educated and helped hundreds of families carry out their own home funerals. It is a separate business practice from Final Passages, which is the nonprofit educational organization founded to educate and train others to do similar work.

Another one of the early trailblazers is Beth Knox, who found herself in a unique position where her heart guided her to take the helm of a home funeral. The story of how Beth came to this work is a poignant tale of her daughter's sudden death and Beth's courage and audacity to do whatever she could to bring her daughter home from the hospital and create a home funeral. She was determined that it was to be her, and not a stranger, who cared for the body of her daughter, just as she had cared for her throughout her life.

Soon after that experience, Beth felt guided to share her knowledge and to enable others to care for loved ones at home. Her friends who shared a kinship with the anthroposophical philosophy offered their support and guidance. She established an organization called Crossings. Beth is another outstanding active home funeral guide, educator, and advocate for home funerals. Mark Harris shares more details of Beth's story in his book, *Grave Matters*.[25]

Numerous critics of the funeral industry have made their mark. Karen Leonard was an early activist who knew and worked with Jessica Mitford and helped in the revised edition of Mitford's book. Leonard also authored the book *Chasing Coffins*. She and Mitford helped form and organize funeral societies that provided information and consulted with funeral consumers to assist in getting fair pricing of mortuary services. Lisa Carlson, author of *Caring for the Dead*, is currently executive director of the Funeral Ethics Organization (FEO), which protects ethical practices in the funeral industry. Starhawk and Macha Nightmare coauthored *The Pagan Book of Living and Dying*. Starhawk is best known as an eco-activist and author of numerous books. One of the earliest ones, *The Spiral Dance*, brought initial acclaim. Her many other contributions are mentioned throughout this book.

Some trailblazers, perhaps greatly influenced by the anthroposophical philosophy heralded by Rudolph Steiner, sat with the dying and their families, essentially helping the survivors experience a gentle home ritual. Nancy Jewel Poer, Heidi Boucher, and the late Tamara Slayton were among those

---

25. Harris, *Grave Matters*, 105–108.

connected with this philosophy and movement. Heidi Boucher, an early film-maker, produced the film *In the Parlor*. The film portrays three families who choose a home funeral.

Selena Fox is the founder of Circle Sanctuary, a nonprofit nature spirituality church and nature preserve. She and the late Nora Cedarwing Young, activists within the community, dedicated a twenty-acre green cemetery as part of the community preserve.

Char Barrett, Lee Webster, Karen van Vuuren, Donna Belk, Jerrigrace Lyons, and Olivia Bareham were among the first to promote eco-conscious home funeral education and celebratory gatherings honoring the dead in a natural fashion.

A couple of early trailblazers in the early stages of organizing their work participated in the PBS documentary film *A Family Undertaking* (available on Netflix). The film features a few families doing their own home funerals. Seeing the film can spark a conversation to further explore one's feelings about death.

Intuition and personal experiences connect me to this work and led me to enroll in Final Passages training. For this reason, I include myself here as a "follower-trailblazer." I offer services as a home funeral advocate and guide. For the past fifteen years, this work has nourished, challenged, and fulfilled my life in numerous ways.

If you wish to follow others on this path, do your due diligence. It is important to get in touch with others, find out what is required in your state, explore your vital records departments, and make connections with others to discuss death in a death café or in home study groups. You then might be motivated to get in touch with one of those trailblazers and enroll in an educational program. You could become another trailblazer!

———

A new millennium, riding on the lyrics of the "Age of Aquarius," was dawning. A number of these trailblazers realized it was time for advocates of home funerals and people with supportive connections to champion the work by forming an association. Conversations across the continent began to take place. In 2009, Karen van Vuuren, Beth Knox, Jerrigrace Lyons, Char Barrett, and several others gathered in Colorado with an intention of joining forces. They made a commitment to keep in touch with each other through email, conference calls, and occasional in-person meetings. A leadership team emerged. The first meeting of the National Home Funeral Alliance was held in 2011, leading to a nonprofit organization whose mission is to educate the public regarding their choices and provide clear information about home funerals.

Many outstanding trailblazers participated in this effort. Today there is a strong association with regular annual conferences, supportive publications, and a volunteer staff. Members consider themselves part of what Jerrigrace lovingly calls "death-groupies." I continue to be a supportive part of the efforts as a sideline grandstand cheerleader. It is time for our mutual efforts to ripple out and provide for others.

Visit the National Home Funeral Alliance homepage, homefuneralalliance .org, and explore for yourself. You will find a wealth of information, including their history, current events, resources for families and home funeral guides, and directories of home funeral guides and others involved in the movement. Supportive membership is free.

The Funeral Consumer Alliance (FCA), another relevant organization, is a national consumer protection watchdog that has been around for decades. In that capacity, the FCA has been involved in monitoring the funeral industry for many years. They monitor trends and advocate for fair practices. They advocate for regulations of the funeral industry at local, state, and national levels. With chapters in most states, they assist groups to form local chapters. Their initial impetus was to ensure itemized pricing of services offered and support fair pricing in funeral establishments. Their support and advocacy continues in multitudinous ways. More information on how to become a member can be found on their websites, funerals.org and FuneralConsumersAlliance.org.

———

An example of how this movement has extended beyond our continental boundaries is found in the story of a trailblazing death guide from Australia who calls herself a "deathwalker." I discovered Zenith Viagro's story during an internet wandering. Utterly impressed, I was drawn to her compassionate and eloquent presence. A wishful fantasy took me across the waters to one of her trainings.

On her website, she explains two aspects of a deathwalker.[26] One is a person who walks their own journey toward their death as openly and courageously as they can. The other is a person who walks with someone else on their death journey, offering guidance and care to inform, empower, and enable them to be as open and courageous as they can be. She notes that in the second instance, a person's death journey inclusively refers to the dying person, family, and friends. Particularly meaningful to me was Zenith Viagro's statement, "We have a birthright and we have a death right. It is our birthright to die, because if you are never born, you can never die. With that, if you are lucky, you get a full journey in between..."[27]

These trailblazers and the supportive organizations that foster natural death care are part of reclaiming actual "traditional" ways of death care as they educate and train others. Just as Jessica Mitford sounded the alarm with her seminal efforts, it is our task to continue efforts by blazing new trails of awareness and intentional practices that reflect sustainable, natural death care, support choices, and respect all beings. A miffed funeral industry's reactive alarm to Mitford becomes past history as we intentionally and respectfully blaze on. We are entering an exciting era of reclaiming what has belonged to us all along.

The diverse cultural expressions and traditions that reach back in time are honored in this movement. Our Indigenous relations are respected teachers and are very needed today. Honoring ancient, Indigenous worldviews and rituals that thread throughout humankind's story is not a "going backward." It is a *re-turning* to what is natural. We turn and re-turn again, witnessing in order to observe, discover, forge, and enact renewed pathways in the "Great Reclaiming Era" of our time.

———

We are indebted to those who blazed the trail of remembering to touch, to feel, and to know intimately death's ever-presence in life. The phrase stated on Final Passages literature about life, including the "miracle of death," conjures a mystical sense of awareness. That realization is key to what motivated many who blazed the trail of reclaiming death's natural and elevated place in life. We

---

26. Naturaldeathcarecentre.org.

27. https://vimeo.com /90256161.

benefit also from further scientific information, a sustainable perspective, and sanitation principles that are essential in our care of the Earth.

This is a worldwide movement. We are connected beyond the scope of our physical vision or geographical boundaries. *We speak of death and death's relevance in our lives.* Now, follow your heart and follow along with an essential mandate. Be prepared for your own amazing journey!

Yes, death is a birthright! *We get to die*—it is one of the privileges of this life. Strangely, this contrasts with today's ordinary life-dulling understanding. Yet, perhaps we allude to an inner sense of this idea when we say a person is "going home," even as we grieve their absence.

SECTION THREE
PRACTICAL GROUND

CHAPTER 8

WHAT IS A HOME FUNERAL
& WHAT IS A HOME FUNERAL GUIDE?

Honest listening is one of the best medicines
we can offer the dying and the bereaved.
—Jean Cameron

A home funeral is just that—a *home funeral!* It is a funeral at home, determined by the people of the home, carried out in the context of a home. The definition is in the name.

A home funeral is a *circle*. It is a circle of family, friends, and love. It is a circle of awareness with the intention of attending to the bodily, emotional, physical, and legal actions needed when a member of the circle passes into the Mystery. The family circle is the entity legally allowed to carry out a home funeral. It may be an open or a closed family group. There may be clarity and ease or conflict and difficulty. The people who make up the circle may be familiar with, and able to carry out, a home funeral, or they may need help knowing what they can and cannot do and *how to take necessary steps.* These issues are essential considerations as how they are mitigated determines the viability of carrying out a home funeral.

Legal Framework

Most often today, it is a mortuary or funeral establishment that handles death care. Such businesses are often cleverly referred to as a "funeral home." A majority of funeral "homes" showcase themselves as the only viable death care option. Yet there is a legal framework for home death care. Legal status for family death care is protected by most states in this country. This is not widely known. However, there are eight states that partially restrict a family's rights to carry out home funerals. They are Connecticut, Illinois, Indiana, Louisiana, New York, Michigan, Nebraska, and New Jersey.[28]

Legally, a home funeral is a family-directed event in which the body of a loved one is cared for in the context of the family, generally in the home of the deceased or in a suitable home setting. It is not a requirement, however, for someone to have passed in the home for a home funeral to take place. A person who is a patient in a hospital or dies in another facility may be taken home after death. An accident victim may in certain circumstances be picked up from the coroner's office.

California's Cemetery and Funeral Bureau pamphlet "Consumer Guide to Funeral & Cemetery Purchases" is available on the state website and given out by funeral homes. Home death care is described as follows:

HOME DEATH CARE

The use of a funeral establishment and funeral director is not required by law when preparing a body for disposition. You can arrange for your body, or that of a loved one, to be cared for, and prepared for disposition, by family and friends at home. If you choose home death care, you must:

- File a properly completed Certificate of Death, signed by the attending physician or coroner, with the local registrar of births and deaths.

- Obtain a Permit for Disposition from the local registrar of births and deaths.

- Provide a casket or other suitable container.

- Make arrangements directly with the cemetery or crematory.

Your local county health department may be able to help you file a Certificate of Death and / or a Permit for Disposition.

(NOTE: Human remains may be kept at home without embalming or refrigeration until disposition. Generally, decom-

---

28. Slocum and Carlson, *Final Rights*, 18–19.

position will proceed more rapidly without refrigeration or embalming.)[29]

A previous edition, however, was worded very differently. I wish to make a comparison between these two editions of the "Consumer Guide to Funeral & Cemetery Purchases" in order to show an example of how watchdog attention and action resulted in change. The previous 2010 edition's wording created a red flag for some that needed addressing. In the 2010 edition, the wording in the pamphlet read as follows:

> The law does not prohibit consumers from preparing a body for disposition themselves. If you choose to do this, you must:
>
> - File a properly completed Certificate of Death, signed by the attending physician or coroner with the local registrar of births and deaths.
>
> - Obtain a Permit for Disposition from the local registrar of births and deaths.
>
> - Provide a casket or suitable container.
>
> - Make arrangements directly with the cemetery or crematory.
>
> (NOTE: Human remains may be kept at home until disposition without embalming or refrigeration. Generally, decomposition will proceed more rapidly without refrigeration or embalming.)[30]

Notice that the statement in part says, *"does not prohibit"* (italics are mine). This rather curious wording seems condescending and could be a deliberate effort to *not empower* a family to do a home funeral. A number of home funeral advocates noticed this wording, saw it as inappropriate, and discussed together what could be done to have the wording changed. What transpired is an inspiring example of how their attentiveness turned to action and effected change.

---

29. State of California Department of Consumer Affairs, "Consumer Guide to Funeral & Cemetery Purchases," revised June 2013, www.CFB.CA.gov.

30. Ibid.

A group of Sonoma County home funeral advocates, led by Jerrigrace Lyons of Final Passages Institute, went to Sacramento to address staff at the Department of Consumer Affairs. They explained that they saw the wording in the 2010 Cemetery and Funeral Bureau pamphlet as misleading and advocated a revision. They were heard, and officials agreed to change the wording, resulting in an improved 2013 edition.

While the parenthetical note regarding refrigeration is slightly different in the 2013 edition, many home funeral advocates would like to see further changes as it could be more supportive of home funeral families doing an extended vigil. A proposed alteration of that notation might be as follows:

(NOTE: Human remains kept at home with the use of dry ice will freeze the body torso sufficiently—colder than morgue refrigeration—for an extended home wake. In many traditions, the average time for a wake is three to five days. The weather, size of the body, and ambient temperature of the home are additional factors to take into account when utilizing and resupplying dry ice as needed.)

The 2013 parenthetical notation about decomposition sounds rather ghastly, contains an unnecessary opinion regarding preservation of the body, and offers no help or suggestions about how to preserve a body in the home. While the proposed note above correctly states that the human remains may be kept at home, it also contains simple information regarding body preservation and gives a helpful suggestion for a family.

Grassroots organizing may not always be immediately successful. However, it is essential to notice areas of concern, discuss our observations, and make grievances known to responsible agencies and advocacy groups. We can make a difference!

―――――

With more understanding about the legality of home funerals, we return to the definitions of home funerals and legalities for more detail. A home funeral is a family-directed event where the body of a loved one is prepared for its final rest in the context of family and friends. In a unique way, it is reflective of that family/friend group, as well as the person who has passed on. It is accomplished within the legal parameters allowed for in the state and county of residence.

The intention of the home funeral scenarios shared in earlier chapters was to illustrate feelings one might experience of awareness, tenderness, poignant sorrow, compassion, tumultuous angst, and a range of emotions, along with connections of spirit presence. A home funeral is all that and more!

Often I've witnessed a dreary space become an exquisite vigil room and an altar that honors and reflects the life and energy of a beloved person. A family's request for a home funeral guide may involve little or extensive participation. A family may only need help in a ritual bath and dressing a loved one or in the paperwork. They may want companionship throughout all the process or a limited consultation. It is up to the family to play the role of "funeral director." That is the legal term and status designation in California, for example. The point is that *it is the family who makes decisions* about what and how much they want in regard to their home funeral. That is the legal allowance made to a family: a designated person is technically the "funeral director" and the responsible party.

If the next of kin is too far away to handle affairs in person, another family member or a community of friends may provide the rallying energy for handling a home funeral. The legally responsible person can designate a proxy to act on their behalf. It can be another family member, a friend, or even a home funeral guide. In this case, a temporary/provisional Power of Attorney (POA) document would be drawn up and filed with the vital records department when the death certificate is executed. In lieu of enacting a POA, it is difficult for another person or community to carry out the function of a home funeral. In this case, the family may need to hire a mortuary. An exception to the next of kin requirement would be if, prior to death, a person designates someone different than their next of kin as their legal agent. This must be in a legal document, such as an Advanced Care Directive, a will, or a Living Trust. It is important for there to be legal documentation that specifically names the person legally responsible and provides written instructions through a temporary/provisional POA document or as listed on the Advanced Care Directive.

Attention—words to the wise for all of us! *Protecting the option to carry out a home funeral is essential!* As home funeral *advocates*, our mission is to protect and preserve this ancient right and our personal rites that are still relevant today! That is why being acquainted with and adhering to your state and county regulations is so important. Accepting what is allows us room to advocate for the changes we consider important within the regulatory structure.

Home Funerals

When speaking of the family as a circle, I am referring ideally to a nonhierarchical body that shares common ground. Congruency supports the ability to discuss different views, beliefs, and ideas with respect for all members of the circle. I am a strong advocate of "circle-ing" as a method of sharing, discussing, and decision-making. On an elder quest some years ago, I became acquainted with Christina Baldwin. In her book *Calling the Circle*, Christina offers an excellent and helpful discussion of the circle as a nonhierarchical entity and contrasts it to an authoritarian entity.

What if the family wants to do a home funeral yet is dominated by an authoritarian energy? If family members acquiesce to a titular head that chooses a home funeral and all give agreement to that person, it can work. If there is considerable conflict and discord, it is less likely to be a reasonable undertaking. Particularly if the declared "next of kin" is authoritarian and against doing a home funeral, it is even less likely to be possible. ("Next of kin" refers to a person's closest living blood relative[s]. The order of legal responsibility for a medical emergency, death care issues, and after-death care is found on page 211.)

This does not mean that if there is any disagreement or distaste for doing a home funeral within a family it will not work. Transformation occurs in many ways. I recall a story of teenage twin girls who insisted that they would run away from home if their parents "stuck" their grandmother in the living room while she was "rotting away." It would be "mortifying"; they could never face their friends again! Their parents insisted, declaring it was Grandmother's wish. Soon the girls were bringing all their friends in to see their grandmother, who looked "so beautiful and peaceful." One might speculate on how future decisions were affected by their experience. In this case, parental authority to carry out the home funeral was purposely enacted, honoring the grandmother and her wishes. The daughters became privileged recipients of an exposure to another way of doing things and experienced a transformation.

Some people say they would rather remember a loved one as they were when they were alive rather than have a memory stuck in their head of their loved one's lifeless body. Surprisingly, this often changes when death occurs. Yet, home funeral guides realize respecting feelings and acknowledging sentiments is an important aspect of allowing transformation to occur. This is why it is valuable to accept statements people make while simultaneously giving time to allow any changes to naturally occur. In this way, we honestly can assist a family to carry out a home funeral if it is their wish and there is a reasonable plan. Remember the example shared earlier of the mother who knew she did not want her son's dead body in her house? As she sat with him after his passing, her perspective changed. She felt a connection and communication with his spirit, even saying the idea to remain in the home came from him. He did not want the separation of spirit and body.

Still, some people will maintain their decision to not view their loved one after they pass. If this is true in the context of a family committed to a home funeral, a home funeral guide can suggest several other tasks—like decorating a coffin, driving the vehicle that carries someone to their final resting place, filling out paperwork, or picking up supplies. Flexibility is important. A person can be vitally engaged and maintain their personal position while also being enriched by the whole experience.

What may unfold is unpredictable and often is a blessing. Perhaps curiosity is what finally nudges a change. Participation often creates a magical spin and alters the experience in a way that enhances and deepens the outcome.

Home funeral participants have confided that a mortuary's "lifelike" look was unsettling and disagreeable to them, as their loved one hardly looked like themself. In a home funeral, the countenance often takes on a relaxed and peaceful look. Natural makeup applied by family is often more appealing than the crafted made-up look arranged by someone who does not know the person. The mortician's art done in a secret mortuary room is not really a "lifelike image" of one's loved one. A natural death countenance is real and changes as the body changes. There is not a pretense of life, but rather the face of one who has died. It is not repulsive.

It is important that home funeral guides have sensitivity to allow things to unfold rather than prescribe a specific perspective or action. A person who was resistant to the idea of a home funeral may change, and they may even be one to spearhead a home funeral at another time.

Avoiding high mortuary fees may be a factor in a family's decision to choose a DIY funeral experience. While this may not be the "best" reason, it may open a window of opportunity for a wonderful experience. A home funeral is a big responsibility, and a home funeral guide's responsibility is to candidly discuss what is entailed and assist a family in making the best, most realistic decision.

A home funeral simply is the act of caring for the body-temple of one who has passed on in the *family's unique, chosen way.* That is why, as home funeral guides, we emphasize it is a *family-directed* event. This is an essential distinction. The home funeral is the family's doing and is not determined by a set formula or an agenda of a home funeral guide.

Lying-in-Honor/Lying-in-Grace

The term "lying-in-state" is frequently used for a public funeral viewing of a distinguished individual. This term is qualitatively different from a term most home funeral families, guides, and advocates prefer. Lying-in-honor and lying-in-grace are two alternate phrases that express what we, as home funeral guides, see as a more real reflection of a family's perspective when exposing the body of a loved one in a wake or vigil. Usually, a family will resonate more with one or the other. These words and the concept they represent are integral to and express how I see what we do. They have come into common usage among home funeral guides.

Home Funeral Guides

What, then, is a home funeral guide? A home funeral guide is simply a person— usually a friend of the family or a person referred by a friend—who is knowledgeable and comfortable coaching a family through the process of their own DIY event. The home funeral guide's task and involvement is to support a family to do what they are *legally allowed* to do. It is a facilitator role. Thereby, they are in a position to assist the family to be comfortable and capable for the tasks involved. Home funeral guides are motivated by a heartfelt connection with the reclaiming energy of hands-on participation and activism in life. Sometimes, guides may also be spiritual counselors, ordained ministers, priestesses, or priests.

A home funeral guide may also be a spokesperson for natural death care. Generally, a home funeral guide is *not* an employee of a professional mortuary or a certified funeral director. Yet home funeral guides appreciate congenial relationships with persons in the industry.

There *are* some mortuary or cemetery businesses that recognize family involvement as essential and offer home-centered alternatives or support a family to carry out their own home funeral and fulfill only the few services the family chooses to have them do. An example might be to only have the business do the required paperwork. A rise in home funeral advocacy is resulting in some new funeral businesses that originated with a natural emphasis from the start. Some funeral directors of such businesses even started out training as home funeral guides while other funeral directors have taken training with a home funeral advocacy group or may embody that mindset as is.

A home funeral guide is familiar with the legal options allowed in their state and county of residence. The family does not need to research legal details at a time calling for personal attention and intimate process. Filling out a death certificate is straightforward; it is an essential piece that must be done carefully and precisely. However, it can be daunting for a family in the midst of caring for the fragile personal aspects of death and grief. It is helpful that the home funeral guide knows how to assist the family to navigate this territory to successfully complete final paperwork and interface with the local Office of Vital Records by accompanying the designated family member to that office in a timely manner. Information related to this task will be covered in another section.

A home funeral guide is a personal coach who assists a family according to the laws of the state in which they reside. The guide offers education and consultation for hands-on death care. At the family's invitation, the guide may also be included in the hands-on care.

Remember to utilize any references to your state's statutes and regulations regarding death care.

Compensation for services varies. Many home funeral guides operate on a gratis to a modest donation arrangement. It is important to remember charges are *not* being made for funeral services. That is the realm of funeral businesses.

Home funeral guides charge only for education. That is their specific focus. They help a family know how to operate within the laws of their state, demonstrate hands-on death care, and manage other essential tasks. A financial exchange agreement typically includes covering expenses (such as dry ice) and a modest contribution for education, time, and energy. This will vary with the person just as each home funeral varies in time and energy. It may also vary with any legal limitations. The desired outcome is an easily negotiated amount arrived at from the heart that is gracious and comfortable to all parties. The work is a reciprocal gift of time and energy.

For me, it is important that any exchange enacted is in balance. I know arriving at an exchange in a heartfelt way is unique in contrast to our mainstream culture and takes special effort. Yet it is clearly my preference. It may be different for others. I've found that as home funeral time is shared, friendships and deep connections are made, which supports energy and financial exchanges to be heartfelt and balanced.

Death Midwives

Sometimes a home funeral guide may also be called a "death midwife." For those who understand the context of this title, it speaks of companionship and support. For others, it can be a confusing term. A death midwife is uniquely able to be present with the dying process and can be a welcome companion, providing spiritual presence for the person dying and for family and friends who also need support.

I have occasionally been asked if it means that I can or will help assist someone to die. Assisting someone to die is *not* what a death midwife does. It is not in the scope of appropriate action. Death is going to happen. Being able to be present with death is a mutual gift of loving support.

In rare and unique situations, a person may ask for help in dying. That is the realm of the person's patient-physician relationship and their inner spiritual relationship. So-called "compassionate assisted suicide" may be legal depending on the laws in the state of residence. For a list of US states that allow compassionate death/death with dignity/physician-assisted death, see page 205.

Personal and collective conversations are essential in this regard. As a society, it is important to consider and navigate new territories regarding these concerns. It is clearly *not the active realm* of the home funeral guide or death midwife.

Prescribed medications for pain or anxiety are often helpful. That assistance also is in the realm of the person's patient-medical team and generally handled in conjunction with a hospice program and/or the doctor and nurse(s) assigned to the person. For many who suffer with a debilitating illness, a medical team is involved.

The assistance of hospice involvement may be enlisted as vital support for a dying person and their family. It has been my privilege to come into contact with heroic, competent, compassionate, kindhearted, and sympathetic hospice personnel. We often become a team of support and find deep affection and connection with each other as we mutually support a person and their family on the path of an ensuing death.

When a person is dying, that person and the family need their closest supportive friends and relations. They need assistance to be comfortable, to find acceptance, and to proceed with what needs to be done in the midst of seeking an ever-illusive peace. They may call for a spiritual counselor and/or a person who is familiar with being in the presence of death. It is as a death midwife that I have been called to companion someone who is dying and to sit with family and friends.

A dying person may call upon a death midwife because they want help in dealing with family members who may be feeling extremely stressed. They may seek help to ease concerns that arise or ask you to merely sit quietly with them to help them accept their death, deal with their anxiety, and prepare for the eventual time of passage. It is an incredibly treasured though delicate time.

Different tasks and foci are connected in heartfelt ways, and there are different reasons for calling on the companionship or assistance of a death midwife. A home funeral guide/death midwife wears many hats, just as those involved face sorrow, dishevelment, logistics, and the beauty of death's appearance in life.

Family Considerations and Interactions with Guides

When a very dear friend of many years called, I was startled to hear her ask right away if I would take care of her "final passage." She asked for my companionship as she navigated through this time. She felt it would help her and those she loved if I were a presence for everyone.

She is one of the people I worked with who, aware of her impending death, chose to discontinue all food and drink in order to expedite a smooth end of her life. In effect, she orchestrated her own intentional death.

While some may call this a form of suicide, it is recognized, medically and legally, as a viable decision when death is certain. There are a couple of official terms used on death certificates as the major cause of death or as a secondary contributing cause of death. The only one I have used on a death certificate is *VSED* (voluntary stopping of eating and drinking). Another term I came across is *PRNH* (patient refusal of nutrition or hydration). This one is more common in a hospital situation. Another term is *palliative sedation*—a medical prescription for severe and unmanageable pain. Websites offer more technical information.[31]

Religious beliefs may also be the reason a family wants a home funeral. An interview will ascertain services essential to their needs. They may be comfortable with the process, only needing to know how long a body may be kept at home legally for a wake or lying-in-honor/lying-in-grace period, or they may want help in preparing paperwork so they can focus on being together and honoring the person who has passed. They may need help decorating a space for the person to be "laid out" when the time comes. These are concerns to deal with during an interview.

It is an honor to be asked to be with a family, a friend, or anyone who knows their time is close at hand. Providing confidence and assistance for a family to do what needs to done and not need to rely on strangers is the key task. It is a unique and unforgettable time of kinship and supporting an acceptance of death, planning for a home funeral, and generally arranging things ahead for the time when death comes.

A home funeral guide assists by being present. In this capacity, it is imperative to clear expectations and let *them tell me* what *they* need. Then I am able to discover what their questions, concerns, or needs are and share available options, as well as explain a family's legal obligations. Discovering what they need reveals the template for planning with them. I can also help them know how to ask their community or family for what they desire.

Whether a family wants to plan and learn how to do what is needed independently or requires assistance, it is helpful to have as much lead time as possible. The intake and assessment interview is especially important to deter-

---

31. www.deathwithdignity.org/options-to-hasten-death,

www.dyingwishmedia.com/faq,

www.dignityhealth.org/cm/media/documents/stopseatinganddrinking.pdf.

mine an understanding of agreements of responsibility and establish an outline of what services are needed. Changes may be made along the way. It is not negotiating a binding contract. It's simply meaningful to create familiar and agreeable ground. It is an important time to fill in important statistics that will be needed on a death certificate. If this is uncomfortable in the moment, a blank form could be left to fill out before another visit. The interview is an essential time. Home funeral guides must honestly evaluate with the family whether doing a home funeral is a reasonable option for them to undertake. It is important to explain that the designated next of kin (advanced care agent, established Power of Attorney, or executor) is legally the acting funeral director and responsible for the legal decision-making—even though, in actuality, it hopefully is a family-group process. When the death certificate is filed, that person's name is written in the box designating "funeral director." Paperwork is addressed further in other chapters and in the Resources section.

A death midwife or home funeral guide becomes a valuable team player with a family. If the family wishes to do a home funeral on their own, the guide can instruct and demonstrate what they will need to know. For example, the guide can explain how to wash, dress, and move a person who has died; legal paperwork they will need to handle; and what local mortuaries or cemeteries are open to working with them when they decide on the final resting place or "disposition" of the body. Written publications that outline the needed process may be suggested. The guide may have material to loan or inform the family where to find or purchase it.

A simple, helpful guide for home funerals is *Planning Guide and Workbook for Home Funeral Families,* by Lee Webster and Donna Belk. The Final Passages guidebook, by Jerrigrace Lyons and Janelle Macrae, is available through Final Passages Institute. Some families have been able to follow a workbook outline and feel supported enough to do all a home funeral entails on their own. A directory of home funeral guides can be found on the website of the National Home Funeral Alliance. More resources are being developed and becoming available in bookstores and online.

A family does eventually need to contact a mortuary, crematorium, private cemetery, or church cemetery for the final committal of the body-temple. A home funeral guide or death midwife may have contact information and know of facilities that are willing to work with families. It is essential to allow a family time to direct their own process, care for a deceased person on their own in their own time, and then hire, when needed, a place for the final committal (legally called the "disposition") of the body's remains. The time a family takes to honor a person's death in a personalized way and to take time to say final words of parting is theirs. *It takes place with the family's timing, not the timing of a business.*

These relationships are the privileged experiences of home funeral guides / death midwives. There is no need for rushing the process. Be present to what is, with reverence and acceptance of what transpires—be it a sweet and gradual decline of active living or a struggle as medical palliative care is supported. I am continually struck by how each experience weaves its way into deepening my soul's awareness.

In any case, a home funeral guide can be helpful with whatever the family needs and what path they choose to follow.

Exceptions to a Home Funeral

Most of the time, when a family's intention is for a home funeral, they have considered how they will do it. However, when exploring the possibility with a guide, they may discover that a home funeral is *not* a feasible option. It is essential for a home funeral guide to be truthful about realistic capabilities of both the family and the guide.

An interview must cover concerns like the size and weight of the person, if the home is accessible, if there are enough support people available to help with lifting and transport, and other extenuating considerations that could deter a home funeral. Caution is important with some issues, such as unsolvable family differences, a lack of people to carry out the work, a severely disfigured person with prolonged time at a morgue or coroner's office, the designation of organ(s) or body donations, the family plot being too great a distance away for ease of transport, or the dead person being a great distance away and needing to be transported home (particularly if across state lines). Some of these may be dealt with creatively; however, it may realistically be too difficult to carry out a home funeral.

A home funeral guide is ideally familiar with local funeral homes that have low costs for direct cremation. Some businesses adjust fees even lower than their standard rate when a family is handling all aspects except for final committal. This information is also available through local chapters of the Funeral Consumers Alliance.

If a burial plot has already been purchased or is in the family, what is possible may depend on prior cemetery arrangements. It could be manageable or not to have a home funeral.

————

An accidental death, a murder, or an unknown cause of death of any sort requires a coroner examination. Accidental death is a tumultuous and traumatic time for a spouse, a family, and often a community. It means that, before family can fully spend time with a loved one's body, the body is whisked away to the coroner's office. The wait that ensues is often agonizing!

If an elder passes naturally but their death was not anticipated, it is often possible to report the death to the coroner and get a referral number without the additional trauma of submitting to an autopsy. Details of the death and a medical doctor's statement regarding knowledge of the person and their health status may be requested by the coroner's office.

If a sudden accident or suicide has occurred, a home funeral guide is in a unique place to help a family and community deal with the shock and trauma as well as possible. With their experience, they may be able to assist with whatever can be done to honor a life snuffed out in such a tragic occurrence.

Many people think such an occurrence would make it impossible to plan for a home funeral and just give up. It is a lot to take on and deserves careful consideration. However, it is not necessarily impossible. It does take strength and patience to be up to the task. It depends on the family's resilience, their decision, and a request granted by the coroner to release the body. Such cases require additional paperwork.

Coroner Involvement

What if the horror of a murder, automobile accident, or other sudden death occurred that necessitated a coroner's involvement? Can a home funeral still be arranged even when the coroner's office is involved? Yes, it can happen. However, it is too painful to write about situations I personally know of. For this reason, I'm inventing an entirely hypothetical scenario to illustrate concepts and experiences that are real and represent what I have actually encountered in various instances.

Here is another way of telling truth, without details of individual and very personal stories, each with its own accompanying raw emotional quality. Everything in the story bears the truth. The experience is based on different home funeral deaths involving a coroner. Descriptions of persons, relationships, and events are drawn from several different times yet are completely fabricated. In other words, the telling is a composite in order to share feelings and process and to illustrate the home funeral guide's relationship with the family.

Death itself is not an emergency. The legal and necessary urgent demand of a coroner intervention has an element of feeling like an emergency due to its time-sensitive, immediate process. Yet for the family, the experience, while often discomforting, is not an emergency in the context of their experience. It is a pause, an interruption, in their process. The nature of a death requiring coroner examination and probable autopsy likely calls forth emergency personnel, though that is their trip, not the family's. The examination also gives a suddenly grieving family time to make adjustments in their disrupted lives.

With even a hypothetical tale, you may feel the effect and wonder why it is important to write about such a death and elicit the raw sentiment of the coroner experience. This emotional road, while tumultuous, is valuable. Your company is welcome in the offering of this hypothetical experience.

———

Mary and I drove in a caravan to pick up Lisa's body from the coroner's office; the others followed in tandem.

A large group consisting of family, intimate friends, and myself—the home funeral guide—waited tenuously outside. A nervous tension trembled through the group. An obsessive need to rehash the sudden and tragic murder that happened when Lisa walked home from a community meeting nearly a week earlier was evident. The group struggled to make sense of it. People hugged and held hands, supporting each other and expressing love for Lisa, Mary, and one another.

The deputy clerk assured us she was familiar with the law that allowed a family to take their loved one home and said it would be only a short wait to get the coroner's signature on the paperwork. Her kindness put us at ease.

Finally, the clerk and the coroner came out. The coroner personally handed Mary her copy of the signed death certificate. With an unexpected show of affection, he took Mary's hand and expressed sorrow for what had befallen her. He knew of Lisa and her work and considered her a valuable asset to the community; she would be missed.

Mary and I hugged as we walked arm in arm to join her family and community. As we joined the others, Fred, her closest friend who was like a brother, greeted her, saying, "Are you ready for this, Mary?"

Mary nodded and smiled. Fred smothered her in a brotherly hug. He had readied his station wagon to carry Lisa's body. Laboratory staff persons were on the way, pulling a rolling cart with a body bag out of the lab and down a ramp.

A lab staff member quietly indicated for two of them to be on one side and one to join him on the other side. A staff person pulled the cart away, and two others joined the bearers to gently slide the bag holding the sacred body into the station wagon. Quietly, Mary said, "Let's be on our way. I'd like to take my sister home."

Mary had asked if I'd stay with her and drive her car. As we embarked, she began speaking softly. "It's strange there are no tears yet. At least not since that night …" She sighed as her voice trailed off. Then, touching my arm, she said, "I could not have done this without you. You gave me strength and resolve when I did not find it in me."

———

This story illustrates the role and value of a home funeral guide in deaths involving a coroner. The home funeral guide/death midwife was *not* there to *do* anything specific, substantial, or legal. The home funeral guide was merely there to provide compassionate support and counsel for Mary, the person legally responsible, to carry out the legal task of interfacing with the coroner's office. Unseen and seen magic transpired. A way was made possible.

———

Thus are the many "hats" of a home funeral guide/death midwife/death doula. The bottom line is that our role, as companions and educators, varies with each situation and aligns with the needs of a given family. Essential attributes of a home funeral guide are to have integrity and be of humble, genuine, authentic service. This role calls upon mindfulness, deep awareness, a willingness to listen, and respect for the ways and wishes of those you serve. It is always an incredible honor to be of such service. It consistently leaves me in awe and with a feeling of being gifted by angels.

CHAPTER 9
DEATH IS NOT AN EMERGENCY!

Life is a great surprise.
I do not see why death should not be an even greater one.
—*Vladimir Nabokov*

Where can we find meaning when a door is closing and death draws so near? *It is now.* What to do, oh, what to do? An unseen spirit hand rests upon my shoulder and a voice softly whispers, *"It is only death. All will be well."* Questions still swirl all around. Yet death *is here*; is it not an emergency?

———

I heard Barbara Marx Hubbard address an audience with a question that stuck in my mind, *"Did you know how to do puberty?"* She spoke of an *inner knowing* we possess, yet it need not concern us; we don't even have to have an awareness of its existence. Puberty happens. I suspect death is like that as well. We know how to do death.

Death happens. It is not an emergency. An impending death calls on one's unwavering presence.

Like an imminent birth or a gripping adventure film or experience, death commands full attention. Yet it is true: there *is* a natural uneasiness about death's approach. A fear of death calls forth an inclination to see it as tragic or as an emergency. A cry for help may rumble in the belly, push its way through the heart and out in a voiced cry or flow of tears. Angst and anguish, fear and sorrow may grip awareness. An innate right and a task are presented and, when not whisked away, we rise to the occasion and find ourselves doing what *will come naturally*. What looms ahead requires action, yet it is *not an emergency*. It is our genuine, real, and essential task—whether we put it out for hire to a business ready for customers or jump in with both feet, heart, and hands and address what is to be done. *There is a choice!*

There are times when it is appropriate to save a life; those *are* emergency or clinical situations. In this chapter, we are speaking of being with someone we know is dying or who has just died. Once death has occurred, it is a "done deal" and there is nothing that must be immediately done.

Death itself is not an emergency. You do not need to call 911! You do not need to call for an official person to pronounce someone dead. Saying this does not alter the profound, sensitive, tender, and emotional character of death's event. Things that must be taken care of can happen in due time.

With an anticipated death, the nonemergency status is more obvious. If there is a sudden unexpected death, circumstances may dictate immediate actions. A person may need to be moved out of traffic, a fire, or other environment. The existing situation itself declares any immediate required action.

Beyond that, it is time to be present with the death. Simply be present.

Of course, you may wonder for a moment—or even longer. There are "those times" we have heard and read about when someone has gone and returned. Those stories are magnetic. A near-death experience (NDE) reveals much about death. It enriches and challenges our precepts. Tales of NDEs are fascinating! They kindle a feeling of curiosity and wonder. Resplendent with expansive possibilities, such tales may prod dealing with fear and encourage curiosity. However, that is another subject.

I smile as I recall speaking on the phone with one of my sons shortly after my mother, his grandmother, passed. Todd asked repeatedly if I was *really sure* his grandmother was *really* dead. He asked if someone, like her doctor, came and pronounced her dead, or did we call 911? He wanted us to make sure we were correct. He could feel his grandmother's presence and wondered if she *could* still be alive. I assured him over and over, yet he needed more reassurance.

Finally, I said, "We were all with her. She had some gargled breath, then after a long outbreath, she stopped breathing. She did not start breathing again.

Her face relaxed, and she now looks very peaceful. Hours have passed, and she still has not started breathing again."

It took saying that much for him to entertain the probability that his grandmother—with whom he had such a sensitive, deep, affectionate relationship—had actually passed. His reaction was natural. He lacked the tangible experience that we had witnessed. For him, it conjured a possible emergency. Emergencies can have saviors. He believed that emergency life-saving efforts might have made a difference in a death he now struggled to accept.

————

Experiencing the moment of death is an opportunity. Something is being offered. Oddly, it is a treasured moment—*this* moment never comes around again. It can call forth a fierce and powerful awakening presence. Whatever feelings are there to be felt, are there. Slow down. Be with the moment. Feel what is. Feel the silence. Feel the energy shift. Feel and see the light in the room change. Feel the relief. Feel the sorrow. Feel the tears. Feel the peace. Feel the wonder.

Often there is the feeling of time standing still and a deep presence. Feeling the pervasive presence of one who has just passed is a sensation that may cascade around you, like an "everywhere-ness." An audible or barely audible sound of wind or air movement may occur. The light in the room may shift. Sometimes it is only stillness. Feel it. Feel whatever it is. Allow yourself to be engulfed in the experience. It is a dip into eternity. It is a time for quietly reflecting and bonding through the grief, relief, and wonder of the moment. *Each death has its own character. Each death is a personal event.* Attunement to feelings validates the momentous nature of what has just occurred.

Recalling the voice of my mother, I was assured of her presence and that she was indeed *"everywhere."*

Sensations are only experienced with awareness if there is a willingness to feel— including the tumultuous and seemingly opposing feelings. There is a raw sensitivity to being in the presence of a death like in no other life event. A place of nonurgency and of unrestrained, fervent awareness assists and supports us to receive *whatever* is there. It is a gift when we open our consciousness to the moment, to the silence, and to the presence of what is.

In silence, we find a gift of keen alertness that opens to the depth and breadth of life. In silence, we open our inner door to transcendent understanding. In the book *Silence Speaks*, Eckhart Tolle illustrates this gift: *"Your innermost sense of self, of who you are, is inseparable from stillness ... Stillness is your essential nature ... You are that awareness, disguised as a person ... When you become aware of silence, immediately there is that state of inner still alertness. You are present."* [32]

———

A dear friend called and asked, "What is the first thing to do when he passes?"

She was referring to the husband of one of her close friends who, like her, lived in an assisted living community overlooking a lake. Spontaneously and without thought, I responded, "Breathe." I heard her relaxed sigh over the phone. She had just done the very act she needed most in that moment. It was also the most supportive and helpful energy to share with her friend when the moment of her husband's passage occurred.

"Sit in silence for a while. There is no hurry to do anything," I continued. There was a pause—a moment of silence shared. Like the Celtic rune, "Wait on the will of heaven," it is about embracing present time.

"Thank you! That's exactly it! You reminded me to just be and not try to escape what has happened, or fix it, or change it. You reminded me to be who I am, and just be present. That is what I really know best."

We continued sharing, allowing our words to just bubble up. We discussed essential oils she had and could share with her friend ahead of time. Anointing the body is a simple ritual without a time frame that offers a *quiet act of doing* that may fulfill a need to *do* something. Anointing one who has passed is a beautiful honoring ritual and can lift the energy in the room. *Anointing rituals* may result in a clearing and healing of energy, as well as supply antibacterial support. It may open up an opportunity for silence to deepen or for people to express a candid, soul-bearing reflection to one who has just passed. It seems Spirit takes advantage of any channel to slip through, transform, and soften grief's tenacious hold.

———

32. Tolle, *Silence Speaks*, 3–5.

If you are attending someone in a hospital or facility, the inclination or expectation may be to call a physician or attendant to pronounce death, to call a designated mortuary, and to initiate aftercare right away. That is one choice. If another energetic space is desired, inform staff ahead of time. Communicate the wishes written in an Advanced Care Directive or any other significant legal documents. Ask that a written order be in place to inform the entire staff in the facility of your intentions. Declare your wishes and ask allowance of quiet space when death occurs so that you may honor your own process. Care institutions frequently face accommodating a family's wishes. If they are reticent, be prepared with reference to your state's statutes and provisions for legal family care of a deceased person.

When attending a person's death at home or at a hospice facility, it is considerably easier to set the stage for family being in charge and choosing how they desire it to be for the dying person and those present. Naturally, one's own home is often preferable.

The one mundane task is to note the time of death, as it will be required on the death certificate. Yet this does not require an exact to-the-minute notation.

If you are called to be with a person and/or family during a death, it is essential that you bring an unfettered presence. Be sure to leave your agenda at the door. You are entering through the servant's door. You are there to be present. If you are acting in the capacity of a home funeral guide, likely a previous interview has clarified what they expect from you. You may be there to set the stage for openness and acceptance, to provide ritual space, or merely to bring witnessing awareness. Be in a state of open, heartfelt awareness.

As a home funeral guide, I generally inform the family they are welcome to call me anytime. Reminding them that death's passage is not an emergency, I instruct if death occurs in the middle of the night to note the time, leave me a message, and call again in the morning when they are ready for me to join them. Usually we wait to address aftercare until morning. Waiting for the right timing to begin care of the body gives family members time to sit with their beloved or perhaps get needed rest. Gathering with the morning light offers gentleness to the sacred process.

The following list about being in the presence of death will capsulize and add to what has been previously mentioned:

- Enter the person's space with curiosity about their energy. It is their time.
- When present at the moment of death, be still, "waiting on the will of heaven" (from the Celtic runes). Allow for a sense of suspended time.
- Breathe—with yourself, the spirit of the person who is passing or who has just passed, and whoever else is present. Waiting Is.
- Allow for quiet. Silence is a gift—a great gift.
- Listen to the person who is dying and to their family. If they are not talking, merge with the quiet space and allow for pauses before you speak.
- Allow time for them to process whatever they are feeling. Sensitivity is primary.
- Be aware of their time frame in regard to awareness of dying and/or transition (from E. Kübler-Ross's classic progression of shock, denial, grief, sadness, and acceptance) and to the transcendent phases (acceptance, release, relief, preparation, curiosity, and readiness). (What I am calling "transcendent phases" is from my own observation. Yet I am not positive it is completely my own, as I may have heard or read somewhere of these phases being called by similar terms. In any case, they are offered here from the collective One Mind.)
- Take to heart consideration of family wishes and perspectives. We each have our own way. You may agree or disagree, and your perspective may differ 180 degrees. However, each person's way is their personal way and is to be respected. Offer your perspective or suggestions if you are asked. Some may desire or be open to discuss and consider options and different perspectives. Be available, yet without judgment of their position.

There are additional factors, important to deal with, that are peripheral to the essential question of how to be in the presence of death. These include the following:

- When called by a family as a potential home funeral guide, it is important to ascertain the position and needs of the family, the situation of the home, and the condition of the person who is passing or has passed. It is incumbent to determine appropriateness on your part to accommodate their needs. You can be truthful without judgment. Sometimes doing a home funeral is not advisable. Be respectfully candid. If appropriate, refer them to another home funeral guide or a funeral establishment that allows family hands-on care.

- As a home funeral guide, custodian trustee, or family member, you may need to ask about family legal documents (e.g., Advanced Care Directive, will, Living Trust) to help answer medical, after-death care, or other pertinent questions.

- An *Ethical* or *Spiritual Will* is another document getting attention today. The idea is bequeathing gifts of energy one wishes to pass on. Such "items" one might include are, "I will my sense of humor to my grandson, Neal," or, "Time to smell the roses in our garden, my beloved wife," or maybe even, "I leave my unfinished scrapbook for my grandchildren to complete." It could be a narrative about one's life that expresses what one wishes to share that has been unsaid. You get the idea. This is a project for anytime in one's life when considering their "bucket list." It might be an engaging project taken on by a family with a dying person to pass time together.

- Often family and friends who wish to help are around. As a guide or friend, it may be helpful to assist people to find their niche. Consider needs for food, water, heat or cooling, covers, pillows, music, candles, altar arrangements, and visiting times. Consider chores or concerns—like housekeeping needs, contacting other friends or family, picking up medications, and hospice / caregiver needs. Remind everyone to be considerate of timing and to ask, "Is this a good time to visit?" "How close shall I sit with you?" and so on.

- A "to-call list" is important, and a family may need help putting it together. The need for this may come after the home funeral. The personal list includes family and friends to be notified with updates and/or at the time of death. A business list includes caregivers, insurance, social security, outstanding bills, and credit cards.

- Remember all-important tasks can be accomplished in right timing. Nothing is urgent except being present.

———

You may ask, "What is it about being with death's occurrence that is most essential to relay?" It is prudent to make choices about death in a timely manner, rather than waiting until it is imminent and feels like an emergency. Putting off significant decisions makes us more likely to act out of fear instead of confident consideration of personal options and decisions. I know of many people who in retrospect wish they had followed a more natural way and taken time to be with their beloved person who died. Some struggle with the infamous question of, "What if?" Such regrets can plague a person and create an internal obstacle that only repeats itself. Making decisions ahead of time creates room for greater peace and can mitigate this unnecessary tumultuous stress. Act now. Why wait until it is too late?

From my experience, I believe *you will forever cherish your involvement and experience with essential tasks of death care that you do yourself, however difficult they may be at the time.* Death is not an emergency, although it is a sure thing. It deserves mindfulness so you act with careful consideration. To act rashly implies an emergency. Give yourself time to consider your choices. It is a gift that helps release your concerns and a valuable gift to those left behind.

———

I felt blessed to work with Pam, the daughter mentioned earlier who lovingly and gracefully created a home funeral for her mother, Sarah. Pam's shining attribute is that she took her time and did not allow any sense of emergency to hamper her actions throughout the whole experience. Everything she did was artful, careful, and unfettered. She had her moments of trembling sorrow, occasionally confiding to me that she was at a loss. Yet she carefully orchestrated her mother's last days both for her mother and herself. In a home funeral resplendent with ease and beauty, Pam created living art, demonstrating a way to move deliberately without generating emergency energy. She sidestepped any effort to act with haste and allowed it all to flow. When all was done, she said that together we had given her mother "the ultimate home funeral."

Pam had some connections with a caretaker of an old church cemetery that was tucked away in a remote community. She contacted him and made arrangements for a green burial. He helped her pick a sublimely beautiful spot, graced with trees and wildflowers. As she felt Sarah's time nearing, she arranged for a gravedigger team.

The morning Pam called to let me know that Sarah had gently "slipped off with her angels," she and I alternated between sacred ritual care, tidying Sarah's room, and attention to paperwork and legal concerns.

We spontaneously created a beautiful shrouding ritual. Pam found a beautiful white lace tablecloth that she wrapped around her mother. I'd brought some white nylon twine, which we circled around on top of the cloth and the body. It blended into the lace cloth, creating a sturdy network that supported Sarah's body-temple. Into that network of twine, we wove bundles of fragrant jasmine vine that a friend had dropped off. Previously, Pam had conceived a brilliant plan to transport Sarah's body in a hammock. We searched and found a white cotton-rope hammock that would work perfectly. Besides using it for carrying her to the car and to the gravesite, we would be able to lower her into the earth by attaching twine on both sides of the hammock. It would be her eco-bed.

The rural cemetery was quiet the day of the committal event. The weather was unusually warm in this near-coastal area, and we relished that warmth as another angelic gift. A few of Pam and Sarah's special friends joined us. The labor crew had carefully dug a grave the day before. They respectfully joined us as well. Gently, we swung the hammock embracing Sarah's body and lowered her into the waiting earth.

We sat alongside the open grave and spoke softly of good times with Sarah and her genuine attitude of acceptance and peace that had colored her last days. It was a blissful morning and early afternoon.

Finally, Pam declared the time to say final farewells. We cast flowers and fragrant herb branches around Sarah's body. We each offered spontaneous prayers and blessings for Sarah on her journey. One of the men who had dug the grave stepped down inside the grave next to Sarah's body. He motioned to us to hand him buckets of soil, which he slowly and methodically poured around her, beginning at her feet, gently covering her body, and finally artfully framing her face. Pam's tearful, exquisite parting words to her mother touched us all. We stood by quietly, occasionally dropping soil with our bare hands into the grave. The crew of men, like monks with a sacred task, finished filling in the grave and formed an artfully crafted mound.

Pam and I lingered, standing alone together for a dip into the eternal present. As she hugged me, she whispered, "It was a perfect day, Jude!"

We headed back to her sweet home, now without Sarah for the first time in many years. We sat near the water tributary that flowed by at the edge of her yard. It was sunny and warm and invited our quiet meditation. Suddenly, a warm wind swirled around us. The wind felt gusty and exuberant, as if playing with our hair and shoulders. We gazed at adjacent yards and the water, noticing the lack of wind elsewhere. The wind seemed to originate out of the land itself and was isolated to her yard and the immediate space around us. Our playful sister-wind felt like a visit from Sarah's joyful, happy spirit. We felt she danced around the garden and us as if to say, "I am joyful and free! Feel and see me dance with you." Pam was transfixed; her mother was letting her know that she was happy and dancing with her angels.

Sarah's spirit dance invited us to drink in the silence. A sweet meditation filled us to overflowing. Pam was blissful and deeply touched by all that had unfolded and the artful display of a love dance from her mother. We both felt a tingle run across our skin. The wind gently drifted away. Warmth from the sun now caressed our shoulders once again. We sat quietly a while longer, drinking in the silence and the beauty. Gradually, a soft pink spread across the sky. It was the close of a beatific day. Angelic energy followed us inside for herb tea.

————

I am reminded often of how in giving, we receive. Our work as home funeral guides is to use our education and planning ability as we enable a family to sidestep obstacles, avoid a sense of emergency, and find a way to honor their beloved in a way that pleases them. The intention is to support ease for the family and friends, helping to provide an experience they will remember as heartfelt and uplifting, even in a time of sorrow. It is a reciprocal experience, as a home funeral guide internalizes an embodied sacred time as well.

We pause. We breathe. We allow the unfolding path of a home funeral to emerge from the center of love and caring. A deep wellspring of spiritual growth may have occurred in the time shared with those involved. Such deepening of spiritual connections may be sustained in ongoing relationships over time.

CHAPTER 10
OFFICIAL GROUND

You take a final step and, look, suddenly
You're there. You've arrived.
At the one place all your drudgery was aimed for.
This common ground.
… What did you want …?
—*David Wagoner*

While a funeral business will provide for "corpse care," there are a multitude of options to consider about the final care of a beloved's body. This "official ground" is referred to legally as the "final disposition." It is also called one's "final resting place." It is personal and must be carried out within the scope of what is legally allowed. At some point this decision must be made, and it will require those responsible to engage a legal entity in the final disposition; a mortuary, crematorium, or cemetery now have their place, along with the necessity of officially registered paperwork. Burial on private land, while not impossible, is rare due to state and local ordinances.

Some people have long held an idea of what they would choose as their final resting place. Others wrestle with choices, juggling considerations of what sounds easiest, cheapest, most elaborate, or simplest. Some struggle between something from a family tradition or a more innovative option. At some point, an appropriate decision must be made, physically and legally. You either deal with this essential choice in life before it is an issue, in the midst of your death, or through others after you die.

What do *you* want? Do you want to be buried or cremated? If you choose burial, do you mean interment in a modern cemetery with gravestone markers, or are you interested in a green burial? Are you interested in new innovative options that are emerging? Whatever you choose, the easiest time to consider your options is now.

Some people resonate with a specific geographical area for either burial or scattering ashes. Purchasing a burial plot involves consideration, especially if one is looking for a green burial site. Cremains have been scattered in numerous places; scattering happens in a personal garden or the ocean, desert, mountains, wilderness areas, or other places a family feels are significantly meaningful. Special locations can be revisited from time to time for picnics or memorial gatherings in the future.

There are many emerging eco-alternative options of interest for both burial and cremation. More details of these unique possibilities will follow.

Cremation

In recent years, the term *cremation nation* has become a frequently heard characterization of current after-death practices in this country. The popularity of cremation is due in part to it being seen as an easier process and clearly because it is considerably less expensive. Additional reasons for cremation vary and are influenced by environmental, religious, humanitarian, and cost factors. Mark Harris in his book *Grave Matters* discusses in detail statistics and predictions of the Cremation Association of North America (CANA). Their director, Jack Springer, indicates that about 30 percent of America's dead are cremated. By 2025, that percentage will jump to 45 percent, and five years later, for the first time, cremations will outnumber burials. Springer also says that in other countries where cremation has taken hold, such as Japan, India, and China, that percentage will be even higher.[33]

Cremation is the least expensive professional treatment method for final commitment of the body. What is called "direct cremation" is a simple cremation with no viewing or services at a mortuary. It is the least expensive and most simply arranged option. In this case, the body is picked up almost imme-

---

33. Harris, *Grave Matters*, 55–63.

diately after death and cremation follows without fanfare. A release for cremation is required.

Occasionally, a family decides to view the cremation. This option is when witnesses choose to be present when the body enters and/or exits the cremation chamber. This can be arranged with most crematoriums for an extra fee.

Following cremation, the cremains are released to the family member in charge or to a designated person. In California, the official destination of cremains is required on the permit for dissolution; generally, the destination is the residence of the acting funeral director (the family member legally in charge). Theoretically, a recorded destination is maintained and, according to most states' laws, must be accounted for over time. However, since it is not a health risk, there is no safety reason to follow up on cremain whereabouts. To my knowledge, there is no pursuit of the cremains. In truth, cremains are extremely sanitary and of no detrimental consequence to the environment. They are not of legal concern.

Families choose various ways to honor the cremains of their beloved. They may buy a memorial urn or make an artistic container of clay, wood, cardboard, papier mâché, or other creative materials. Cremains may be kept in a mortuary niche, buried on cemetery grounds, or honored in various more personal ways. Some are elevated on a family mantel or altar, worn in a locket, or fashioned into jewelry. Many are scattered in a garden, at the ocean, lake, or waterway, or in another favorite family spot. Cremains are less often tucked away on a closet shelf, yet even there they are honored as a family treasure. These variations often provide a family with an opportunity for another ritual gathering in honor of one whose memory is treasured in their hearts.

Persons doing a home funeral frequently utilize the direct cremation option unless they are choosing a burial. This makes it easier and clearer for the funeral business as direct cremation is listed on the required itemized price list, making a charge for their efforts with a home funeral understandable. Fortunately, some funeral homes familiar with working with home funeral families will accommodate families further with an adjusted rate. This may be especially true if the funeral home is not processing the paperwork. In a home funeral event, the family either transports the body to the crematorium, if allowed in that state, or a funeral home or transport service transports the body for subsequent cremation.

Although cremation has been a favored option, the process has negative environmental impacts such as burning fossil fuels to attain extremely high heat and releasing carbon dioxide and other potent toxins into the atmosphere. Many states and counties have instituted regulatory emission standards. Although the cremation industry claims to comply and monitor emissions with better technology, many toxins are still potentially released, including nitrogen oxide, carbon monoxide, sulfur dioxide, particulate matter, mercury (major source from dental amalgams), hydrogen fluoride, hydrogen chloride, and other heavy metals.[34]

Traditional Burial

As we have repeatedly noted, burial has long been the most common practice. It is still considered by many as the most natural and ecological choice in contrast to cremation. Doctrines of major religions, even today, generally favor burial. This is notably so with Islamic and Jewish faith practices.

Until this past century, it was the norm for a family to prepare the body and arrange for the interment on their own land or in a local church cemetery. With the advent of professional undertakers, this has become more commonly the domain of a funeral business. Still, small and large cemeteries and memorial parks dot the nation's landscape. Large monuments and gravestones must be maintained, or they become crumbling structures in older cemeteries. The preference today is for smaller, uniform monuments or even markers that are level to the ground to make mowing and maintenance easier. The increasing cost of acquiring grave plots will continue to grow. It has made burial less popular. Also, burial on private land is more difficult due to land use laws.

Awareness of valuable land use, coupled with strong sentiments regarding the tonnage of metal, concrete, and potentially toxic chemicals deposited in the earth, has become a major concern for many people, not only environmentalists. The "Green Council Report" from the Green Burial Council (an online organization) reports that American funerals are responsible for 30 million feet of casket wood, ninety thousand tons of casket steel, 1.6 million tons of concrete for vaults, and 8 million gallons of embalming fluid and other toxic

---

34. Harris, *Grave Matters*, 55–63.

chemicals that are dumped in the earth every year.[35] All this, along with a huge percentage of land use that is not multiuse, leads to many essential questions of modern funeral practice.

Green Burial

Environmental activists and advocates who favor keeping death in balance with the natural process of returning a body's physical resources to the earth promote this option. Minimal environmental impact and protection of natural landscapes are the key factors. People who ascribe to a religion's doctrinal mandate on death care may also be committed to green burial options.

Green burial choices vary from a designated green area on established cemetery grounds to newer eco-concepts of a green burial site in a natural surrounding landscape or even in a wilderness sanctuary space. Our Indigenous relations speak of "sacred burial grounds" that continue in perpetuity. That concept suggests that such sites hold land open and are to be cherished and respected by not building on them or desecrating them in any way. This idea could merge naturally to use of public wild lands (such as national forests and Bureau of Land Management (BLM) land or private conservatory land) where a marker could be as simple as a GPS coordinate listing, a fruit tree, a special planting, or a natural rock tribute.

The Green Burial Council, founded in 2005, offers standards for green burial sites. It also provides education and supports a broad spectrum of people, organizations, and funeral business. Their vision may be characterized as a return to old ways, yet it is supported by modern science and organic concepts of respect for the Earth. Mark Harris, author of *Grave Matters,* champions green burials for their simplicity and the return of old-fashioned values.

Green burial is gaining popularity because more people are concerned about the impact they leave on the Earth when they die. Some mortuaries and cemeteries now provide sections to allow for green burial. Green burial sites have also been set aside on both public and private lands that incorporate multiple uses. On page 201, you will find a list of green burial cemeteries and the standards promoted by the Green Burial Council.

---

35. greenburialcouncil.org.

Decomposition is ultimately seen as beneficial to the ecosystem because it creates greater microbial and plant life diversity. I call decomposition Earth's "yummy feast," as our vast, complex ecosystem is abundant with life and responds to decaying matter with glee in the process of autolysis, which is triggered by the decaying matter itself. In death there is life! I loved basic biology class where I learned much about this basic life-death process! Decomposition is our friend, allowing our physical remains to return to the great cycle of life, death, and rebirth. These sentiments are of primary interest to people who hold a reclaiming mindset.

Ramsey Creek Preserve in Westminster, South Carolina, is the first official green burial site in the country.[36] Since it opened in 1998, many more sites have opened. The option of walking around in nature in a soothing environment is gratifying to many who choose this comfortable multiuse alternative. My active imagination envisions ways green burials can create sacred burial grounds akin to our Indigenous relatives' practices and preserve land—from parklike facilities to wilderness areas—for generations to treasure and enjoy.

Innovative "New" Alternatives

While burial in the earth is probably the most common mode of final disposition, throughout our distant to recent past, all of the elements—earth, fire, air, and water—have provided innovative approaches to final death care. Fire is likely the next most frequently utilized mode of disposition. Cremation, with few exceptions, must be done in a licensed crematorium. Today, with concern for lessening environmental impact, it is a highly regulated industry, especially related to temperature and filters of toxic elements. It is out of the eco-concerns of today that many of the new innovative approaches have arisen.

A budding interest in emergent eco-alternative options is catching on. Many new innovative ideas are being marketed online. Some are reminiscent vestiges of ancient practices and Indigenous traditions. Some options of interest are quite curious, like a mushroom bodysuit and aquamation (alkaline hydrolysis). Traditional options like a shroud or pine box are reemerging in popularity. These choices are lending themselves to great variations of personal artistic

---

36. www.memorialecosystems.com.

expression. For those intrigued, I encourage an internet exploration. A few brief overviews, from my limited exposure, are relayed below.

Shrouds—A shroud is generally a lengthy piece of cloth called burial clothing, a burial sheet, grave clothes, or winding cloths. Beyond wrapping up the dead in a sheet, the shroud lends itself to broad creativity. I've seen the use of exquisite fabric patterns and various types of cloth. I recall a heavy fabric with a dragonfly pattern, expressing a personality aspect of the deceased. Another, featured in another chapter, was one of lace, tied with twine and interwoven with fragrant boughs of jasmine. Those choosing a green burial will utilize natural fabrics like hemp, linen, organic cotton, or wool. An internet search reveals companies that design and sell beautiful shrouds. Also available online are patterns for sewing your own shroud.

Wooden Caskets—A plain pine box or a homemade wooden box of any wood type are a frequent consideration. In an earlier chapter, there are details of the one my brother, Paul, built for our mother. A friend in our local community has a business of building custom-made caskets. Directions can be found online of patterns to build your own casket. YouTube videos are also online with detailed live instructions. Caskets may be made of a wide variety of natural biodegradable materials that will decompose quickly in the earth and not leave a toxic environmental impact. Materials used include a variety of fibers such as reeds, bamboo, hemp, willow, bark, and cardboard. Search the internet for more ideas and companies that sell ready-made natural caskets.

Mushroom Ingestion—A few products are available that use mushrooms as a catalyst for rapid decomposition. Coeio (coeio.com) is one company that produces an eco-garment shroud infused with mushrooms and microorganisms that aid in decomposition and work to neutralize toxins found in the body as well as transfer nutrients to plant life. Since such mushroom species do not eat live flesh, the suit can be tried on while a person is alive. When the person dies, the mushrooms activate. Due to the fungi's ability to deactivate and mycoremediate toxins, the environment is not affected negatively. This eco-option is legal and of particular interest to those interested in green burial. More information and videos can be found on Coeio's website.[37] Incorporating these types of mushrooms is of great interest to me, although I would personally favor the mushrooms' direct use into the soil. Rather than purchase an expensive suit, my choice would be to merely add these mushrooms along with red wiggler worms from my compost to the soil for my green burial.

Alkaline Hydrolysis—In this option, the body is placed in a pressured vessel that utilizes lye and heat. The result is liquid and soft, porous bone remains that can be dried and made into a white powdery dust. This dust can be returned to the family. The liquid is either disposed to irrigate a garden or into the waste water system. This process is also called biocremation, resomation, aquamation, water or flameless cremation, or green cremation. It is not readily available in the United States, though it is an inexpensive option in some British crematoriums.[38] More information can be found on the internet through many informative sites.

Memorial Reef—Another new option is for cremains to be made part of a man-made reef in a beautiful underwater structure. This enhances habitat and supports sea life. Cremains are mixed with natural concrete and either formed into a pod or a capsule to be added to the man-made reef. Two companies, Eternal Reefs and Neptune Memorial Reef, provide this service off the southern Atlantic coast. Both companies' websites have videos that capture the beauty of an underwater, sustainable man-made reef that enhances habitat for marine life.[39]

Sea Burial—Sea burial is another past tradition that is a rekindled option for some. Sailors and sea lovers might consider being "tossed to the deep waters." Strict laws for sea burial require a permit, issued through the EPA under the Marine Protection, Research, and Sanctuaries Act (MPRSA). Also, a destination of at least three nautical miles from shore is required; there, a weighted-down body may be dropped over the continental shelf. While a personal boat may be used, generally chartering a vessel, crew, and sea cap-

37. Coeio.com.

38. fcaofmn.org/alkaline-hydrolysis-green-cremation.

39. eternalreefs.com and nmeef.com.

tain is needed, making for a rather expensive event, albeit a legal one.[40] Perhaps this is why cremated remains are more often taken to a high cliff over the ocean or a bridge over water and cast to the wind and water.

Other options—Countless innovative options are emerging. Here are a few others that may kindle your interest: A biodegradable burial pod that integrates the body into a tree is called **capsula mundi**.[41] **Promession** is freeze-drying the body in an environmental way, utilizing liquid nitrogen; the body becomes brittle, is reduced to a powder, is buried in a biodegradable container, and finally turns into compost. Swedish marine biologist Susanne Wiigh–Mäsak founded Promessa, deriving the name from an Italian word for "promise."[42] **Celestis** provides a way to shoot your ashes into space. It is the only company to have successfully conducted memorial space flight missions. The cremains are actually in a sealed space capsule. The capsule burns up on Earth reentry, reaches an extraterrestrial destination, or goes into deep space, leaving our solar system. Celestis was selected by NASA to honor one of its scientists in this way.[43] **Recompose** is another very new innovation I heard about when attending the Bioneers conference in October 2019. It seems the most encouraging and exciting possibility to emerge related to green practices. Katrina Spade, the company CEO, presented a method of composting deceased bodies in a safe, sanitary, and very beautiful manner. She has been working within legal channels to establish legality for the process and has created a beautiful facility for a pilot project.[44]

Thus is an incomplete overview of some innovative ways elemental disintegration transpires. More options and innovative ideas will arise. Our molecular elements—earth, air, fire, and water—in myriad ways ultimately re-turn to the interconnection of all things. The spiritual and religious may explore and conjecture how the fifth element, called Spirit, returns into the Mystery and its harmonic relationship to the cosmos.

---

40. epa.gov.

41. capsulamundi.it.

42. promessa.se.

43. celestis.com.

44. recompose.life.

Other Factors

An internet search for natural death care, natural caskets, casket-building, and home funeral guides will lead to many articles on death perspectives, training programs for those interested in green solutions to death care, alternatives to what the funeral industry offers, DIY plans, and even products such as woven baskets or artful organic urns. However, it is not easy to acquire a plain, sturdy cardboard coffin online. Many companies only sell to licensed funeral businesses. However, today there are a few independent, eco-centered firms that sell cardboard caskets and other biodegradable containers to anyone. Federal law prohibits a funeral business from not allowing people to purchase or build their own casket.

The best way to find a cardboard casket may be to contact a home funeral training program. Another option is to find a local casket maker. Some people appreciate being intimately involved, decorating the casket even though they may not want to participate in hands-on body care. In a comfortable and pleasurable group activity, people can find a deep connection with the home funeral process. Pictures of the process and the finished masterpiece can be considered treasures.

Required Paperwork

Death Certificates and Permits for Disposition

These are paperwork essentials that must be done legally and filed before final disposition, also called the committal act, can be done. It may necessitate a sometimes tedious and laborious hunt for required documentation and the making of multiple copies to get final legal approval. Ultimately, flawlessly executed documents are to be submitted to the county Office of Vital Records/statistics for final certification. Accomplishing this, however, is not an impossible task for a family to manage. In California, families are permitted to handle the entire home funeral process. It is wise to contact your county office for assistance. A guide being able to assist with filling out these forms is an exceptionally appreciated skill that should be made available for the family.

A statute that defines the status of this process is generally found in the health and safety code of your state. Information about a specific state may be found in the book *Final Rights*. For example, California allows a family the right to prepare their own dead for disposition. A *Certificate of Death* and a *Permit for*

Disposition must be filed before disposition occurs (i.e., before a body is moved or taken to a cemetery or mortuary). A mortuary or cemetery generally asks to see a copy of the certified death certificate and will require all four copies of the disposition permit, one of which they keep while the others are sent to the county vital records department as a verification. Mortuaries generally file via electronic transfer, and some states require that filing be done by a registered funeral director. If your state allows you to do the paperwork, it is advisable to contact your county office for assistance. If cremation is being done, the establishment will also require a release for cremation, signed by the authorized family member.

The Death Certificate (DC)

I am most familiar with what is required in California and will utilize that information here. Be sure to research your state requirements and acquire a copy of your state's official death certificate to use as your initial template. In California, this official document must be either printed in black ink or typed precisely. All information must fit within the outlined designated space without touching the lines of any box. No erasures or whiteout may be used. It must be clearly legible and all information must be completed prior to submitting to the Office of Vital Records (OVR) for approval. (*Handy Hint:* Purchase a few archival pens at an art supply store in a couple of point sizes—medium, to fine, to extra fine. These are invaluable as they do not smudge.)

Death certificate information includes, in part, the following categories: decedent's personal data, usual residence, informant's data, spousal and parental data, funeral director/embalmer and local registrar information, place of death, medical information from an attending physician, cause of death, and the physician's certification. In the personal data section, one line requires "decedent's race." I discourage the use of the term *caucasian*, as it is not usually an accurate designation. In support of my opinion on this, please refer to an online article titled, "Why Do We Keep Using the Word Caucasian?"[45] The California death certificate allows up to three ethnic identities to be recorded. I encourage families to fill in personal ethnic origins as it declares our rich ethnic heritage and is more accurate than using terms like "white" or "black."

---

45. Moses, "Why Do We Keep Using the Word 'Caucasian'?" http://www.sapiens.org/column/race/caucasian-terminology-origin.

In the case of a home funeral, the name of the person legally responsible is entered in the box labeled "Funeral Director." In the box labeled "Embalmer," write, "NONE." For additional notations regarding paperwork, see page 209.

A good idea is to initially fill out the information on a practice worksheet, either during an initial intake interview or at a convenient time during the vigil. A few practice copies are often necessary before preparing the actual death certificate for final approval. You must go to your local OVR to acquire the legal form of a death certificate. (Official death certificates are not given out casually nor are they available online.) Inform the OVR you are helping a family who is planning a home funeral. Keep a low profile until you get to know the OVR personnel and their procedures for individuals doing home funerals. Over time as you become acquainted with office personnel, they will understand your role in helping the families carry out their legal rights. It is important, however, to prepare needed documents as soon as possible and get them to your county OVR; it can be a lengthy process to get approval and must be done before moving the body.

The information from the attending physician and/or coroner can only be acquired after death. It is good to establish contact with the physician beforehand whenever possible. A doctor may only be familiar with how a mortuary handles documentation and not realize that the home funeral process is legal and different. In assisting a family with the paperwork, you naturally become an emissary and educator. Know your state's statutes so you can inform and allay concerns that doctors or hospice personnel may have. Death certificates require getting information in regard to the cause of death and then acquiring the doctor's actual signature in person *after* OVR approval. The doctor must have seen the person within the previous twenty days and be familiar with the person's condition (assuming this is not a coroner case, detailed below). If the person has been under hospice care, this step is generally facilitated with ease as the hospice nurse and physician are in regular contact, and thus the physician has up-to-date information about the patient.

Coroner Involvement

This is required in a death that is related to an accident, drugs, occupational hazard, contagious disease, suicide, crime, and unusual or unexpected circumstances. Most of these cases will require a coroner examination and often an autopsy. Occasionally, this can be avoided if the accidental death happened to an elderly person or someone who died of an apparent and obvious natural cause substantiated by their primary care physician. The coroner will use his discretion in allowing a physician to make this determination even if the doctor didn't see the deceased within the required twenty days. In this case, the coroner must still be contacted and will review the death certificate and determine if a coroner's case number can be entered on the death certificate in lieu of a physical exam and autopsy. This is my personal understanding and in accordance with my experience as a home funeral guide in the state of California, county of Sonoma. For other information and legal questions, refer to your state statutes by contacting your state's Department of Consumer Affairs, reading *Final Rights*, or visiting the Final Passages or the Funeral Consumers Alliance websites. In California, another essential reference for confirming legal allowance of family involvement is the "Consumer Guide to Funeral and Cemetery Provisions" from your state.[46]

The Application and Permit for Disposition of Human Remains

This also must be filled out in black ink with the same cautions/limitations as stated above for the death certificate. In California, a PDF with instructions for filling out this document is available online. For detailed questions and concerns regarding exact regulations about cremated remains, you can consult the Cemetery and Funeral Bureau's *Cremated Remains Disposers Booklet* as well.[47]

Filling out these forms is fairly self-explanatory, although exact wording or specific abbreviations are required, and sometimes what is acceptable may change. The process can take time and OVR offices are only open during normal weekday hours. Also, some offices have specific time slots for reviewing and approving the paperwork. This is why preparing the forms and faxing them to the OVR as soon as possible is critical, especially if a family wants to accomplish everything within a specific time frame.

The information the physician must supply (including the cause of death, related information and timing of care, signature, etc.) is critical and must be provided in a precise manner. The OVR must approve a draft of the entire

---

46. www.cfb.ca.gov/consumer/funeral.

47. "Consumer Guide," cfb.ca.gov.

death certificate document (with physician's declared cause of death and other significant factors) before the physician actually signs it. Then the completed document can be submitted to the OVR for final certification. Technically, this is the responsibility of the family member legally in charge. Yet a family involved with their hands-on home funeral and their own grief may find it too cumbersome to deal with this exacting process. A home funeral guide's familiarity with and competence in helping to manage this detail is extremely valuable at this difficult time.

Once final approval is obtained and the physician's signature is on the document, you can proceed to make an in-person appointment with the responsible family member to deliver it for certification. While a guide may schedule the appointment in the family member's name, the actual person responsible (POA, executor, right of kinship in legal order) must go to the appointment. A home funeral guide may accompany that person, which is something that is both acceptable and helpful. Filing fees for the death certificate and the disposition permit are paid at this time as well as requests and payments for the number of certified copies the family needs. The copy or additional copies can also be ordered by phone to come by mail.

Another more detailed description of how to fill out each line of these forms can be found on the previously referenced Final Passages website in the section titled, "Abbreviated Instructions for California End-of-Life Documentation."[48]

I encourage anyone interested in home funerals to join the National Home Funeral Alliance (NHFA) as a guide or supporting member. Members can access NHFA resources on the organization's website.[49] If you are interested in being available as a home funeral guide, I strongly urge you to pursue training with one of the educational programs available.

———

The information offered here is specific to the state of California. Be sure to research your state and local county for documents required by your locale. Familiarize yourself with local funeral homes willing to support a family who wishes to keep their deceased family member at home for any period of time.

---

48. "Final Passages—A Complete Home Funeral Guide," finalpassages.org.

49. homefuneralalliance.org.

Even if your state has laws that require a funeral home to handle all "corpse care," most still are willing to allow time for a family to be with their family member at home before picking them up. If the body is picked up soon after death, either from the home or where the body was found, most funeral homes will allow for a preliminary viewing before other arranged preparations. They may insist on some things regarding closing the eyes or other simple cosmetic adjustments before allowing any viewing of the body.

Even if a death is not imminent, being acquainted with your local funeral homes and their policies can be very helpful in preparation for the unknown.

SECTION FOUR
CREATING SACRED SPACE

CHAPTER 11
READYING THE BODY-TEMPLE

Death, like birth, is a secret of Nature.
—*Marcus Aurelius*

Each experience of being in the presence of death is different. Yet for all its differences, my experience repeatedly is this: at the moment of death, it's as if the *universe holds its breath*. There is a pause when a tumble of feelings may collide, even explode, and then there is a nanosecond of quiet acceptance. Awareness is keen and heightened.

Let's imagine …

The moment has arrived. Someone just died—someone whom you care about. You have been called on to assist the family with their home funeral. You are prepared. You shared many special moments with the dying person and their family. You interviewed the family, discussed concerns, and anticipated this time coming. You've agreed on how to be of service to them. Calligraphy-lettered signs saying, "Enter Quietly" and a cardboard casket have previously been delivered to the home.

The stage is set by your acts of kindness. Now it is time to enter their space and assist them in their final hands-on care and tributes to their beloved family member. *We are a team in this true-to-life hypothetical scene.* We will do this together.

———

"Roland" had been strong and healthy for nearly ninety-seven years. It's been a remarkable gift to share many visits with him and his family. He experienced a gradual decline that progressed to his nearing death. With his family, he made necessary plans for his end-of life-choices. He was, and is, at peace. His wife, Rita, and sister, Veronica, were with him when he passed early this morning, and his son, daughter, and grandchildren will arrive soon.

We pause before entering and join hands as we allow a shift in our energy, dipping into sacred awareness. We enter empty-handed so that we may be with what is, before taking specific action. Veronica and Rita greet us. A tangible sense of presence and awareness is silently shared as soft tears wash our faces.

Veronica comments on the peace visible on his face. Friends echo the sentiment. They talk about the morning events with wonder and admiration in their voices.

We gather around Roland's bedside. Veronica tells us how she sat vigil through much of the night. She wanted to let Rita get some needed sleep, assuring her she would rouse her when she noted signs the hospice nurse told her would occur. As dawn approached, Roland's eyes fluttered repeatedly; his breathing became labored. Veronica woke Rita. They sat on either side of Roland; each held a hand as he had asked. He smiled at each of them as he shifted his body a little and drifted in and out of awareness. It was a gentle passage.

We await cues that Rita and Veronica are ready to begin preparing the body. Veronica implores us to take the lead and help them know what to do. I nod to you. You exit to bring in the items we left in our car.

Early this morning, Veronica tidied and cleaned the room while Rita sat by Roland's side. Rita whispered of her love and gratitude for their life together.

We notice the closeness of the two women and their ease in balancing each other's energy. You move quietly in and out, arranging our kit in a designated spot. You carefully handle the dry ice container, knowing how important it is for dry ice, even in a cooler, to be on a surface it will not burn and damage. Their bathtub is a perfect spot. Padded gloves and brown paper bags are with the dry ice.

We prepare a rolling cart with washbasin, cloths, cotton swabs, herbal and essential oil soap, cotton balls, plastic sheet, pillows, towels, cover blanket, long tie-scarves, candles, essential oils, and other items. You fill a basin with warm water, an herbal soap, and an essential oil blend Rita previously chose. Rita asks a friend to softly play some of Roland's favorite music. Some friends are busy housecleaning and preparing food in the kitchen, and the smell of cookies baking flavors the air. Anticipating the arrival of grandchildren adds excitement.

Rita and Veronica want to do as much of the hands-on care as possible, yet they ask us to guide, prepare, and help them along the way. Previously, we'd discussed many of the how-to logistics of moving a body, proceeding with a ritual bath, and other techniques that could be helpful. We'd demonstrated and practiced with Roland's wife, sister, and Roland's daughter. We had asked about forms of ritual they resonated with. We found common ground.

Rita asks that we hold sacred space and initiate ritual throughout the day. She wants to be free to be with her husband while others' work goes on.

With the cart bedside, we are ready to begin. I take a few moments to feel Roland's tangible energy, pervasive in the space. I light a votive candle and allow spirit energy to speak through me as I invoke sacred space honoring Roland, his ritual bath, his body-temple, and this sacred vigil. Silence embraces us as we connect with each other.

Conscious of sacred energy surrounding us, we begin. First, we tuck a plastic sheet beneath him and cover it with a cotton sheet and absorbent pads. We position his body and slightly elevate his head. I squeeze warm water through washcloths and hand them to Rita and Veronica, who gently and tenderly wash Roland's face and neck, making sure to wash ears and crevices.

I assist by holding his head to guard against fluid escaping while Veronica does oral care with swabs and cotton balls. We set coins over his already-closed eyelids. His mouth reveals a slightly open, peaceful smile. We tie a scarf around his jaw temporarily to ensure his relaxed smile will continue. We work smoothly with each other, each of us uttering caring words, as if Roland is here with us. His presence *is* felt.

We enjoy watching the two women who previously had expressed reservations about doing this task. Their soft chatter is filled with love and joy for a good brother, father, and husband. They move and work naturally together, washing the front of Roland's body. Rita covers Roland's genital area as she lovingly washes her husband's private parts. With a coordinated movement, we turn Roland to the other side to wash his back and buttocks area. Again, I support his head to prevent drainage. Rita laughs, recalling her husband's comfort with his body; he was never overly modest. Still, we keep him covered except for the area of his body being washed, as part of a respectful ritual.

It is nearly time to place the dry ice under and over him. Fortunately, the weather is moderate and the room is cool. He did not die of an illness, so body odor is not strong. We remove the damp plastic sheet, replace it with a dry one, and cover that with a clean, dark blue sheet Rita had saved for this purpose. We excuse ourselves to prepare the dry ice packs, leaving the women alone to do an anointing ritual with essential oils.

A padded glove protects my hands from burning as I handle the dry ice. I pick out three pieces from the twenty pounds purchased earlier. We will likely need another twenty pounds in a day and a half, depending on the weather. You ready the brown paper bags. We insert dry ice in three bags, fold them neatly, and wrap each in an absorbent towel. We place these ready packs back in the cooler and return to help dress Roland.

Aware of sacred space, we quietly enter the room. Roland's spirit is pervasive throughout the entire home. Still, the focus is on this sacred event. Rita and Victoria are meditating and speaking softly with their beloved Roland. The aroma of frankincense and cypress oils fills the room. You and I each take a turn anointing his head and feet with frankincense. We speak prayerfully, honoring remembrance of the rich time we spent with him.

Rita retrieves colorful clothes she and Roland previously handpicked for him to wear. Roland wanted it to be easy to dress him. Together, they had chosen a shirt that Rita had embroidered for him during their courting days over fifty years ago and a loose pair of trousers. As he was a gardener and loved to go barefoot, Roland had asked that his feet be left bare. Veronica brings out a quilt made by their mother long ago.

It is easy to put on this outfit. At other events, it has been necessary to cut fancy clothes up the back in order to dress someone or wrestle arms into sleeves. Roland and Rita had practiced this part of the ritual, so she asks for only a little help. His hair was washed the day before, so we do not need to use the dry or wet shampoo from our kit. Rita combs his hair as he liked it and adds his garden cap to top off the look. Veronica muses about how to arrange the quilt. We shuffle, turn him again, and drape the quilt over his shoulders and around his arms and flare it off to his sides. Veronica comments that he looks ready to hop up and head out to his garden.

It's time for the dry ice. We lift and roll his torso to one side—again, holding his head higher so as not to allow fluids to drain out. We place two larger pieces beneath his torso—upper chest and lower back. Rita gets his hand pruners for him to hold. We place the smaller piece under his hands. Something is needed to camouflage the height of the dry ice under his hands. A pillow under his knees helps balance the prominence of the dry ice. Rita giggles and retrieves his garden tool belt and a large, brightly colored handkerchief. Creative fiddling manages to adjust the dry ice over his abdomen, cover it with the handkerchief and garden belt, and put one hand on top of the other, allowing the top hand to hold his pruners. Rita is delighted imagining him in heaven's garden already, creating beauty for the angels. Veronica remarks that his peace now is our peace. She offers a spontaneous prayer as we clasp hands, lingering for a moment. It is a beautiful and tender moment shared.

With Roland's body bathed, dressed, and cooling, we turn our attention to the room. This inviting personal space is where friends and family have comfortably sat bedside to visit. Now it needs a new arrangement. It is time to transform the space from a dying room into a sacred sanctuary space; Roland's body-temple is to be "lying-in-honor."

When asked about a color theme, Veronica and Rita simultaneously say, "Deep blue and green!" Our collection of altar fabrics in color-labeled bins—along with miscellaneous containers providing everything from pushpins to crystals and altar items—is in the hall. The sisters head for the bins to choose fabrics and items to beautify the room.

In near silence, the four of us dance spontaneously, as if choreographed by angelic presence. Our simple communication is subtle and exquisite as we create a sanctuary altar space. Veronica removes the eye coins and unties the scarf around his chin. His gentle smile and relaxed eyes remain. Gentle tears and laughter flow like a river of love through the dance in memory and honor of Roland.

Synchronicity magically fosters our realization of completion. Simultaneously we sigh, stand back. Mutual smiles proclaim satisfaction. We are filled with awe. The room is radiant with soft candlelight, a deep blue-green hue of color, and memorabilia of a life well-lived. The altar and body-temple of Roland is deeply honoring. We take hands, embracing the silence, and feel spirit presence. A vibrational feeling of chills sweeps throughout my body. Prayerfully channeled words of tribute are voiced in honor and blessing. Here lies a gentle man who is crossing over the threshold ahead of us who remain here to celebrate, witness, and mourn his passage.

Veronica brings in a couple of chairs to accommodate afternoon vigil visitors. The room feels ready to receive guests. You and I quietly slip out. Rita and Veronica stay in the room. We hear soft mumblings indicative of a conversation with Roland.

We put away extra materials and connect with the rest of the household, waiting for Rita and Veronica to rejoin us. We will take our leave or stay to help depending on what they wish. Rita emerges and expresses her gratitude. She asks that we stay, hoping we will be present with visitors. She'd like us to reply to anticipated questions, rather than her or Veronica. They simply wish to be with Roland and friends to share love, joy, and sorrow.

We stay, honored to be part of the afternoon as visitors slowly trail in to pay their respects and bring offerings of food, flowers, and stories of their love for Roland, Rita, and Veronica. Family arrives, and children add buoyancy and an obvious affection for their grandfather. The kindergarten boy, Lucas, tells us his "Gramper" told him that, *"Everything* is part of the earth and the soil and is *never, ever lost!"* Further, Gramper said that whenever Lucas missed him, Lucas could go out in the garden or snuggle in his bed and call Gramper. Gramper would come give him a hug. He said it might feel like only a breeze or a tickle from a plant or appear as pretty colors in a flower or glowing in a sunset or even a twinkle from a star outside his bedroom window—yet it *would actually be him—his Gramper!* It is obvious the children spent many happy hours with their grandfather.

Lucas leads his cousin Emma, weaving in and out of what he calls the "silly room of Gramper." As we share a cookie, I ask him why he called it the "silly room." He explains that Gramper told him that the body he left behind to go into the earth was just *"his silly body, not his real body!"* In a serious and knowledgeable voice, he explains that Gramper told him his real body was invisible and that it would stay around forever. This obviously made Lucas very happy and left him untroubled by seeing and touching his Gramper's "silly body." As he and Emma "noit" Gramper's head with a kiss and the "good smelly" oils their grandmother let them pick out, I overhear Lucas illuminate his cousin. Her constant attentiveness is obvious and so sweet. These two wise and loving cousins express joy and a feeling of being in right relation with all that is. Their presence definitely is a significant part of the living legacy and ritual that is taking place.

A spectacular autumn day is coming to a close. Visitors were in and out all day, adding to the energy of a beautiful and vital vigil. A feeling of community and enduring love is conspicuous. Close friends are preparing dinner for family who will linger for the night. We check the dry ice and coolness of his body and share a brief check-in with Rita and Veronica. Rita confirms how much the grandchildren loved being with their Gramper. This evening, they will have a story reading from a surprise book their grandfather wrote for them. We both remark how this day is such a beautiful reflection of Roland and the life he shared with his amazing family and friends.

"It was perfectly how Ro wanted this day to be," Rita shares as we revel again at his peaceful smile. We laugh as I recount the spiritual lesson about the "silly body." Rita imagines a new sign will be made, illustrated by Lucas and Emma, saying, "Gramper's Silly Room."

Lucas certainly adds to my understanding of death and its ongoing-ness. Now I, too, have Gramper and Lucas to help me explain death to another child or adult.

The weather is quite cool. We will be back to pay respects and check the coolness of Roland's "silly body" tomorrow afternoon to determine when more dry ice is needed. With a prayerful closure to our day, we speak in turn; a collective prayer cherishing the beautiful vigil time is a benediction. The vigil will continue until the final committal ritual. Meanwhile, we encourage Rita and Veronica to enjoy family, get needed rest, and feel free to call us anytime.

Reflections and Guidance

We will return to Rita and Veronica since we are still responsible to help them complete their lying-in-honor event. Yet as they rest, we take the opportunity to evaluate where we are.

If only each home funeral unfolded this easily. Not only does that not happen every time—in truth, we would not want it thus. All lives are vastly unique and different, as is the experience of each death.

How each home funeral is orchestrated is unique; that is its beauty.

A Guide for the Guide

No list or exact protocol can encompass all essential aspects or ways to do this work. That is not only because every death is unique to each person, it is also because *the primary acting entity is not the home funeral guide.* The family unit is what provides the template for what ultimately will create a one-of-a-kind experience. The home funeral guide is a catalyst, a facilitator, and an assistant to a multifaceted, layered, and often complex live group of players who are the *heart of the home funeral—the family.*

In that context, here is a guide for the guide. Likely, with each home funeral event undertaken, you will encounter a new problem or issue and a remedy to include in your prep-kit. The learning curve is an ongoing adventure.

Following the guide are other considerations of what one could encounter and need to factor in when helping a family. There is a combination of items needed and possible actions to take. See page 207 for bulleted lists of items needed for a home funeral kit.

————

Have your kit ready and easily accessible. I have a *small kit* of bare essentials and a *larger backup kit* with extra things to refresh the smaller kit as needed. For example, my small kit has soap, basin, washcloths, comb, hairbrush, shampoo, plastic sheet (one large bed-sized and many smaller ones), essential oils, coins, shoestrings, cotton swabs, cotton balls, gloves, gauze rolls, scissors, tweezers, adhesive strips, absorbent pads, and crazy glue (to close eyes or mouth if desired). A larger kit that stays in my vehicle has more towels and cloths of different sizes, absorbent pads—both cotton and ones called "chux" (paper with one plastic side)—basins, cotton sheets, plastic sheets of various sizes, rolls of paper towel, rags, belts, larger gauze rolls, plastic bags, small and large pillows, scarves, ties of many lengths, makeup kit (with light and dark foundation, eye pencils, lipstick, and a couple of colors of nail polish), combs of different sizes, brushes, body-sling carriers, and backup items for the smaller kit. A divided plastic tray is handy for small items. A folding cart with wheels and a compact music box are great extras.

It is prudent to have a *designated cooler for dry ice* accessible. I suggest it not be the same one you use for picnics, as a picnic cooler could be in use when you need it for dry ice. *Know where you can easily get dry ice.* Be familiar with as many places as possible and know their protocol. Most suppliers in grocery stores want to handle it themselves. However, if you tell them you need to pick out particular sizes, you usually can convince them to allow you to hand-pick what you want. Be prepared with your own padded mitt. They will weigh your dry ice before it goes in your cooler. Twenty pounds is usually enough for the first day. You may need that much for each day or day and a half. If the weather is extremely hot and/or the person is very large, more ice will be needed. Be sure to place the cooler in a safe place to not burn through and mar a wood floor or other surface. A bathtub, shower, or outdoor covered cement area is an ideal place. Dry ice evaporates quickly; it needs to be purchased at the time of need, not far ahead of time. Only the torso, where vital organs are located, needs cooling. Generally, two large square pieces of dry ice are placed under the torso—one under the rib cage at the level of the heart, and one under the lower abdomen in the area of the gut. One additional smaller (though substantial) piece is placed over the abdomen, usually under the placement of the hands. Decomposition occurs first in the vital organs rather than the extremities, where it is much slower. Dry ice is the easiest and most convenient to use of other alternatives. Since dry ice is solid carbon dioxide, it evaporates rather than melts and easily freezes the torso very quickly. It is much less messy than regular H_2O ice, which needs more attention due to melting. Another alternative is the newer option of "Techni-ice," which is a layered ice pack frequently used as a substitute when dry ice is not easily available. Techni-ice is reusable and good to have on hand for immediate need. It is better to use than gel packs.

Altar fabrics and altar items are useful to collect. A family may have special fabrics, blankets, and treasures they wish to use. However, often there is not enough. Have fabric in many sizes and colors. Long fabrics are especially handy as they can wrap a bed or massage table and hang to the floor (a great place for storing items), cover bookcases and dressers, or even drape walls and windows. A canopy can hang from the ceiling and create a magical effect. My fabric is kept in large plastic bins marked by color (blues-lavenders-purples, oranges-reds-pinks, whites-blacks, unique prints, and wall hangings with figures). A smaller bin has items like crystals, figurines, vases, candles and candleholders (think safety!), box of pushpins, adhesive tape, small hammer and tiny nails, and scissors. I also bring a couple of lightweight, small tables.

I keep one cardboard coffin on hand so there's no need to make a rush order. This is available to the family for reimbursement, not as a profit sale. A coffin/casket, shroud, basket, or wooden box are all other options for a family to consider. Online references are plentiful with referrals for green burial options and DIY instructions for building caskets and making shrouds. (Finding online sources for cardboard caskets, however, evaded me. All the websites I found sold only to funeral establishments. Contact home funeral educational institutes for a possible source.)

Develop a list of people to assist a family. Often family members want to be helpful in ways other than directly dealing with the body-care aspects of a home funeral. Consider making a list of people to help with house chores, pet care, regular jaunts for shopping, post office pickups, garden chores, notifying neighbors, and planning for parking. Part of assisting a family with a home funeral is finding supportive ways to create ease during a stressful time. Family members and friends may wish to be enlisted for needed tasks.

A portable CD player and CDs are valuable items to include. Have soft instrumental music and environmental sound CDs. Family or friends may have plenty of favorite music. Soft music playing in the altar space with the person lying-in-honor will create a quieting ambiance that affirms the sacred vigil's nature.

Regarding body washing: The family's wish in this regard is most important to address and agree on before the time arrives. For many, it is a *sacred ritual.* Who participates may be what is most important. The bathing ritual can be one of the most special aspects of a home funeral. Home funeral guides may find that they become part of a team with a hospice crew. Yet when assisting with plans for a dear friend's home funeral, I recall the dying man saying he wanted his wife and me (his friend) to be the only ones to do his ritual bath. He emphatically stated he did not want the hospice team to do this, even though he appreciated their palliative care. Special attention to the genital area is imperative to address and mitigate with sensitivity—something that is best to discuss ahead of time. For some it is "no big deal," and for others it is more awkward. This is not a complicated chore, just a delicate and sensitive one. If a catheter has been inserted, the hospice team will likely be glad to remove it and also assist with genital care. In general, urine cleansing is easy with plain soap and water, essential oils, and changing of undergarments and sheets. Excess in the bladder is addressed simply by putting pressure on the lower abdomen/bladder area. If bowel care has been regular and the person has not been eating, fecal accumulation is absent or minimal. Yet it is easy to check with a gloved hand and remove any fecal matter present; follow this with soap and water cleansing.

Essential oils are helpful; however, they alone do not eliminate the cause of odor. Hygienic bowel and genital care is essential when a person is to be lying-in-honor for a vigil viewing.

Regarding body care and changes: Stiffening of the body (technically called "rigor mortis") is a dynamic process that is not exact in timing, onset, or duration. Usually shortly after death, the body is relaxed and flaccid. Stiffening can begin in a short time or not occur for an hour. Therefore, rigor mortis, sometimes called a "third stage of death," cannot be definitely predetermined for planning the greatest ease of movement or ability to bathe and dress a body. Generally, one can consider it easiest to bathe and dress a body shortly after death, although that is not always possible. The cause of death, a person's weight, their size, and how long they have been bedridden may be factors in the onset of rigor mortis.

Onset of stiffening does not preclude handling, bathing, and dressing. It is possible to work around the fluctuation from relaxed to stiffened. It is helpful for at least two to three people to be involved in this process. That is one reason it is valuable for home funeral guides to work as a team and/or for willing family members to do the work (remember you are helping them). It is also important to educate and engage a family in how to bathe and dress a deceased family member ahead of time. Another important factor to address is the relative change in weight of the body after death. Remember the personal example of "dead weight" told of in chapter 2. This is another area where teamwork is important.

If there is a pacemaker, it must be removed in the case of cremation. Any other drainage tubes or shunts that are exterior can be removed (although sometimes that may not be necessary). In doing this, however, it is important to know that there may be drainage of fluid. An emesis basin is useful to catch drainage, along with extra cloths. Also, have gauze dressing material and plain Band-Aids at the ready. If a hospice team is engaged, a nurse or aid may help with this process or do it for the family. Still, it is not impossible for the family to perform this action with your help and guidance.

Be sure to note jewelry being worn by the deceased and inquire how the family wishes to deal with those items. If there is to be a burial, the family may choose to leave jewelry and artifacts in the coffin. However, if a body is to be cremated, the cremator will ask that unburnable, plastic, and toxic materials are not included with the body.

If you are participating in bringing a body home after a coroner examination and possible autopsy, there are some additional things to consider and to prepare a family for. When the coroner knows a family will be bringing a body home, they may put in extra effort to make the torso incision clean and neat. If there is a possibility that toxic chemicals or drugs contributed to the death, the coroner will have probably opened the skull to examine the brain, and the cranium may still be open. This means there will be more body fluid to deal with, and super glue (ethyl cyanoacrylate) will be your saving grace. It is essential to have a home funeral family team of two or more who are comfortable with this situation and able to work together with home funeral guides. It is essential to talk with the family about how tedious this process may be beforehand. You must be sure that they are prepared and that a designated family member or friend is available to also be a primary worker.

The potential for complications may discourage a family from deciding to have a home funeral. Be honest and candid with them. Tutelage with the designated person(s) ahead of time is essential. Items that are important to have on hand (along with the super glue) are gloves, plenty of absorbent cotton balls, gauze and disposable cotton rags, shampoo, plastic bags and plastic sheets, more wash basins and a container for catching washing fluid (this can be carried out to nourish a garden or drained in the tub or shower), a makeup kit with matching skin foundation, long ties to hold the skull together, hats, headscarves, and any personal items that would camouflage the possible head shape being altered.

This is a delicate situation, and it is essential to speak frankly with the family beforehand. Nevertheless, it is entirely their choice. They *do* have the right to handle their loved one's body. However, they need your honest assessment and experience as a home funeral guide to confirm one way or another if they are able to handle a more intense dealing with body fluid and the emotional experience that will certainly be part of such an endeavor. Be gentle with everyone regarding this concern.

Sometimes when helping a family evaluate whether they are good candidates to manage a home funeral, it may become evident that it is not an easy or reasonable fit. In such cases, it is important for a guide or advocate to honestly decline participation in a home funeral. That is another reason it is helpful to know of local funeral establishments that are agreeable, comfortable, and accommodating to a family who desires to be as hands-on as possible; it is also exceptionally valuable for home funeral guides to ensure their connections and working relations are respectful. Some funeral homes offer moderated and itemized fees to support such families. Ask these businesses for any forms they need when a family is planning a home funeral.

Planning ahead for the committal event, the family needs to consider whether they wish to transport the body in their own vehicle or arrange for a friend to transport the body (depending on your state laws). A seventy-two-inch length is needed to accommodate a cardboard casket. If a different type of casket is being built or purchased, be sure the space in the vehicle is long enough to accommodate it. In most cases an open truck bed is acceptable, though the body must be covered.

If there is to be a procession to the committal site and the family wishes for all to stay together, there is a commonly known practice of all cars turning their headlights on in the procession. Today, however, many people leave lights on in daylight, so confusion could occur. A sign saying "FUNERAL PROCESSION" can be copied for all vehicles to post in side and back windows.

Be clear and honest about your available hours for being called upon in the home funeral process. I tell a family they may call anytime and inform them what hours I will be close to my phone. If I miss a call, I will return it as soon as I am able—usually within ten to fifteen minutes. They are even welcome to call in the middle of the night and leave a message. If you have a home funeral partner working with you, make sure that person is also clear about their hours of availability. It is a good idea to have other backup numbers available—for example, a family or close friend who would likely know your whereabouts.

We Return to Rita and Veronica and the Vigil Wake for Roland

Let's check in with family and determine how Roland is looking. There is more activity going on as we enter; more people are milling about than when we left a day ago. A very active group clustered around the cardboard casket is creating a masterful art piece to honor their friend. Laughter and stories, alternating with quiet focused time, happen as people demonstrate love through art. Other young children have joined Lucas and Emma, and happy feet are scurrying around. The children come in and out to draw on Gramper's "silly body box," as Lucas terms it. Mostly, they play and work in Gramper's garden, which was apparently one of the favorite activities they shared with him.

I marvel at precocious Lucas, who loves to explain Gramper's spiritual philosophy to other children and even to some adults before they enter to view his Gramper. He also takes on the task of keeping other children in line to be respectful of his grandfather. Emma eyes Lucas with obvious admiration. These children are enchanting!

You and I enter the now officially christened "Silly Room." A colorful sign is added above "Enter Quietly" at the doorway: "Enter Gramper's Silly Room." It is beautiful and obviously made by the two youngsters. Roland's countenance has barely changed, with only slight color variations evident on his skin. His soft smile and mostly closed eyes show little change. I remark to you how this is a unique example of someone being in relative good health with death's passage. We stand quietly by his side, again admiring his relaxed, even beatific expression. You initiate a brief prayer, calling for his celebrated crossing over and reception into the Mystery.

Together, we measure and feel the evaporation extent of the dry ice. Roland's body is exceptionally cold. His torso feels quite frozen and there is no detectable body odor. We can tell that anointing of essential oils has continued by the aroma that permeates the room, even wafting outward. Someone has wisely opened two windows just a wee bit, allowing some cool cross ventilation. Lighted candles have been refreshed and are strategically placed away from the windows, curtains, and edges of tables. New pictures of Roland through the years have been added. The music has changed to quiet instrumental New Age melodic harmonies. It is a beautiful sacred space. As we stand reverently beside Roland's body, we anoint him with the rose oil, now the predominate aroma offered on the nearby table.

Rita is excited to tell us of progress for the planned committal of a green burial on a nearby small private church cemetery. Roland's family has lived in this county for years and this church cemetery was a quiet retreat place for him as a child. He knew that he wanted to be placed in the earth there when his time came. The church is still maintained by a deacon, who approved the burial and acknowledged his responsibility to accept and keep paperwork on file in the church office. The deacon honors Rita and Veronica by suggesting they consider the church sanctuary for a memorial service later. This is very touching to Rita. She tells us she plans to make a donation greater than the fee requested.

I can tell from Rita's bubbling excitement that she is running on endorphin energy of love and presence for her "Ro." I know she will greatly need support from her family and friends in the weeks that will follow these few days. I make a mental note to talk with you about her remarkable energy, the glow that is lighting her way today and naturally softening her grief for the moment and her needs in days to come. Grief has a dynamic face that changes, surprises, and requires vent as it unfolds. The seeming lightheartedness Rita is exhibiting now is a reflection of that changing face of grief. I will follow up on the initial interview promise I made her that she can call upon me for support in the days and weeks that follow.

It's time to address how Roland's body is holding up. We determine that since Roland is quite cold, this evening will be soon enough to change the dry ice. We linger for a few more quiet reflective moments. The sun is drifting behind the trees. We take our leave of grandmother and grandchildren who are quietly cuddling together and go inside to introduce ourselves to Catherine and Stephen.

All four of the grown cousins want to participate in what they spontaneously call the "Silly Ro ice ritual." We make a plan to return in a few hours, after their dinnertime, with fresh dry ice. This is unfolding to be the sweetest home funeral I could ever imagine!

The lying-in-honor vigil is nearing completion. We enter a quiet house with the dry ice. A quiet Silly Ro ice ritual is easily shared. We blow out candles and bid them rest and sweet dreams.

Tomorrow they expect a quiet day. They express anticipation of the final committal gathering. We let them know we can be called anytime. We plan on only a brief check-in time tomorrow and then again before the gathering on the following day, when we will gather for a committal ritual in the garden. We pause, ending this saga for now.

———

Assisting a family is dear to the heart. Even as I write an "imaginary" scenario, I form images of the experience that feel tangibly real. I have experienced with you the lying-in-honor ritual and the family community related to Roland. I trust you gained an understanding of how to help a friend or family member with a home funeral, if this is on your horizon.

Each death is its own unique event—no matter how difficult, awkward, agonizingly sorrowful, peaceful, beautiful, or strange. Yet there is a magic that creeps in, in spite of everything. I am reminded of a Leonard Cohen song. His song relays to us that there is a crack in all things and that it is that crack that lets the light in.

By sharing this unique honoring of Roland's life, we've been given an opportunity to feel part of what is entailed with death care and a home funeral. I imagine you also felt a celebration of the light that slips through the crack of reality and embraces all in its path. Revel in that light. Integrating our experience is part of deepening our understanding and promotes skillful preparation for the many ways of being with others in their home funeral. I recall a favorite line from the thirteenth-century Persian mystical poet and Islamic scholar, Rumi, who reminds us, "Let the beauty we love be what we do. There are hundreds of ways to kneel and kiss the ground."[50]

Blessed be.

---

50. Rumi, *The Essential Rumi*, 36.

CHAPTER 12

THE COMMITTAL EVENT

Death—the last voyage, the longest, the best.
—*Thomas Wolfe*

A final act of love is the commitment of the body to a final resting place. It is a decision made by a person before their death or by their family after their death. The enactment of this commitment to honor someone who has passed is referred to here as the *committal event*.

I resonate more with this term than the more commonly used legal term *disposition of the body*. Committal, a relatively old term, comes from Latin and means "to entrust." The dictionary definition says it can refer to the burial of a corpse. I am not sure when I first came across the term; I recall hearing it used at a graveside many years ago and pocketed it then in my memory. In the context of this writing, it makes more sense to use *committal* than *disposition*. Committal is descriptive and honors the specific action and ritual more than the legal term, which is about "disposing of" or getting rid of the body. Even so, clearly there is the body, and it must be dealt with appropriately, physically and legally. The focus of this chapter is about honoring a loved one who has passed beyond.

The question remains: What do *you* want? How do you wish to be honored? How do you choose to honor those who go before you?

A final resting place and the commemoration of a committal event are the last rituals with the body-temple of one's beloved. Some people refer to this time as "a last lingering look." Now we shall participate in an example of a committal event as we return to our work with Roland's family.

Recall from the last chapter that Roland's commitment was to have a green burial at a nearby church cemetery, a place he frequented as a young child. Now as we return to this experience, let's check in with his family in our mutual event.

Returning to the Roland Committal Event

The time has come to set aside body care and tender socializing and handle the paperwork. Although it can be tedious and distract from a desire for intimate family to just sit vigil and be with their guests, it is Rita's intention to do this task. As their guides, we focus on making it as easy as possible by gently shepherding the process.

We find a quiet corner to sit with Rita and Veronica. You, as an apprentice, prepare a mock-up document, while Rita, Veronica, and I fill out the death certificate form with personal identification and data on Roland. A call to Roland's personal physician gets Rita the medical information she needs for the form. A call and fax approval of the document from the local records department is needed to acquire the doctor's signature. We acquire that easily, as Roland's personal physician is also the attending hospice doctor and part of Roland's men's group. He is a lovely man and relates stories of his escapades and rich times with Roland. This provides a welcome reprieve for Rita and Veronica.

At the Office of Vital Records (OVR), we meet with a helpful person who is familiar with us and working with home funeral families. She does the final approval and records the official death certificate and Permit for Disposition. Rita signs for them, requests the four certified copies she needs, and pays the required nominal fee. As we leave the OVR, we all utter a sigh of relief and burst into laughter, releasing our nervous energy. Rita, waving the envelope with the death certificate and disposition permits, says, "Let's take a lovely ride to the church and meet Deacon Evan."

Deacon Evan greets us warmly at the quaint community church. He proudly shows us the burial plot he has marked off and tells us he will be there later when the men's group arrives to dig the sacred earth for Roland's grave. He tells us he will be present for the graveside ceremony. Rita leaves him with her generous donation. She keeps the paperwork, as it needs to be in the car with the transport of Roland's body. Deacon Evan will need the disposition permit copies at that time to record and return a copy to the OVR. Exhausted, we return home and are greeted with friends who have prepared dinner. You and I make a brief entry into the Silly Room to pay respects and check on the condition of Roland's body. Fortunately, the cousin team has replenished the dry ice. Roland's skin tone is darkening slightly, though his face still holds its peaceful look, and the room feels comfortable. We anoint him with frankincense once more, in respect and to cover any untoward smells. With a loving glance to Rita, Veronica, and family enjoying their sumptuous meal, we take our leave. Tomorrow will be a full day.

The morning promises a bright, sunny day. We arrive early, knowing there are essential tasks to handle in addition to being present with the sensitive energy of the family's last lingering look and committal ritual of their beloved Roland. We feel a deep connection with everyone here, recognizing how important this family has become to both of us. We join our new friends and enjoy coffee and delicious fresh bread. Today will be mostly a matter of coordinating lifting Roland's body into the coffin and carrying it to the garden. Rita asks that she have time to sit with her Ro in the Silly Room alone for a while. She says that when she is ready, she'll invite Veronica and family to join her, and when they come out, it will be time to transfer Roland's body. The plan feels right to everyone.

In our initial interview, we learned that Roland and Rita discussed having a brief parting ritual in their garden before moving to the burial site. The energy today is reflective. Various friends are moving about, preparing for this next event. We join some folks who are creating additions to the cardboard casket. We inscribe our love messages, mixing in with the artful décor being created.

We await a signal to help with the transfer of Roland's body from altar to casket. Someone rings a bell, and as a group, we spontaneously carry the decorated casket to Gramper's Silly Room. The children proudly line the box with a beautiful blue and green bedspread their grandmother gave them for that purpose. The four cousins take charge, moving Roland easily from his altar to the coffin and carrying the coffin outside to the picnic table, allowing room for people to gather around. It is a lovely setting.

In order to view the display of loving art on the coffin cover, one of the men ties the cover to a tree branch extending over the picnic table. It creates a captivating focal point, drawing friends near the open casket. Fragrant boughs of rosemary, lavender, and sage from the surrounding garden are laid around the coffin. The outside altar is another exquisite and personal display that honors Roland, his family, his friends, and, naturally, his garden.

As people trickle out to the garden, they gaze lovingly at Roland's body, adding fragrant herbs around his "silly body." His smile is still evident and looking quite peaceful. Many quietly address him. I offer a greeting and an invocation. His men's group's members facilitate the rest of the ritual, enlisting each family member to speak. They add depth and humor and keep the parting ritual flowing. The stories of Roland's life, death, and passage expand on a life of love, service, and deep connection with his family and his "tribe." The family sings a closing benediction and others join in harmony.

Roland's garden truck is at the garden entrance right by the compost pile. The cousins lift the coffin, carry it to the truck bed, and set the coffin lid firmly in place. Stephen and Craig pull the truck onto the road. Family and friends join in procession, some in cars, others walking the short distance to the church cemetery.

The burial site provides for yet another last farewell gathering. The men's group move the beautifully decorated coffin to the graveside. Family and friends cluster around the coffin and grave. Many are holding hands or snuggling with each other. The men begin one of their favorite chants. A group of women gather spontaneously and sing another chant. The harmonious duet is awe-inspiring. As the chants continue, a few men jump into the grave and bear the coffin gently to the ground. When the men climb out, boughs brought from the garden are tossed on the coffin; handfuls of earth cover the sacred remains. Men, women, and children sing one song or chant after another, ending with a song of returning to the earth. Some wander through the lovely church garden-cemetery while others finish filling in the grave and creating a raised mound to which plantings of herbs and flowers are added.

Who says a ceremony must be solemn? A beautiful, full-bodied, multilayered ritual ceremony full of laughter, solemn moments, tears, and joy brings us together in a dignified, authentic celebration honoring Roland. His distinguished "silly body" is committed to returning to the earth, with a shared recognition, on his word, that his "real body" will be around forever. Thus is our experience; a committal event of great beauty and respect has transpired before us.

———

This rich participatory tale is about a green burial. Yet clearly there are many ways this event could transpire. It could be very simple. It could be only a brief time with or without any formal or informal ceremony. Again, it is as varied as the people who participate in this event. If there is a cremation, the ceremony may be as simple as people transporting the body to the crematorium. Unless a viewing of the cremation has been arranged, those who have transported the body will leave the body in the care of the cremator. If a viewing of the cremation is arranged, that might constitute the committal ceremony. Or a family may wish to plan another ceremonial gathering to scatter the cremains at a favorite site. Sacred sites for scattering ceremonies are so varied; I have attended many, from scattering at the ocean, in a forest, around a special tree, along a river, and more. Our family hiked a mountain trail on family land, scattering the cremains of our Grandmommy Anna along the way; years later, we scattered our Mama Iris, and later, with our cousins, our aunt and uncle, too. Hiking that trail remains a sacred walk. Many funeral businesses with a memorial lawn are glad to allow a family group to be on the grounds for as long as they like. They may also inform a family of the approximate time when the cremation will take place. Some families like to return at that time to be present on the grounds while the cremation is occurring. There are many options to consider.

There truly are so many ways up the mountain. I anticipate you have questions swirling in your head as you consider what you have learned and envision the possibilities. Ask yourself, What would you orchestrate? Get a copy of the Advanced Care Directive and Five Wishes. Discuss and write down what you want and how you want your body handled medically, if that is in question. Let your family know if there are particular ways you'd like to be celebrated.

Then surrender. Remember that how you are celebrated is something your family and those you love will choose. They are the ones who will live with the loss; they are the ones who will feel the emptiness of your absence. It is their need to quell their sorrow and grapple with a life without you.

The committal event can be one of the most tender and lingering moments for a family and community. This "last lingering look" matters. It is a unique time and deserves its place in the last physical honoring of one's beloved. The cycle of birth and death and renewal has been enacted.

One could say the "party," or rather parting, is over, yet in many ways it has just begun as well. As the year unfolds, there will be many memories related to a cycle of personal dates and seasonal rememberings. Life and the world have changed. At this time, there may be a feeling of relief now that this sequence of activity is accomplished. Yet the impact of the loss and personal grief may arise with fervor. The grief of bereavement with loss of a family member or an intense grief in losing a close friend needs its own time to unfold. That may be a reason to pause and allow grief to express itself through the emotional and physical body. As a home funeral guide, one may support and encourage this time. It is important to be present to your own grief as well, since you may either already be a personal friend or have become one in the process of guiding the family. Still, it is vitally important to be respectful of personal family space and their need for privacy.

————

If you are on your own or assisting in making the choice for the final commitment, take time with yourself or with each other. Has the one who has passed either left direction for aftercare on a legal document or expressed to you and others how they would like their body-temple honored? What is the way most fitting for this person? What legal considerations are there to deal with?

Now that the committal event is complete, what is next? In the near future, another event will likely happen—that of a memorial gathering for the family or a larger event for family and community to honor and remember one who has passed. A person may or may not have left ideas for their memorial. Yet this is a time that matters most to those who remember and mourn a loved one's passage. Fortunately, there's no rush or time line for this event. Some people like to have a gathering within a very short time, others wait a few months, and others postpone it for a year or more. Besides a scheduled memorial gathering, other special times of honoring one who has passed may arise through the years. The ritual of honoring our ancestors as way-showers remains our heritage and our legacy. Blessed be!

CHAPTER 13

RITES, RITUALS
& REMEMBERINGS

Take care with the end,
As you do with the beginning.
—*Lao Tzu*

As home funeral celebrants, we envision and approach rituals, rites, and rememberings in unique ways. While we may work with formal scripted liturgies, we also find and honor space for rituals that happen spontaneously in the course of a home funeral unfolding, and also for ones that emerge in the midst of a detailed, planned memorial event.

Spontaneity of Spirit has a way of arising; often it seems to magically transpire. It is an offering of grace. Unexpectedly, such a miraculous and mystical rite was revealed in the face of one who had just passed. The story is relayed below. Those of us privileged to be present became beneficiaries of an internal reenactment of Spirit presence that was awe-inspiring.

———

His gaze riveted up and to the right. Everyone entering the upstairs room to pay respects was compelled to look toward the man's apparent vision. His peaceful countenance calmed them. Visitors only imagined what had engaged his attention.

A friend, who had sat vigil and meditated with the dying man through the night, reported they had together proclaimed "last rites." Then both entered a meditative silence. Shortly before dawn, a soft utterance of awe and then a gentle last outbreath alerted the friend of the dying man's quiet passage.

The look in his wide-open eyes and transfixed gaze held. The dead man's engaged, uncanny, and inspired vision at his point of death remained. No one, especially his family, wanted to close his eyes.

I, too, gazed upward every time I entered the room, attending to my after-death tasks. I desired to see what he saw and felt as well. Spirit, it seemed, had graced and inspired a divine caress.

————

Rituals become the magic by which we honor and memorialize those whom we cherish and carry in our hearts. Being touched by Spirit in ritual enhances the joyous celebration of a baptismal rite, a marriage dance, or a sorrowful remembrance of a death. Ancient rites, ritual celebrations, and death memorials can all elicit a simultaneous solemnness and ecstatic energy that remind us we are more than the flesh we live in.

Rituals transform what is happening and give meaning to important moments. A ritual may be as simple as a daily lingering over morning tea or coffee, a yogic stretching midday, or an aperitif at close of day. It may be as complex and layered as a ceremony in a temple, church, or mosque; a Pagan ritual circle dance; or an orchestrated event of honoring and remembering.

We ascribe meaning to the commonplace, transforming it into sacred consciousness imbued with elevated importance. In both rituals and rites, a marriage occurs between the common and the sacred. A magical formula creates balance whereby all is sacred, even as all is common. Envisioning with a sacred perspective, we find a depth of awareness in ordinary time and place and remember who we really are. In other words, common ordinary acts carried out in a framework acknowledging sacred nature become a meaningful act of spiritual awareness. Such meaningful rituals offer healing and peace. This becomes particularly true as we commit the experience to memory and embody its significance.

Below, I share a poem that channeled through me as I recalled lingering and lying beside one of my dearest friends of over fifty years. The experience became an intimate "parting ritual"; a last rite was shared in this sacred moment.

————

A sacred moment out of time …

Her soft pink gown—a delicate fabric,
brushing over her comfortably curled body
resting on her side.
Facing me, lying beside her.
A rosy pink auric glow radiates around her.

Affection and stillness, tangible between us.
Mature, wise face, soft blue-green eyes
seeing all the way through me.
Feeling love vibrating so deeply inside.
Palatable, fathomless knowing, in full measure
to a vulnerable and transparent core.
Completely undisguised.

Undetermined time lapsed dipping into eternal well.
Drinking deeply.
Caressing her cheek sinking into the pillow
framing her familiar face.
Sliding hand over soft hair and down over shoulder,
across delicate skin of arm.

"Is this okay?"
"Yes, your touch, always, you know … me."

Time, slipping through fingers of eternity, lingering.
"I shall not say goodbye, dearest Jean Rose."

"Oh goodness no! Until we meet again, beloved friend."
—Judith Fenley

———

The ordinary-ness of life and the spiritual significance of life are inseparable. Rituals can be deeply powerful. They can change perspective and outcome. A ripple of a tingling sensation flowing over our skin, the soft tears that wash our face, or the silent hum heard and felt in our body confirms an awareness that what is occurring is more than a superficial experience. It weaves its awareness deeply into the core of our being.

I have been present when a feeling of the sacred is filled with raucous laughter, sobs of anguish, or even prolonged, deep silence. Rituals may be planned or spontaneous. They may follow a written script or develop spontaneously as if guided by Spirit.

Our society puts much effort into making death invisible. Formal services or rituals in a mortuary chapel or church-for-hire, officiated by a stranger, can feel stripped of significant meaning. We may sit gazing vacantly out a window or absentmindedly at the back of the person in front of us. Perhaps our most authentic act at such contrived events, after filling tissues with tears, is to leave wondering what happened.

There is a difference between an act that is performed mindlessly when people are not truly engaged and one where there is an authentic presence in a rite or ritual. In the first case, watered-down meaning leaves no tangible connection with Spirit. We may be dumbfounded sitting in a church, mosque, or temple where we have become spectators watching a performance-celebration. Gatherings that debase into drunken parties or elaborate glitz, sidestepping real interaction with those present (not to mention spiritual presence), may leave us feeling a bottomless void. In the second case, with authentic presence, participants experience a depth of meaning that affects their deep sensibilities of truth.

This latter case—where the people present are soulful participants—is what I care to explore. The presence of Spirit that comes from a ritual imbued with meaning is palpable and touches those present in amazing ways.

How does this relate to home funerals and to the practice of holding space as a home funeral celebrant? What guidelines can I offer?

Our task as home funeral guides and celebrants is to witness, accept, honor, listen, and assist in an energy shift toward an authentic, peaceful understanding and harmonious process. That itself is a ritual. It need not be identified, yet, like an invisible cloak, we are in the unique position of being a conduit for Spirit energy. When death happens or is in process, emotions may spill over around the dying person, family, and friends. A contagious effect may demoralize or uplift a group; people may realize they need help finding a way to be more centered.

While our feelings are also part of the mix, we are not usually in the midst of personal grief and, therefore, are free to act as a more neutral channel for Spirit's guidance. We can bring transitioning energy and guidance to those who trust us to help them face their own death or the death of a loved one. The gift of creating space, allowing and acknowledging what is happening, receiving everyone, and inviting those present to shift their awareness and connect with the sacredness of the moment can be a profound experience.

Initiating rites and rituals is an important aspect of the home funeral process. They may be incorporated into the home funeral itself and/or may become a separate function facilitated by a celebrant priestess or priest. A planned and detailed event will usually come after a home funeral and when planning the rememberings of a memorial.

I feel a unique kinship with the way a home funeral unfolds spontaneously. The simple art of intuitively feeling the energy and allowing rites and rituals to emerge organically and naturally in the context of whatever is happening in the moment is demonstrated in the ritual below.

———

We maneuver down the narrow hallway, carrying the lifeless body of our dear friend; Annie, a woman of seventy-four years, now weighs as little as she did as a child. The shirt she chose to wear says, res ipsa loquitur: *as it seems, a Latin phrase she had picked up in law school that we had found humorous countless times.*

Annie lived her last months and days in bed. She loved looking at the wild landscape outside her window, enjoying the season's change. We called it her "room with a view." Light streams in through a window that looks out on the scenic rolling hills.

The five of us (Anabela, Glenn, Grant, Walter, and me) don't have far to carry her slight frame as we proceed with her committal ritual.

The hall windowsill frames that wild landscape view and serves as an altar; it is lined with tiny animal figures that speak of her affection for all creatures of the animal kingdom.

She had been a mentor and true friend to each of us who now bear her dead weight to the awaiting casket decorated with painted wings, symbolizing letting her fly free. This home is still full of her courageous and once-active life energy, even though she had depended on a wheelchair to move about for years.

Of the self-appointed pallbearers, two she had referred to as her adopted children—a man and a woman, now grown adults. They both know profoundly the positive impact she had on their lives, knowing, too, that their youngsters will also be recipients of Annie's legacy.

Anabela, the young woman, will soon live in this house with her young family, as Annie had left this home to her. Anabela had picked greenery from outside. She lines the inside of the coffin with a soft blanket and the greenery.

My son Glenn reads a story he says reflects Annie's questioning nature. We appreciate the wisdom it embodies and how it reflects our "Great Questioner" friend.

Walter, a close friend and one of Annie's doctors, adjusts her body, remarking that now, for the last time, she is well-adjusted and will make it onward. Our laughter echoes off the stone fireplace.

Grant relays his appreciation of the counselor and personal coach Annie had been for him, especially with regard to his romantic relations with women.

I speak of the pivotal place she played in my life for twenty-five years and the deep impact of this past week.

Her distant family and other close friends are with us in spirit.

We stand around the casket, continuing to share stories from our unique places in Annie's life. Our attention is focused, honoring her body-temple and feeling her spirit.

Anabela, teary, speaks of how beautiful she looks and how much she will miss her. Grant's shaky voice remarks that she's not the only one who will miss her. We will all miss her annoying questions and her sound advice, and we vow to treasure her gift of attentiveness.

Anabela brings closure, touches Annie's cool hands, and plants a kiss on Annie's forehead.

This completes a loving commitment I made to my friend: I would companion her last days and hold her hand as she passed.

Anabela and Grant spontaneously close the casket together.

A moment of silence embraces us; we taste the sweetness of tears. It is time for her final journey down the hill.

Thus there is a momentary touch of closure; our parting ritual, sponta-neously enacted, comes to a close.

———

Ritual space may be planned for while leaving the actual unfolding to evolve spontaneously. Sometimes recognizing we exist within sacred space makes any moment available for a spontaneous ritual. It's as if every sacred breath is a rit-ual. There are times when we may only realize a ritual has occurred in retro-spect—like the parting ritual, which is scribed in a remembrance poem honoring my dearest friend, Jean Rose. She had not been actively dying, yet she realized it was her time. She declared her desires for her last rites to her close-knit family. Then she stopped all eating and drinking. In the following two weeks, her adult children deliberately orchestrated an exquisite flow of multiple last rites for their beloved mother of ninety-six years. Intentional decision-making conversations with her children, a parade of friends, a choir singing, visits with intimate friends, grandchildren's visits, and quiet meditations all flowed by until her quiet release to Spirit.

Music in Ritual

Jean Rose and I often spoke of the magical union of God-presence in all things. In earlier conversations, I recall how we often softly sang the words of a favor-ite song recorded by Buffy Sainte-Marie that expressed the equation of magic's vitality and divine presence. The song reveals the transformative power of the mystical experience, reminding us of Spirit presence in the ordinary—merger of magic, God, and ordinary life. That is a ritual. On Buffy's website, she says that music and song can be more effective than four hundred words or marketed news stories.[51] At times, music is more moving in a ritual than long eulogies.

Music is a natural vehicle that can create a deep feeling of the sacred. Clearly there is magic in music. It is ritual when it penetrates and touches our senses as it bursts forth and alters our perception, either spontaneously or in well-rehearsed memorials. Music has the power to transform experience from confusion and despair to joy and transcendence.

———

51. http://buffysainte-marie.com.

Choir members from the Unitarian Church sang to Jean Rose for more than an hour one evening. A choir member asked if she was tiring. Her reply: "Oh not at all. It is nourishing and preparing my spirit." They continued singing until my friend said, "One more, please." A spirit of ease and acceptance touched all of us present in the room in such a vulnerable time. Music had indeed soothed our souls. The volunteer Threshold Choir's bedside singing is another example of music as a source of ritual, often without need for spoken words at all.

Music is medicine and plays a significant part in ritual. It may provide important transformative energy for the person who is dying as well as for those who surround a loved one who is departing. It can be soothing, calming, uplifting, inspiring, quieting, exciting, and awakening. Music is a universal language that transcends words and thoughts and can invoke Spirit and sacred presence, evoking memories and mood. It can be conducive to letting go, releasing, and peacefulness. Music can provide transition from one aspect of a ritual to another.

As a vehicle for the movement of spirit, music can facilitate separation of spirit from the body, enabling it to move on as if on a transporting "stairway to heaven." When a person is afraid, upset, frantic, distraught, or agitated, music can shift the mood. Music being played in a room where a person is in transition can soothe the body and give space for Spirit. It will also help set the stage for a sense of quiet and gentleness for those who sit in vigil with a person who is dying or has died.

What type of music is best to use in ritual? There is not one answer to this question. It varies from favorite current music to music from days gone by—to what a person liked in childhood, teen time, or courting days. It depends on the situation and the energy. Intuitive awareness is key.

Music connects us with our life. It connects us with others and with events in our lives. I have seen it bring people to laughter and to tears. As a home funeral guide, I keep music of different genres with me—soft instrumentals, New Age, and gentle, uplifting melodies. I also look around a home for what music might be appreciated. I ask about a person's favorite music. I have been surprised by the magic that is created when just the right piece is played. Sometimes by discovering or establishing a context, an experience deepens and expands in the moment. Below is an example of that magic.

———

My sisters and I were perplexed when our brother Paul insisted that playing Neil Young's "Harvest Moon" would fit in his part of the memorial service for our mother. His wife assured us it would work. Paul didn't want us to know what he would say ahead of time and asked that his part be near the end of the service. He spoke of what he knew of our father's love for music and imagined that, if he had lived through the sixties with us, he would have liked much of our music, playing along on his harmonica. He introduced the idea that our father, who had drowned forty-three years before, was welcoming our mother, and painted a picture of them reuniting and dancing together. "Harvest Moon" began playing for the uniting two lovers. The feeling of our father and mother dancing above our heads was a phenomenal experience. It evoked a deeply emotional and tangible body sensation.

Creating Rituals with and for a Family

How we help make the dying process a sacred event is open to a family's creativity. It is personal. Every situation is different. There are no specific guidelines on how to be present with someone who is dying or with the family of someone has just died. The emphasis is on listening and being aware of the clues and stories in a family environment.

I ask questions to understand as much as I can about a person and their family, their background growing up (geographically and energetically), their religious or spiritual background or nonreligious and/or spiritual upbringing, their interests and hobbies, the activities or sports they play or watch, the books they read, and what programs or movies they watch. In other words, I seek to know as much as possible about their ordinary and extraordinary life. All this helps understand context and how to craft rituals that fit the person. I may also rely on information picked up by the surroundings in the home: books on a shelf, art objects, wall art, style of furniture, outdoor space, kitchen artifacts, and food on hand. It is surprising how much one can come to understanding about others from their environment.

Many Kinds of Rituals

What kinds of rites or rituals are called for in a particular home funeral setting? There may be a need for a **letting go** ritual, a **cleansing** ritual, a ***preparation to*** *die* ritual, or a **being at peace** ritual. These are the most frequently requested or called-forth rituals, either as a spontaneous ritualized moment or in a planned memorial ritual. Frequently, I find that the material for a ritual or a rite is readily available. It might be a symbol of something the dying person has voiced or given as a clue, an object in a room for them to hold, words of comfort that someone has uttered, a picture of family, a cuddly stuffed animal, a doll, a childhood toy, a tool, or an object used as part of a favorite pastime.

A home funeral guide colleague told me an endearing story about a dying woman who was difficult to relate to. She had become very disoriented and even antagonistic at times. She was failing in health and had dementia. She asked the home funeral guide if she had brought her a gift. My friend had noticed a beautiful antique doll in a glass case in another room. She retrieved it and gave it to the woman. A delightful smile crossed the woman's face as she reached for the doll. She began talking and entertained everyone in the room, recounting stories of her childhood. She spoke about her mother and how she longed to see her again. She found a way to open an internal door for the release of her spirit. She soon passed. Everyone felt she was in her mother's arms once again.

A valuable time may occur when a dying person is aware and expresses their wishes and needs. If you are a privileged presence, take time to tune in with them. What do you sense is happening for this person? Are there fears, anger, or anxiety riding on the surface? If you sense tumult, you may find a way to encourage the person to give voice to what they are feeling and what could alleviate discomfort. This may inspire the creation of a spontaneous ritual that could free up their energy and assist in allowing whatever movement needs to manifest.

If a person is dying or has died in a hospital room, there may be fewer things around as clues to inspire you, yet what is available will surprise you. Artifacts and treasures can be brought in by the celebrant and the family to create a sacred atmosphere. Keep eyes open and call on intuition. From common objects to words or phrases picked up, unique ideas are everywhere. Magical-mind thinking/seeing will turn simple items into meaningful symbols. When a home funeral or a memorial takes place in a personal home, many more ideas, artifacts, and clues to what is significant abound. Look and listen.

Even when a person's state is compromised or the person is in a coma, the family or the environment may provide a key to unlocking body tension and creating a relaxed readiness that enables someone to move on. What if there is agitation and anger and someone is fighting death? Sometimes pain can keep a person magnetized in the body. Letting go is a dynamic process. Be watchful for a clue that will help them find a safe release for their angst, enabling a more peaceful death transition. Here is an illustration from a favorite film:

————

In the film Resurrection, *staring Ellen Burstyn as Edna Mae, you may recall the very adversarial relationship that existed between Edna Mae and her father.*

The father had been very mean-spirited with Edna Mae when she was growing up. He had become a bitter and grudge-holding man. She returns to be with him as he lies dying. He carries on in his old ways, creating a rather disturbing and lingering death process. Finally, Edna Mae crawls up on the bed with her father, tells him she forgives him, and starts describing a beautiful scene of going into the light and seeing his wife and other friends. A remarkable shift occurs when he suddenly cries out in obvious awestruck awareness and dies.

————

Sometimes someone dies alone. An accident or a sudden or unexpected death leaves so much unknown. It is sad and may be very disturbing for family when this happens. It may exacerbate the grief, stir up stressful images about what might have happened, and leave many questions unanswered. A ritual to honor and release their sudden departure may alleviate undue angst and perhaps allow for a more peaceful release of spirit for the departed and for their intimates. If a home funeral guide is also a shamanic practitioner or calls on one, there may be a releasing ritual done for the one who passed. A shamanic journey may assist the person who passed in unknown ways.

It can be helpful to offer to a family group a guided autogenic relaxation-meditation ritual; it may allow them to envision and feel a peaceful place of comfort in their own bodies, easing the pain of not knowing. It could allow a letting-go of anxiety and perhaps assist the release of one who is dying in a troubled process. It is essential to be sensitive to the family dynamic, not just relying on your collection of scripts.

We all wonder what death itself is like. What if someone told us what happened as they were dying? In the book *This with My Last Breath*, Meridel LeSueur, a dying woman, describes her sensations on scraps of paper left on her body, telling of her experience *as she died*. Meridel LeSueur, a famous author and activist of the early and mid-twentieth century, was a woman of immense presence and wisdom. We're allowed a unique peek into her character as revealed in this enchanting book. It was compiled by surviving members of her family. We learn how her daughter, Rachel, came upon Meridel's last gift of authorship and pieced together her deeply profound poetic rendering composed as she passed through death's door alone. An indication of incredible self-awareness and assured consciousness in her dying process is evident and speaks for itself in the brief portion of Meridel's words shared below.

———

This is like adolescence—all your body is
changing … the glands … the center glandular
shift … fast changes.
substance tempo another kind of sleep …
my reality seems different … I am a stranger to
myself … where are these alien feelings coming from?

O come to me … I am entertaining
Some other person and nothing is familiar to me.
It's not sleep … I am simply gone …

It is strange you are taking
on a new personality …
a stranger … alienated … unfamiliar
I write differently …
Then I seem to be gone
My body inhibits … immobile …
an empty house. I am sitting here as no one
absolutely no one. The wind blowing.
into your valves and caves and habitat.

We've taken off our persona and
Removed a dress to make a study of bones.

Death
Who is that with you? ... [52]

———

The entire poetic narrative is enchanting. I am grateful to my friend and Meridel's daughter, Deborah LeSueur, who introduced her mother's "colorful and vibrant life" to our women's circle. Over the years, she shared many of her short stories, poems, and even a film featuring the life of her mother and her social concerns.

———

Sometimes a family member may be the one who is holding back the energy of someone who is at death's door. It is unlikely a spouse would wish to prolong suffering, and yet they may hold on to one they love, feeling they cannot bear to lose that person. They may be praying for a miraculous recovery, even as they realize the impossibility of that to occur. The person who is dying may be holding on as well because they are in touch with that person's feelings. This is a delicate matter, yet a ritual for letting go may allow the release and peace of passage that can free up both people. Below is an example of such an occurrence.

———

A man was nearing his passage in the hospital. His wife had been vigiling with him for days. She would hardly leave his room. At one point, I suggested we go for a cup of coffee in the cafeteria. Her husband gave her hand a pat-pat as permission to go.

I felt he was holding on for her. As she sipped her coffee, she spoke honestly, facing her tenacious hold. She knew there was something she needed to do for him, yet did not know what it could be. I confirmed her knowing with a pat-pat to her hand, mimicking her husband's gesture.

---

52. LeSueur, *This with My Last Breath*, 29–32.

We returned to his room to find he had slipped away. His facial expression told her he was at peace. For a moment, she was distraught at not being there. Then she realized that he had given her permission to leave and that it had allowed his release. Her cries as she laid her face against his chest were soft sobs of release.

Her exit from the room, with his permission, became her ritual of letting go. He found the way to free himself and enable his departure and to free her from being present to his death. He apparently needed the quiet solace of aloneness for his parting ritual.

———

Sometimes a tender relationship with dying is between a human and their nonhuman intimate. Many of you may know of, or have experienced, the deep connection of a pet or "familiar" and the heartbreak when their life ends before yours. To them, we are the immortals. A letting go ritual may be needed on either side of this relationship. The story of our friend Lloyd and his canine companion exemplifies this kind of connection.

———

We called her Sniffer. She was a most patient and endearing dog. Her companion, our friend Lloyd, devoted his attention and his care to Sniffer through long months of her failing health. Sniffer finally let Lloyd know that she had to go.

Lloyd was beside himself. He accompanied her as the vet caringly euthanized Sniffer. His pet of many years died with Lloyd at her side. Lloyd did not know what to do next. He was not sure that he could bring himself to bury her and yet was uneasy and unsure about having her cremated.

It was evident he needed a letting go ritual and help in caring for the committal of his familiar. I held him in a long therapeutic hug.

"We can do this together, Lloyd. I can do the digging, and she will have a comfy resting place under the trees on the bank."

"Really?" Lloyd's teary voice reflected gratitude and relief. "I just am not able to bury her by myself, yet a resting place by those trees feels more like what Sniffer would like than anything else. She loved to sniff around up there."

Others joined as we dug a beautiful circular grave. Sniffer's body curled into
the space, and she looked perfectly at peace. A beautiful mound with rocks and
fallen wood outlined her grave.

We said prayers and blessings for Sniffer's joyful run to freedom.

Sniffer and Lloyd now were at peace.

———

There is such variety to rituals, rites, and rememberings, and I love to tell of them. They are symbols of life and death. I find it is helpful to hear and share stories. They soften impact, give ideas, and connect us with real situations and feelings. They may even foster our imagination for a peaceful dying. If you are involved with death work, you may find that a memory altar will grow with your life-death experiences.

Ritual Considerations

There are two primary things to address:

First, it is imperative to consider above all the one who is dying. If that person is still alive, it is their time. What is happening is the only thing happening for them. What rituals do they need? If they have already died, what will best characterize who they are?

Second, it is important to consider what the family and intimate friends of the dying person need. The family, whether in waiting, transition, or passage, is primarily focused on what is happening for their loved one. What rituals do they need in the course of the home funeral? As that time passes, their unique needs are addressed again from a different standpoint. Their grief after a loved one's passage is then focused on what is happening for them. Their grieving is often center stage for a year and beyond. It is likely a home funeral celebrant may be called on to assist in planning a memorial after the home funeral, when a family's grief is also important to honor as well as the one who has died.

———

So far, in planning rituals, rites, and rememberings, the emphasis has been to discuss and give examples of rituals and rites that are spontaneously and extemporaneously experienced in the moment. It is important as a home funeral guide and as a celebrant to be sensitive to what is occurring and to be capable of creating a ritual spontaneously and of planning more formal events. It is an art form—a sacred art form. It may take time to cultivate this skill, yet it becomes one of a seasoned home funeral celebrant's abilities. We are assisting a family in turmoil and grief to find solace and relief in the midst of a hectic and emotional time.

Being able to cultivate and develop sacred space and create ritual that acknowledges sorrow yet elevates one out of despair is a valuable gift. This is true whether a ritual is taking place with a person who is dying, with family and friends in a home funeral, at a graveside or cremation, or at a formal or informal memorial later in time.

Having inspiring resources handy—a liturgy book, prayer books, a collection of poems and readings, or perhaps one's own *Book of Shadows* (a celebrant/witch's collections of rituals)—is valuable. Yet most important is that rituals be natural and not contrived, reflecting the unique life and energy of the actual person who is dying or has died and the family who memorializes that person.

Unless a family desires a prescribed religious liturgy within the context of their religious practice, a home funeral celebrant may naturally assist a family to initiate personal ritual(s) during the home funeral. The home funeral guide might also be asked to help plan a formal memorial event at a later time.

There is a basic sequence for planning a ritual with family and friends in preparation for an honoring vigil, meditation, last rites, transition ritual, or for a burial, cremation, or remembrance ritual. The sequence is essentially the same in all these instances as well as for a memorial service that may occur at a later time.

First—Prepare by Centering

Assist those present to be ready for the task by acknowledging who is there and what is occurring. It may be a focus on the dying person or, if they have passed on, the family and friends. I like to begin in a nondirective way; I like to visit with those present, inquiring as to their relationship with the person who is dying or has passed. I orient myself to the surroundings, getting a feel for the space and what might be needed to invite a natural shift into prayerful or quiet mode. This allows a space for me to feel comfortable, appropriate, and effective in making a suggestion for preparation and purification for the dying person and/or the people present. Prayer may be a good way to center and bring people together. Depending on the situation, I might use music or a ringing bell to call attention to the moment.

Prayer is an aspect of ritual with many different styles. It may be religious, though it is not necessarily so. Prayer is an affirmation of sacred space and time. I find a quiet centering moment is facilitated with prayerful energy. It may be with words affirming those present and a reflection on what is occurring from a spiritual perspective. It may be silently focusing my energy and setting a tone that others can feel. Creating an opening ritual with the use of incense, sage, rose water, anointing oils, or candles may also be helpful.

Second—Create Sacred Space

I see this as both attention to the physical space and creating an intention for an intangible spatial dimension. Sometimes I begin by general housekeeping. Because a dying person and their needs come first, clutter may have accumulated, resulting in a feeling of chaos. Clearing physical clutter allows time to notice what special treasures, unseen at first, are in or around the space. Ask about special objects. Once the surrounding area is clear, use fabrics to cover tables, walls, or shelves; arrange candles, art, and sacred objects; create a sense of cloistered space by closing doors or draping fabric over an opening. I may be clearing and arranging a space either with people or alone. Others may decide to join the effort and provide personal touches. It is often a good time to put on soft, instrumental, inspiring music to create an intimate space and room to honor the sacredness of what is happening.

Third—Create an Intention

An important aspect of initiating a ritual includes voicing an intention that calls people together. It serves to connect participants in an idea of ritual sharing with a common purpose. How this occurs may depend on what is happening and on the spiritual and/or religious context of those present. I may initiate a "call" nonverbally by merely reaching out my hands, inviting those around me to take hands with others and me. Pausing and stating the person's name declares intention for a sacred moment. This may be enough for others to speak out, in the context of their framework, to honor the person with a memory, a prayer, an invocation, and/or reflections on the meaning of this time. If this does not manifest an intention to take time together, I may make a verbal suggestion or communicate to a focal person aware of the energy to do so.

Fourth—The Ritual

This calls for creativity relative to what is happening—whether it is a last rite, a release of emotions, a preparation for a gentle passage, a purification in preparation for transition, the need of a dying person, or the remembrances of a person who has recently passed. If a person has already passed, it could be a prayer for their journey, a song or chant, a reading, a poem, or silence. Tailor this to the presence of those gathered, whether around the person who has died or in remembrance of that person in relation to those present. The ritual may be an adaptation of religious ceremonies like breaking bread or a ritual bathing, anointing, or an informal holding of hands in a circle. This could be a very participative time, or it could rest on a celebrant to carry it off. Intuition and listening are key.

Fifth—Expressing Gratitude in Preparation for Closure

Give thanks to all present who cocreated the ritual and/or contributed a sense of unity and strength to the process. Give thanks and praise to divine energy/God/Allah/universal presence or collective consciousness—whichever is appropriate. It is important to acknowledge that which is beyond our understanding in some way. Participants may wish for a collective sharing of gratitude. A song or chant or passing of a sacred object may facilitate a feeling of closure. If the dying person is present, singing to that person, having a laying-on of hands in a blessing, or allowing an opportunity for each person to quietly speak directly to the dying person may be natural. This is a wonderful opportunity to invite a local Threshold Choir group to join if that fits with the people and situation. Recorded CDs are also available to learn some of their songs.

Sixth—Closing Sacred Time and Space

Just as an opening statement or invocation may begin a ritual, it is important to close the space with words of benediction, breaking held hands, blowing out candles, or a chant/song. The closing may be lengthy or very short. Sometimes a safely placed "eternal flame" is left burning for a time. A song, a hug, a circle with a shared breath, and a drawn-out and repeated *om, aum,* or *ah* can also complete a ritual.

Megory Anderson in her book *Sacred Dying* writes of preparation for death vigils and rituals. I found our language and outlines merge in a similar way in preparation for a death vigil. Her work is here acknowledged as elements are woven together. I found kinship and convergence with her work.[53]

Memorials and Rituals Many Years Later

Memorials, or what I like to call "rememberings," are usually the conclusion of the planned formal or informal gatherings to commemorate a life. A memorial can be planned ahead for days, weeks, months, a year, or even years after the passage of a loved one.

A memorial event continues the honoring of the loved one who has passed, yet the emphasis has shifted. It is now significantly important for survivors and friends, perhaps as much for survivors as for the loved one they honor. It is the survivors who must carry on in spite of their loss. Sometimes a person who died has left instructions regarding a memorial service, such as how formal or informal the ceremony should be or specific music and messages to share. This gives valuable ideas and aspects to consider. It may help those who are planning and carrying out the service. In a special way, however, the service is now most keenly for those left behind who are dealing with the absence of the one they love and their ongoing grief.

Sometimes as time passes, there is a desire for a commemorative ritual years beyond the passage of the one remembered. A long-ago loss may have found grief rekindled or simply new depths of understanding that are part of one's growth. The following narrative illustrates that it's never too late for another memorial ritual, no matter how much time has passed.

―――――

"Has it really been fifty years since Daddy drowned?" my younger brother, my youngest sister, and I asked nearly simultaneously.

―――――――――――――――――――――――――

53. Anderson, *Sacred Dying,* 39–40.

Our sister Lindajoy invited us to her home for a fiftieth-year memorial cel-ebration for our father. Albert George Fenley was our father and also the com-mander to those who served on the USS Boyd, a US Navy destroyer.

Lindajoy had been researching details of our father's life for a book and wanted to have a special memorial exactly five decades after we lost him in our lives. We were all too young when he passed to have graduated to using a more grown-up word like dad; we all still referred to him as our "Daddy Al." I was a young teenager, about to turn fourteen years old; Lindajoy had just turned ten; and Gini and Paul were six and four, respectively. Throughout the years, my brother and sisters relied on me, the oldest, to fill in memory gaps about the man we wished we had known better.

Sister Lindajoy now had gathered a lot of facts about our father. She also carried an emotional depth of feelings for her Daddy Al. After our mother passed, she spent countless hours going through Daddy Al's journals, logs, and letters, some written when he was only twenty-two. She interviewed each of us and some of his former shipmates as well. Our father had served on several naval destroyers after enlisting during WWII. He had skippered two of those vessels as captain of the ship.

Lindajoy had been Daddy's girl. As a young girl, she isolated herself for years after he died, grieving for the special adventure her daddy had promised her. This day was a "coming-out" for Lindajoy. Over the years, her grief had dimmed. She was happier, more extroverted, and wiser as to whom she was now in contrast to how she was as a child.

She set the stage with family pictures placed around her living room and passed out short excerpts from her book for each of us to read. We found an opportunity to remember not only our tragic loss—we learned more about our father and ourselves. We laughed and cried and wondered. We wondered whom and how we might have been had our father lived. We wondered what his death meant to his spirit. We wondered and honored the memory of our father. We honored our lives with and without him. We shared an emotional catharsis and an ecstatic honoring of who he was to us now in the wholeness and fullness of our lives.

This fifty-year memorial of his passage was healing for each of us. With gratitude to our sister, we relished each other in celebration of our parentage *and our connection with each other. Our gratitude is as enduring as our love for our Daddy Al and our Mama Iris.*

Planning Memorial Remembering Services

Here are some ways and items I find helpful as I plan and/or help facilitate rituals:

A Ritual Kit

It is helpful to keep materials on hand. My kit includes candles, matches, sacred objects, fabric in an array of colors and sizes, lightweight tables to create altars, hangings with beautiful mandalas, designs, and sacred figures.

Prayer

I may read from prayer books for inspiration, although most of the time I tune in to the energy around me and then, with a moment of silence, call on Spirit to speak through me in ways appropriate to the situation and for those present. For a formal memorial service, I may write out or note key points for a prayer.

Poems and Readings

Collect materials that you like and are appropriate for various situations. A few selections for an event are helpful to begin brainstorming.

Predesigned, crafted ceremonies or guided, spontaneous events offer different options whether an event is cocreated with a family/community or if the design is left up to a celebrant. It is almost always a collaborative effort. The way a ceremony is orchestrated depends largely on the family and how formal or informal they wish it to be. A family may have selected a reading from religious books or have special poems or readings. Involvement in a home funeral or memorial means eliciting as much family participation as possible to best reflect and honor the person who has died.

Depending on the situation, I write out ideas, rehearse them in my imagination, or, if viable, hold ideas in mind and heart and allow for inspired guidance as part of a group process.

An In-the-Moment Litany

This is a wonderful thing to create as part of a group process. Listen for a phrase that is repeated among people present as they speak of their beloved one who has passed. It could be, "She had such wisdom and strength," or, "He always knew how to show his love," or, "He was so courageous." That phrase can be spoken by the celebrant and repeated a few times to gather attention and momentum. Call for the phrase to be repeated by the group. Follow with key phrases about the person, like, "Her family knew they could count on her to be there for them." Now, invite a repetition of the phrase that was repeated previously, such as, "She had such wisdom and strength." As a celebrant, add other statements and allow more to emerge from participants. The initial phrase is repeated following each statement made. A litany has evolved that is very personal and vibrant. It weaves magic into the moment.

Musicians and Places for Memorials

A contact list for people and places that are available is an extremely helpful resource. Live music is especially conducive to invoke sacred energy. Often a family member or friend wishes to participate and make the service very special by offering their music.

Having a small music device is useful. Today's smartphones and electronic devices make it easy to prepare playlists of inspirational songs and chants. The Threshold Choir's CDs are great resources. Have a collection of song sheets to choose selections from. I often rely on a song or a chant to communicate what is called for and to invoke a peaceful, supportive atmosphere. A song or chant may emerge from another person's awareness as well. Spontaneous group singing can be supportive and unite a group consciousness.

Presence of Pictures, Mementos, Personal Art, and the Urn

Items of remembrance bring a deep personal touch of warmth, memories, and connection to the person of honor. Family, friends, and volunteers who wish to be included in the service are good sources.

Candle Lighting Ritual, Gongs, and Bells

These are a few more considerations that may add a distinctive quality to a service. Candle lighting is a sacred symbol of the *light of divine presence* and a beautiful symbolic beginning. Sound instruments are especially appropriate for opening and closing the service.

Invite attention and silence in unique ways, sometimes without the need for words. Below is an elegant candle lighting ceremony that was carried out by our mother's two young grandchildren for her memorial.

———

Coaching my young niece and nephew as ceremonial candle lighters provided an exquisite and regal opening for our mother's service. Marissa, who was ten, and Aaron, who was eight, wished to be part of their Grandmother Iris's memorial.

They practiced. To open the ceremony, they walked in unison down the isle; step together, pause, step together, pause, step together, pause. Deliberately and slowly, they moved in unison alongside each other. Before ascending the steps to the altar, they paused again, then simultaneously ascended each step. They paused before the tall white candles on the altar. They turned and nodded to each other and then lit the two candles. There was a hush of awareness from those present in the room.

A person on the side sounded a Tibetan bowl. The ceremony began …

Parts of a Memorial Service

The parts of a ritual or a memorial service are similar. A memorial is often more formal and planned out in greater detail than the spontaneous rituals we have discussed in the home funeral. A memorial service may be arranged in various creative ways. There are general parts that flow in a sequence: an opening and a welcome, an invocation, an honored focus, and an adjourning or closing benediction. Ideas and details follow.

An Opening and Welcome

I like to introduce the idea of the community, addressing everyone present as participants in remembering and honoring a life, interacting with each other and the spirit presence and memory of the person of honor. I like to use the full name and/or nickname of the person of honor, depending on which is most appropriate.

A Candle-Lighting

This may come before an opening or as part of the opening or the invocation.

An Invocation

This is a positive statement declaring and calling upon sacred/purposeful space and intent. Spiritual and/or religious beliefs, or absence of specific beliefs, will color what is said.

An Altar

Containing sacred objects and often a prominent display, with a large picture of the honored person, favorite items from the person who passed, or other sacred objects that offer a focal point of attention. I recall a surfboard being a focal point of one altar.

The Remembering—A Eulogy

This recounts the person's life from birth, or it may only include highlights, current life energy, and events, or it may just touch on generalities. One person or a number of persons may be part of this delivery.

Songs, Readings, Poems, Speakers, Music Performers, Prayers

Live performances and group singing are very meaningful and can communicate in magical ways.

Group Sharing

This part and the parts above are fine and very acceptable to mix and match. With Spirit guidance, a natural progression can and will unfold. Be attentive to the process so it maintains flow. And yet trust, too, in the process unfolding in unexpected ways.

Closing Benediction

Simple closing words that leave the group honoring their loved one serve as a reminder to carry the remembrance as they go on day by day. I often like to refer to the participants as the "living legacy" of their loved one. Their part is that they now carry that legacy of being forward. Another personal favorite is one I discovered on a tombstone while meandering in the memorial park during my mother's cremation:

> *To live in hearts we leave behind*
> *is not to die.*

A Program with a Picture

Creating and producing a program is an important consideration. Including pictures of the one who has passed, along with sayings and brief messages from them, gives personal meaning. A printed program is a cherished memento that means a lot to friends who attend. It also can be mailed to others who were not able to attend. I treasure and keep many memorial programs, often placing them on my personal altar for a period of time and when I am thinking of that person or honoring a special time with them.

Momentos

Some people like to include a memento in addition to the program. Items may be bookmarks with a picture of the one who died, a copy of a poem read, a laminated copy of the obituary, a CD of pictures covering the deceased's life, a miniature casket with a carved name of the beloved, flower seeds, or a whimsical item reflective of a life joyfully lived. One of the most frequent mementos, if one has been cremated, is a portion of the cremains. People have made clever decorative containers that hold a small portion of cremains; they become treasures to keep as an altar item, a special scattering ritual, part of a friend's garden, and so on. A friend carried one of her special friend's cremains and scattered them at many sacred sites throughout her visit to Europe.

Announcements

If announcements need to be made during a service, do this with simplicity while maintaining the integrity of the service. Mundane things that might need addressing are restroom facilities, parking, food placement, chairs for special family or those who need assistance, and mementos available for guests.

As a Celebrant

When you have been asked to be the celebrant for a memorial remembering, take time for an extended interview. Find out how your role is seen by those who have called you to serve. Sometimes a family will wish to plan the event and want a celebrant to officiate partially or only during the opening and the closing. Sometimes they want a celebrant to help them plan the service and carry the flow throughout. Sometimes they ask for the celebrant to plan the entire service. An interview is very helpful. A celebrant can bring ease and continuity to an event. It is helpful to understand your role. Clearly your role is unique; if you are a longtime friend, your role is different than when you have been referred for your service. I love both situations for different reasons. As a friend, I am seen as part of the family and community. Here there is common experience and memories to draw from. When I have been referred and do not know the person or family to whom I am called on to attend, it often becomes a deep dive into the person, family, and community. I have found this to be a very rich and rewarding experience. Family history, wonderful memories, quirks and never-told-before escapades and all manner of family secrets may be revealed. I become a privileged journeyer. A family who lets me in helps me facilitate a personal celebration that truly honors their special person. Each opportunity is different and special. The magic of rites and rituals and rememberings can be created anywhere. All is sacred. Serving another on their dying bed or in their transition deepens who I am. Serving a family and/or group of friends is as uplifting and nourishing as it is tender and sorrowful. Service is a full-circle gift.

———

When there is Love and Compassion, with the Divine resting on your shoulder, there is room for neither argument nor angst. Divine presence is confirmed by sensation of fullness in the heart, allowing one to let go and let be. There is equanimity in acceptance of all beings. Love, Compassion, Divine Energy shows up, manifesting Divine Order out of chaos.

Dancing Dragonfly Dancer (Judith Fenley)

And so it is.

SECTION FIVE
IN CLOSING

CHAPTER 14
COMMON VALUES

We will be known as the culture that feared death and adored power,
that tried to vanquish insecurity for the few and cared little for the
penury of the many … We will be known as a culture that taught
and rewarded the amassing of things, that spoke little if at all
about the quality of life for people.
—*Mary Oliver*

The time of renewal is at hand. As an advocate for natural death care, I support the idea that *everything is connected*. That is the essence of my message. All issues for healing our world converge in any one cause.

How we treat anything is how we treat everything. The means are the ends; the ends are the means. Thus, how we treat and understand death and how we treat the living soil are examples of an "anything" of relevance. Being present with persons and families as a death midwife and home funeral guide is one of the essential ways that I participate in Earth-healing.

Writing about experiences with death and sharing my growing understanding of natural death care is a privilege. I feel abundant gratitude for being a recipient of experiencing the miracle, the Mystery, and the transformation of what occurs in the presence of death.

Death is a point on the life cycle continuum. It is a point of departure into another realm. Experiencing natural death care can allow us to open ourselves to the flow and to see death for what it is—a transition point in the great ongoing life-death cycle.

We are created in the image of life, whether you call it the Divine or a mysterious gift. We are life and we are death. It is time to reassess what is imagined by many to be a downward spiral looming before us. Examining and viewing history and prehistory provide an opportunity to view and translate our pre-conceptions and to choose to live more authentically and with more joy. As we live in joy, even in the face of death, we are freed of much of our fear, sorrow, and pain.

———

A precious memory of my father, Daddy Al, who exited from this life in my early years, is the memory of him sitting bedside, telling us stories as my siblings and I drifted off to dreamland. His stories gave subtle instruction in life's ways, often relating to events of the day. In this honored tradition of storytelling, I will spin a tale to help us picture what could be, with a vision reflecting what many of us carry in our hearts as conceivable. It may assist us and free up our imagination. It could allow us to imagine and create what a reinvented "new way" could be. Our story will speak of death as part of life, honoring its natural place in the Mystery.

To begin—all that really exists is present time. Past, future, and this moment converge in the *now*.

———

Once upon a time, in the nearby distant land of infinite time…

Two sister goddesses, Gaea Mother Earth and Anna Perinna, initiated a forward turn of the wheel of life. They felt an urgency to assist mortals reluctant to change at a pivotal time. Their intervention resulted in a spontaneous catapult into a future where ancient, modern, and spiritually enlightened wisdom converged. These wise beings noticed many people of Earth had lost an active sense of common values and decency. Yet the Wise Ones also knew that nothing is ever really lost. Even though common values seemed lost from ordinary consciousness, they recognized that the distractions and "inter-fear-ance" of a power-over stance shielded a truth that still existed.

In truth, universal values for common good never really vanish. The Mystery that some call the Divine is always present and embedded in all beings and in all things; so it is that the existence of common values never really left the collective unconsciousness and the overall field of consciousness.

Voices of women, wise elders, and Indigenous leaders prophesized the return of a higher consciousness with deep caring for others, along with the recognition of the unity of all beings and all things. Their voices echoed through the winds of stillness and turbulence, whispering in the ears of those who would listen with heart and mind. If we listen even now with our inner ear, the prophetic voice is heard in this very moment. It is the truth that abides in each of us. It fosters honoring the wonder of nature and a desire to live in harmony with all beings and the Earth.

Yet the goddess sisters saw the disintegration of such values was pervasive, and greed operated as the dominating default mechanism. Dominator beings had vied for position, wealth, and power-over, fueled by greed and corruption. A great shaking and upheaval occurred on the Earth. There was a period of long suffering and seemingly endless wars. Earth peoples had to face themselves and their own demons. Finally, the dominators were shaken of their position and control.

As the sisters turned the wheel of life, a time of renewal came to planet Earth. A miracle of sustainable regenerating life began again. After a period of wild chaos and migration, Earth peoples remembered their truest selves. Greed crumbled on its own accord. Violence against life crumbled. Obsessive commercialism crumbled. Care of the "Earth spaceship" nest was rekindled. Nature and a natural egalitarian, local-focused, cooperative consciousness was reinstilled as a mode of living. People found ways to "re-organ-eyes" and share a renewed life-giving paradigm.

Death became seen again as a natural part of life. Joy and inclusion became rampant. Transformation and rejuvenation were again viewed as part of the natural order. Everything trans-formed and re-formed in the cycle of change and renewal. Change was embraced as the vehicle of everything wonderful. Nature once again became the primary teacher for living fruitfully and joyfully.

Local councils encouraged sensible relationships for living in harmony with a global awareness. Tribal communities took responsibility for their locale and worked out territorial issues in cocounsel with other tribes or communities. Restorative justice was key for orchestrating disputes or differing views. Caring prevailed for all people. Communication was seen as the river that flowed to the sea, embracing the unity of all that is.

Earth people gently vanquished the selfish governance that had held people in bondage to those who utilized power-over in order to be seen as superior and worthy of taking more than their share of wealth while treating anyone in their way as pawns. Diversity was welcomed and celebrated. Recognition and appreciation was exhibited for those who had previously been referred to as subservient to and/or lesser than the wealth-grabbers. Concerns were addressed with grace, equity, and harmony. Slowly, a spirit of cooperation and egalitarian balance became acknowledged as beneficial to all. It was a win-win of daily philosophy and practice.

The concrete jungle crumbled. Natural geographical diversity of Earth's terrain was respected. Wilderness areas were restored, cared for, and protected. The commons was cared for with respect for nature and all living communities. Nature Spirit beings companioned and supported everyone. All was a wonder to be seen.

Thus, a gradual, natural transition to honored common values emerged as practical guiding wisdom for life. Indigenous wisdom of Earth elders was valued. This wisdom had been there all along, waiting in the magical realm to be called forth.

In the previous era of greediness, people believed that only what was logical and scientific was reliable truth. The intuitive dimension and invisible truth were often relegated as less valuable. While each had its place, the full truth was less attainable. When the scientific facts overruled moral judgments, ecological disasters ran rampant and were not sustainable. Concepts of superiority and division had taken precedence. The people let go of these false narratives that had limited them. A balance of integrated brain function with the empathetic understanding of the heart transpired, creating a dynamic balance.

The idea that there were separate races or that a variety of gender expressions were diseased or wrong was now seen as humorous stupidity, limiting the reality of oneness. Everyone knew and understood everything always existed on a wide, dynamic spectrum expressed in numerous ways.

Existence of great diversity manifested in vast creativity and diversity of the One-life as it affirmed prolific options for all expressions. This spectacular diversity and a respect for all were celebrated. The Great Turning occurred. Earth beings rejoiced.

The Wise Ones, the elders, the wizards, the priests, priestesses, the jesters, the peasant folk, the playful ones, the medicine shamans, the two-spirit and trans beings, the Indigenous caretakers, the carpenters, the builders, the water bearers, the fire tenders, the food growers, the forager gatherers, the dancers, the music makers, the song carriers, and more emerged and found each other.

They shared their stories, their knowledge, and their visions. Wisdom and tales of love triumphing were sung in circles, around firesides, and all places people gathered. There was challenge and support to live fully. Traveling bards, songsters, and storytellers carried tales as they migrated and shared village nests around the Earth. The belief was that variations of spiritual understanding added depth to a panorama of joy and a celebratory way of life.

Death, a natural part of life, was portrayed and recognized for its ultimate significance. In earlier days of chaos, many truth-sayers spoke out, attempting to bring solace and wisdom to the people. Now, shamans, spiritual teachers, and religious leaders—all with varied tribal, cultural, spiritual, or even religious doctrines—acknowledged that the truth and a common thread existed and were expressed and present in all variations of spiritual life and in all religions. An experiential awareness of daily life reigned as the greatest value. People prepared for death in a variety of ways and celebrated it as part of eternal life. Grief and loss of physical presence were honored, yet an awareness of Spirit-presence bridged the chasm of the tender moments of loss, anguish, and heartache.

A shift occurred in death practices. People honored and celebrated death in various, simple, ancient ways that respected the dead as simply those who had passed on to their next phase. Reorientation of countless Earth life practices rekindled a natural peace and harmonious interactions among the people.

Thus, the Great Turning came about. A turning of the wheel of life continued perpetually as a natural flow. The gift of change was recognized, accepted, and celebrated. Mother Earth rejoiced in her children's re-turn. Father Spirit breathed freshness in the winds of awareness.

A chant, frequently heard in celebrations everywhere, rang out...

She changes everything She touches
and
Everything She touches changes...

Thus a tale ends, and our part together begins.

———

The purpose of this fantasy tale is to support merging with your intentions and to encourage creative imagination that will enable renewed expression for sustainable living and natural death care. May this writing strengthen our mutual resolve. Why else would I take time to write about natural death care when our country and our world are in the midst of so many crises that show up every day? Assisting others to care for loved ones in their own way and being an advocate for natural death care is fulfilling an aspect of my purpose in this life and demonstrates my respect for the Earth.

I've emphasized a mandate to be prepared! By this, I mean more than merely having your Advanced Care Directive filled out and your final wishes discussed with your loved ones (although I mean that, too). I mean, above all, being in touch with your spirit, your spirit guides, your intuition, your core beliefs, your fears, and your spiritual purpose. I mean finding teachers that foster your deepest values and assist you to prepare for death in a meaningful way. I mean standing up for the freedom to deal with death in one's own way. I mean all this with a heartfelt purpose.

It is true; I also have a particular personal bias that I advocate. I am advocating belief in nature and natural ways of physically dealing with death. I am advocating natural green practices that do not negatively impact the Earth. I am advocating green burial, particular in open-use ways, rather than single-use cemeteries. I advocate as well for newly emerging alternatives that are respectful of the Earth. I advocate a reorientation to how we live on the Earth, with respect for all life.

Picture green rolling hills, forests, plains, or deserts as sacred burial grounds, embracing multiple uses of land. As you wander, notice in your mind's eye a natural stone—subtly marked or not—an apple tree, a redwood tree, a rock pile, a mushroom outcropping, a bench, a labyrinth, and a medicine wheel. Imagine many subtle ways of marking and adorning a cherished spot, yet leaving the area open. That is what I mean. If we want to establish in perpetuity where someone's remains/cremains are buried or scattered, reliance on GPS technology can indicate an exact location.

I advocate multiuse sacred land for family and community gathering places: places for picnics or to sit and remember a loved one, places for concerts or playgrounds or to sit and meditate and invite ancestral connection. This, too, is what I mean. Further, I mean with any of these examples to respect the concept of sacred burial grounds.

I advocate taking time to connect with the stillness in any way that fosters spiritual awareness. I am advocating that everything be honored as sacred, even as it is common to us. I advocate everyday rituals to share our collective mind/heart/spirit. *Everything is simultaneously sacred and common.*

————

In closing:

Listen to the voices of Indigenous peoples' wisdom, reminding us to consider all actions for seven generations ahead in all that we do. Wisdom from ancient writings honors the concept to *do no harm* and that *everything you do returns sevenfold*. Observance and obedience to what is referred to as the *Golden Rule* would support right living and could be the only law we need for existing respectfully. It would lessen the existence of greed and the need for so many written laws. A version of the Golden Rule appears worded differently in most religions and philosophies. It is a connecting thread that would serve our return to a divine nature.

Light is shed on our path. I am grateful to the trailblazers, watchdog organizations and associations, training programs, books, articles, and conversations supporting the righteous path of reclaiming natural death care. In the name of respect for our Earth home and death as part of life, I am grateful to this life.

We can honor and care for our beloved dead in many meaningful ways. Wanting death care to be different is not enough. Our trailblazer kin opened doors of perception. It is time for us to become follower-trailblazers and continue the journey. I invite you to be part of this advocacy.

We are the trailblazers, forging again along ancient paths that became overgrown and obliterated, yet are still here for us to uncover.

REQUIEM FOR A PRIESTESS
by Oberon Zell

She lived a Priestess
She died a Queen
She rose a Goddess!
—Susa Morgan Black ("RavenMage"), speaking of Morning Glory

When Morning Glory, my beloved wife, priestess, pyrate queen, and lifemate of forty years, was dying, Judith came to assist and help navigate the legal parameters for a home funeral and green burial. After eight years of Morning Glory bravely battling a relentless cancer of blood and bones (multiple myeloma), the doctors told us there was nothing more they could do to reverse the ravages of the disease, so we brought her home for her final week, setting her up in our goddess temple with a hospital bed provided by Home Hospice.

Many, many dear friends, family, lovers, waterkin, priestesses, and priests came by over the final weeks in the hospital and at home to lend support, prepare meals, clean house, share stories, and generally take care of everything for everyone. Some stayed on, pitching tents in the yard or sleeping on pads on the floor. Reverend Judith Fenley, a home funeral guide, was one of those who joined us as we held vigil and embraced Morning Glory in her passage. Judith especially became part of the circle of women tending to the care of Morning Glory and the space surrounding her. Judith was also there supporting me and holding me up emotionally and as a consultant for the legal matters that required my attention.

I was completely useless throughout this ordeal. I had spent four to six hours at the hospital with Morning Glory every day during the weeks she was in there having dialysis, apheresis, radiation treatments, and other attempts to restore her fading health. Our fortieth wedding anniversary passed while she was in the hospital. And her sixty-sixth birthday would have been a few weeks later.

When we brought Morning Glory home, everyone told me that all I needed to concern myself with was being there for her, and they would take care of everything else. And so they did, while I stumbled around in a daze, frequently breaking down into tears. Meanwhile, Morning Glory's devoted handmaidens bustled about, organizing the space, feeding everyone, cleaning up, putting stuff away, playing music, singing songs and chants, answering phones, managing visitors, and—most movingly—embroidering the lovely burgundy velvet fabric for her coffin.

On Tuesday, May 13, at 5:42 p.m., as I held her in my arms, my beloved expelled her last breath. One of our friends held a stethoscope to her chest, listened to her final heartbeat, and intoned, *"The queen is dead."* I broke down, sobbing uncontrollably as everyone in the house responded in one voice, *"Long live the queen!"*

Her last words to me were, *"Don't let it die!"*

The women took over to wash her and dress her in her handmade sea priestess robes and drape the bed (now a holy dais-altar) in the burgundy fabric they'd embroidered. I placed her Galadriel crown upon her head, with gold Sacajawea coins on her eyes for the ferryman, and another friend reverently placed her fencing saber, *Heartshorn,* in her hands. As Morning Glory lay in grace and honor through the following day, she looked like a legendary warrior queen of ancient myth. All the lines and wrinkles disappeared from her face, which became as smooth and beautiful as when I first met her. All who came bowed in reverence.

Thursday evening, the women wrapped her body up in a golden shroud, bound and tied with the ribbons upon which everyone had been writing blessings since her Celebration of Life Day at the hospital a month before.

Throughout these final phases of home passage and funerary procedures, Judith was a continual presence, bringing her considerable expertise to guide and direct the process. A major concern to us had been the final disposition of Morning Glory's body. Both of us remembered the "Burning Times" all too well, and the idea of cremation horrified us. Morning Glory and I both desired to be laid to rest naturally, without toxic embalming, in a green burial on sacred land; to be returned to the Mother, with a tree planted on our grave, as in Gwydion's song, "I'll be Reborn," and Oscar Brown Jr.'s "A Tree and Me."

Our church, the Church of All Worlds, has a fifty-five-acre sanctuary in Mendocino County, California, consecrated by Gwydion as *Annwfn—Welsh Land of the Dead*. Ever since Gwydion's death in 1982, Morning Glory had tried to have the land declared a legal cemetery, as Gwydion had intended. But she could never get the application process past the county authorities.

As Judith researched the desire to carry out the wish and mandate of Morning Glory to be buried in the beloved soil of Annwfn, she was struck by the reminder given by a sympathetic and caring mortuary owner that church cemetery property was not under jurisdiction of cemetery law. That cinched it and gave her and the community the verified legal action that could be taken. The Annwfn caretaker and acting church deacon simply had to receive the multiple copies of the Permit for Disposition with the Church of All Worlds as the legal entity identified as the cemetery/ground of the burial. A copy of this had to be filed in the Church of All Worlds' records, another mailed to and filed with the county of death, and another mailed to and filed with the county of burial. Thus, the beloved soil of Annwfn, the Church of All Worlds' sacred cemetery, became the final resting place of our beloved priestess.

On Friday, May 16, with the shroud closed around her, we placed Morning Glory's body in the cardboard box that everyone had decorated over the past week and drove her up to our church's sacred land of Annwfn in Avilynn's black four-wheel-drive Kia (the license plate reads "Hekiate"). Motherbear's son Emrys met us at the upper parking lot by the dam with a beautiful, open, redwood-bark casket he'd made for Morning Glory, and we reverently placed her into it on the burgundy velvet liner. The children brought a basket full of flower petals, which they spread over her, and people added more gold and silver coins to assure her passage. Then she was carried by six pallbearers across the dam to the campfire, where she was laid in the center of the circle.

The ceremony was small and private, attended by immediate family and about thirty of our closest friends. Julie Epona, our devoted paramour for the past twenty-two years, served as priestess, beginning the ceremony by singing the moving blues song Morning Glory had written about her illness, "The Cancer Train." Motherbear crafted the ritual and also served as priestess throughout these final rites.

As Motherbear intoned the beautiful Circle Casting she had written for Morning Glory, Brad Lee drew the Circle with Morning Glory's sword, which had been made for her by Ace, her fencing master, lover, blacksmith, and Captain of the Cardiff Rose. After the casting, Ace laid the sword upon her body to be interred with her. Hades and Hecate (two of her patron deities) were invoked, and Julie sprinkled sparking faerie dust over her. Then I passed a drinking horn of her favorite whiskey (Tullamore Dew) around the circle, and each person in turn told of what Morning Glory had meant to them. All spoke of her unconditional love and inclusiveness and the profound effect she'd had on their lives.

Then we carried her up the hill and lowered her into the grave that Emrys had dug for her. Starting with her granddaughter, the children began tossing flowers into her open coffin, in the oldest burial custom of humanity—begun over sixty thousand years ago by our Neanderthal predecessors. As we filled the grave with handfuls of dirt, Kiri sang RavenMage's beautiful Morning Glory lyrics to "Amazing Grace," and Corrine sang "May It Be" by Enya from *The Fellowship of the Ring* movie. I planted an apple tree over my beloved's great loving heart, so that someday her substance may return to us all as sweet nourishing fruit. More chants and songs were sung, and many tears shed.

In years to come, the soil of Annwfn, the cemetery of the Church of All Worlds, will be honored resting ground, embracing others' sacred remains. What we bestowed together, honoring our beloved Priestess Morning Glory's burial, is an example of the beauty of honoring the ongoing cycle of life and death.

This book is dedicated to sharing the idea of honoring life and death naturally with others so that they may find their natural and unique way to honor ones they love.

Oberon Zell

August 12, 2020

GRATITUDE &
ACKNOWLEDGMENTS

It is said that no one person writes a book.
—Did I say that, or was it many others?

My inner vision perceives a drop in the stillness of a lotus pond with a ripple of gratitude radiating out in all directions. I feel immense gratitude for what has brought this book to fruition. My gratitude reaches back in time from young years to current ones and encircles so many people and events close to me.

Many childhood memories remind me of the deep regard for all people that was fostered by my parents and embedded in my psyche. That set the stage for the wide breadth of experience in my life that led me to care about how life and death are seen. I am eternally grateful to my parents, both of whom exhibited equanimity for all life—Iris May Evans Fenley and Albert George Fenley. To my "Daddy Al," whose sudden death gave me an opportunity to experience death at a formative age and to get very personal with my feelings, I give reluctant thanks. Also, thank you, Daddy, for bedtime stories that always demonstrated genuine esteem for nature and a sense of cooperative spirit. To my "Wild Iris Mama," I am ever grateful for the closeness and candid quality of our relationship. I cherish your loving tolerance, practical wisdom, and even your annoying phrase, "Let that roll, like water off a duck's back." I also appreciate how cleverly you still correct my grammar from a watchful angelic cloud.

Deep gratitude to my grandchildren (Ivy, Vaughn, Liam, Conor, and Clara) and great niece and nephew (Willow and Arrow), who bring joy and remind me of an ongoing commitment to the future. My one-year-old granddaughter and I frequently go to the Academy of Science in San Francisco. There, we are surrounded by a diverse mix of people, some speaking in languages other than English. One of our favorite places to sit is in the Skin Exhibit room, where a huge wall displays beautiful smiling faces in an array of skin tones, genders, and ages. We gaze with delight as the faces randomly light up. Our enjoyment is often infectious, as other children and adults linger with us. Clara's exposure—even sans words—is enhanced by the magic of diversity everywhere. On an unconscious level, she is integrating this exposure.

Regarding the actual writing of this book, the inception of the book idea is pivotal. A tender and poignant time with Oberon Zell and his community during the passage of his lifemate, Morning Glory, had just transpired. Up to that point, I knew Morning Glory better than Oberon. I treasured intimate conversation with her at gatherings in the home of our friends Anodea and Richard. One afternoon in the weeks following her home funeral, I remarked to Oberon, "Shall we write a book about natural death care and home funerals?" He was enthusiastic. While the idea had occurred to me before, this time it seemed more possible and perhaps an easy thing to do. What was I thinking?! Allow me to comment on how erroneous that "easy" thought was.

I am grateful to Oberon, who said yes to the book and connected with a publisher. Our time and experience vacillated with satisfaction, frustration, and results as all unfolded. It turned out differently than expected. Thank you, Oberon, for your wisdom, encouragement, and support of this work, and even for your annoyance with me at times. It helped prod me on. Also, thank you, Oberon, for sharing your TheaGenesis hypothesis, its timing, and the true spelling of the goddess Gaea.

A deep and abiding gratitude is attributed to Morning Glory for the opportunity to serve her in a most sacred time! Morning Glory, your passage lifted new heights of spirit awareness. The opportunity to confront creatively your green burial expanded my horizon. Your own audacious energy miraculously reached through the veil of your passage and truly spurred me on!

To the numerous others I have been allowed the honor to serve in this way, I feel humble gratitude. In unique and personal ways you gave so much, whether as the one who passed beyond or as family and friends so intimately involved. Many of you are represented within these pages, veiled in pseud-onyms. Your valuable part is greater than is measurable. It is unfathomable! Your stories are testaments to the legacy and unique trail you blazed for those of us left in the wake of your transition. I can only thank you on a prayer-ful thread I send beyond, yet you remain with me. Your death touched an understanding of my death and imparted truths that resonate and continue to deepen. You remain sacred ancestors to whom I am eternally indebted. Grat-itude deepens also to the many friends and family members served. Many of you are part of my community of close friends.

————

There are a few exceptions to those dressed in pseudonyms. My family members are called by their given names and gave permission to use their real names. They are acknowledged in various places throughout the book.

To my dearly loved three Taurus sons, Greg, Todd, and Glenn, who came through my body, and a Libra "step-"son, David, I consider each of you my great-est teachers! In countless unique ways you each challenge, support, and spur me on! You generate so much fullness and deep, immeasurable love in my life.

A particular shoutout goes to son Todd, who spent countless weekends with me readying our family home of forty-plus years for sale. Evidently that had to occur in the midst of book writing! Dang! Special thanks to his wife, Reed Aline, for putting up without him around their home and also for manag-ing to arrive many times to pitch in. Thanks to Glenn, who contributed finan-cial support to enable me to hire extra workers. What a difference that made. My son Greg helped me realize how vital it was for me to let go and move on. My brother, Paul, and close brother-friend Lorin worked great magic on our old redwood deck and completed the ornate redwood baseboards that my hus-band, Michael, and I never finished. David, too far away in Seattle, offered his verbal support and "hurrah" over the phone. My long-time plumber, Neil, and his team did more than I ever expected. Whew! The house sold and I survived!

Of incredible importance are the siblings in my family of origin—Lindajoy, Virginia Iris (Gini), and Paul Albert. You are, in so many ways, the biggest sup-port in my life. In individual and collective ways, you make life worthwhile! I would not have made it through some difficult struggles or even some happy times and events if not for the numerous times you pitched in and helped me through the physical, emotional, and plain ol' ordinary reality! A particular dose of gratitude goes to sister Gini and her husband, Jerry, who made living space for me in their already-full home after the sale of my home.

———

A huge thank-you to Amie Hill, one of my dearest friends and one of the very best housemates one could ever ask for. Our sisterhood is part of my blood and bones! Your encouragement, reviewing, editing, and offering sound advice gave me courage. Thank you for saying, "What you have to share is valuable; just write like you are talking to me." Thank you, Amie, for your amazing skill, acquired naturally, as well as for your years as a staff editor on *Rolling Stone* magazine. How I enjoy and am entertained by your colorful stories!

I have tremendous appreciation for another close best friend, Kathleen, who cheered me on through many sit-still times as I read aloud to her. Kathleen, your feedback and well-put questions were so helpful. She is the one who read me the wonderful Steve Martin quote. Thank you, Kathleen, for your wisdom and caring encouragement!

Thank you to a dear Gemini-sis friend, Gail, who not only traded massage, but arranged my turn to be on a Friday so that I could join her and her partner, Steve, for a delicious meal and provocative conversation. They offered valuable critique to early writing efforts shared.

Great appreciation goes to Anodea for deep friendship along with the richness of her mentoring. I enrolled in the Chakra Intensive seminar she offers and worked with her as an assistant in that training for many years. It was a soul-enriching time, particularly as it began on the heels of grieving the passage of my mother. The outgrowth of this work converged and enhanced becoming an advocate for conscious death awareness as well. Anodea is the one who coined the word *co-heart*. I love that visually wonderful word. For the deep dive into how a study of the chakra system impacts my life and understanding of others, I am so grateful. Thank you, Dea!

Thanks to my housemate, Michael B., who for many years shared my home, performed great kitchen witchery, and sweated in mutual garden efforts. One hardly ever needed to ask Michael to do home chores as he was always on it, leaving the kitchen ready for the next act and gardening with gusto. Thanks, Michael, for your good nature and responsible support! You, too, gave space for writing.

Also a sweet appreciation to Michelle, girlfriend of Michael at the time, who moved in with Michael, and together we became a fun "us" home team for as long as she was there. I loved our meaningful and supportive talks. Thank you, Michelle, for your loving friendship and the wisdom of Oriental healing arts, shared with grace. You, too, gave space for my work.

Rousing applause to another Gemini-sister-friend, Nancy, who arrived from Florida to explore living among us and stayed awhile. How I love the way you grappled with issues we spoke of and elicited belly laughter. Intimate talks about life and death and what the heck to do with folks in our lives added insight and generated ideas to put on paper. Now will you please return from Kenya for more? A special gratitude to Diane Darling, who prodded as a tickler-muse and called on me to be there for Morning Glory in right timing.

I feel immense gratitude to incredibly intimate sisters in our Sacred Women's Circle, who, for over twenty years, have been a source of support and encouragement. I am so grateful for each of you as you nourished and upheld me in tumultuous times as well as held sacred the interactions of our intimate communication. You have a special place in my heart. Thank you Deborah, Grace, Nancy Ramah, Constance (who made up our five pentagram starter group), Bobbi, Gabriella, Leela, Pamela, Jerrigrace, and Diana. For the wisdom of our Circle, I am grateful! May our love continue to ripple outward, honoring all beings and our Mother Earth.

Jerrigrace Lyons, one of the sisters in this circle, deserves a special mention as the founder and director of Final Passages. As the one who mentored me in gaining a practical grasp of what it meant to be a home funeral guide through her tutelage, training programs, and close friendship, I give enormous thanks. Without that training and the experience it provided me, this book could never have become a reality. Thank you, Jerrigrace, for your unique place of friendship and collegiality and for writing the Foreword to this book.

How could I possibly have made it through without the beloved Yogini Sisters Yoga group? Gratitude to Marisa, who leads us, sharing her lovely home and supportive guidance on our Wednesday mornings. The time is a goddess-send for the over-fifty healthy women friends who occasionally call what we do "groaning yoga!" The intimacy of that group as we nurture our beautiful, aging bodies together is such a gift! Thank you Marisa, Nancy, Jeanne, Lani, Bobbi, Jerrigrace, Constance, Diana, Sheldon, and Denise.

I owe a significant debt of gratitude to Ernestine, an amazing professional therapist and personal friend. Thank you, Ernie, for your wisdom, deep understanding, penetrating questions, and stubborn insistence on being real. You support my quest for deeper, personal, authentic personhood. Great value expands even more in the T-group of Ernie's design that meets monthly. Thank you, Ernie, for inviting me to be part of this group! Special gratitude to Stuart, Anne, Ritama, Bonita, and Ernie, for your authentic presence and deep sharing, which enriches my life!

A number of dear friends read parts of this book, offered feedback, and, along with others, gave support in unique ways. I trust you know how I appreciate you. You are part of an amazing community of remarkable, compassionate beings. Still, more than a nod goes out to a few of you: Mark Hill (husband of Jerrigrace and "co-heart" of Final Passages), Anodea Judith, Susan Campbell, Marla Charbonneau, Tori Pratt, Kate and Richard Cordell, Diane Darling, Farida Fox, Gary Hansen, and Connie Cook. Extra gratitude I extend to Michael DeVore, husband and father in our young family. Michael's past-to-current presence in my life is a sustaining intellectual, spiritual, and sweet supportive relationship, even though we are no longer wedded partners.

———

A how-can-words-ever-say shout-out from a mountaintop goes to my sister Lindajoy, editor par excellence and my greatest champion in the process of writing this book. She spent innumerable hours in detailed editing and more editing. Her meticulous efforts and talent were enhanced by her journalism training and impeccable grammar skills. I value her Piscean direct, yet kind, ability to make valuable and even harsh criticisms that enhanced readability of my wordiness. Thank you, sis, for your no-holds applause for good work when it was appropriate. Lindajoy, you clearly are the MVP of this endeavor. Words really cannot express my gratitude for the goodwill and countless hours you extended to me. Thank you for treating me to the writer's conference, for the "Do Not Disturb—Writer at Work" sign, and for hours and hours of coaching, encouragement, and calls to "Focus!" Your skill in editing and utilizing a program wherein I could accept or reject changes also assisted me in learning needed skills. From the fullness of my heart, I am so grateful to you! This book would definitely not see the light of day without what you gave to this project!

Clearly not least is acceptance of our proposal by Llewellyn! What a gift to ride on connections of Oberon Zell, who already is a respected author. Llewellyn took me on with his recommendation. I am certain that, time-wise, living up to expectations was a thorn in the side, as life events intervened too often and slowed us down considerably. Elysia, the initial primary contact person, offered support and challenge in the initial process. I am grateful for your nudges and trust in the eventual publication of this work, and the value it offers will redeem sense of time lost along the way. To Heather, who picked up when Elysia moved on, I offer a special thank-you! I feel tremendous gratitude for your patience in reaching me and for your encouragement throughout. Your direction with technical formatting was clear and helpful. I appreciated our candid conversations about the book. I revel in your sharing that, while you had long been interested in death's role in life, the idea of hands-on care and home funerals was both new and exciting to you. Special appreciation to Sami Sherratt, my editor, for her precise editing, gracious understanding, and patience with me. Sami, thank you for your ease of communication and helpful suggestions for making this work clearer. You rock! Thank you to Kevin R. Brown for a beautiful cover that invites people to pull this book off the bookstore shelf and to Donna Burch-Brown for her beautiful book design. Thank you to Andy Belmas for cooperative editing on the back cover. Thank you to all the Llewellyn staff for doing what is called for to get this work to print.

The list of those to whom I am ever grateful would not be complete without expressing heartfelt gratitude to readers near and far! To those who discover a new way to think about death in general, their own death, or a loved one's death, or who follow up to encourage family and friends to also explore their relationship with death, I'm grateful for you, wherever you are. I pray for an amazing rippling effect that will transpire and be of value in the world. I am certainly grateful to those of you who will be motivated to learn more about hands-on natural death care and follow your heart to become a natural death care advocate or to seek training and find meaning as a home funeral guide.

There is no one here except us. Together, we can and will be the change toward a more sustainable way of being on our planet Earth.

Blessed be.

RESOURCES

Home Funeral Advocates, Guides and Natural Death Care Advocates and Related Services

Persons, organizations/associations, programs, and other resources related to home funerals and natural, sustainable death care.

Compassion and Choices

800-247-7421

www.CompassionandChoices.org

A nonprofit organization committed to helping everyone have the best death possible. Offers free consultation, planning resources, referrals, and guidance for end-of-life options.

Crossings: Caring for Our Own at Death—
A Home Funeral and Green Burial Resource Center

Beth Knox, Founder, Director

7108 Holly Avenue

Takoma Park, MD 20912

crossings@crossings.net

crossings.net/index.html

Doorway into Light

Rev. Bodhi Be

Pauwela Cannery

375 West Kuiaha Rd., #5

Haiku, HI 96708

808-283-5950

End with Care—A Resource for End-of-Life Care
241 Country Club Road
Newton, MA 02459
617-686-0220
contact@endwithcare.org

Final Footprint
PO Box 2726
El Granada, CA 94018
650-726-5255
www.FinalFootprint.com
Provides natural death education for advocates. Mainly supplies environmentally friendly caskets and urns.

Final Passages Institute of Conscious Dying, Home Funeral and Green Burial Education
Jerrigrace Lyons, Founder, Director
PO Box 1721
Sebastopol, CA 95473
707-824-0268
www.FinalPassages.org
finalpassages@sonic.net
Offers extensive training in a three-level certificate program and a graduate practicum program with eligibility for personal mentoring. A short YouTube film featuring Jerrigrace: "Green Burial | KQED QUEST"

Fitting Tribute Funeral Services
Amy Cunningham, Owner and Licensed Funeral Director
1283 Coney Island Avenue
Brooklyn NY 11230
amy@fittingtributefunerals.com
Blog: TheInspiredFuneral.com

Funeral Consumer Alliance (FCA)

Joshua Slocum, Executive Director for media, legal requests, and interviews,
   802-865-8300

Natassia Strackbein, Office Manager, 1-800-765-0107

33 Patchen Road

South Burlington, VT 05403

802-865-8300

funerals.org

funerals.org/about

funerals.org/affiliates-directory/-CA

www.funerals.org

A nonprofit federation dedicated to consumer protection for meaningful, dignified, and affordable funerals. Previously identified as Funeral and Memorial Societies of America (FAMSA).

Green Burial Council

Kate Kalanick, Programs Officer

PO Box 851

Ojai, CA 93023

1-888-966-3330

info@greenburialcouncil.org

www.GreenBurialCouncil.org/

Environmental certification organization. Sets standards for green burial sites
in North America. Issues environmental certificates for funeral homes, cemeteries, and product manufacturers.

Harmonizing Sacred Pathways—
Honoring Rituals of Passage

Rev. Judith K. Fenley, Spiritual Counsel and Ceremony; Member of Final Passages Core Council; Owner of this private practice honoring birth, marriage,
home funerals, and memorials

PO Box 23

Graton, CA 95444

707-823-4976 (magicJack message only)

707-322-0405 (mobile message or text)

jkfenley@gmail.com

Home and Family Funerals

Jerrigrace Lyons, Owner

707-849-5959

Private practice guiding home funerals for families for twenty-five years.

In Loving Hands

Heather Massey

Cape Cod, MA

508-457-1612

lovinghandshomefunerals@gmail.com

International End-of-Life Doula Association

69 Montgomery Street #287

Jersey City, NJ 07303

201-540-9049

info@inelda.org

Lifespan Doulas

Patty Brennan, Doula Trainer, Author, Owner

722 Brooks Street

Ann Arbor, MI 48103

734-663-1523

patty@lifespandoulas.com

Melissa Weaver, Home Funeral Guide and Celebrant

707-823-3235 (landline)

707-520-0233 (text only)

Summerland Light Minister serving Sonoma County, California.

National Home Funeral Alliance (NHFA)

11014 19th Ave, SE, Ste #8, PMB #155

Everett, WA 98208

www.HomeFuneralAlliance.org

info@homefuneralalliance.org

media@homefuneralalliance.org (for media information)

Provides connections and resource information for home funerals. This is a very detailed and maintained site and is valuable to explore.

Natural Burial Company—Serving a More Natural End

Cynthia Beal, General Manager (US)
PO Box 2026
Eugene, OR 97402
503-493-9258
Peter Rock, International Sales (UK)
46 Matlock Road
Brighton, BN1 5BF
Phone: 01273-508207
www.NaturalBurialCompany.com
Biodegradable coffins, eco-friendly caskets, and ash burial urns for North America.

The Natural End Map

www.NaturalEnd.com
Connecting families with funeral directors and service providers offering simpler, more natural end-of-life options. This site is sponsored by Natural Burial Company.

Natural Transitions—A Resource for Green and Holistic Approaches to End of Life

Karen van Vuuren, Founder, Executive Director
780 Quince Circle
Boulder, CO 80304
720-432-2296
www.NaturalTransitions.org

Oceana End-of-Life Doula

Oceana Sawyer
1547 Palos Verdes Mall #334
Walnut Creek, CA 94595
415-336-4479
oceana@oceanaendoflifedoula.com
www.OceanaEndofLifeDoula.com/

The Order of the Good Death
Caitlin Doughty, Mortician, Founder
c/o Undertaking LA
5300 Santa Monica Blvd Ste 320
Los Angeles, CA 90029
www.OrderoftheGoodDeath.com
A group of funeral industry professionals, academics, and artists exploring ways
   to prepare a deathphobic culture for their inevitable mortality.

Rev. Dr. Shé D'Montford
PO Box 3541
Helensvale Town Centre, QLD
Australia 4212
+61(0)402-793-604
Officiates at Pagan funeral services in Australia. Prepared or individualized
   services that can include a personal Pagan eulogy and chants.

Sacred Crossings—Funeral Home and Institute for Conscious Dying
Rev. Olivia Bareham, Founder, Death Midwife
Los Angeles, CA
310-968-2763
www.SacredCrossings.com
olivia@sacredcrossings.com

A Sacred Moment Funeral Home
Char Barrett, Founder, Director
1910 120th Place SE
Suite 102
Everett, WA 98208
425-316-8290
info@asacredmoment.com
char@asacredmoment.com
A pioneer in home funerals and green burials in a funeral home.

SevenPonds—Embracing the End-of-Life Experience
Suzette Sherman, Founder
PO Box 28
Sea Ranch, CA 95497
415-431-3717
suzette@sevenponds.com
www.SevenPonds.com
SevenPonds maintains a beautiful, comprehensive end-of-life resource
   on the web.

Threshold Coaching & Consulting
Sally Shannon, Founder
Serving Marin County, CA
415-713-1477
www.SallyShannon.com

(This is an incomplete list. More people and organizations are continually being added as this service to others grows. Updated information of other home funeral guides, other educational services, and related information may be found on the NHFA site as well as other sites.)

Green Burial and Alternative Scattering Sites

Green Burial Sites—See NHFA's website. Go to "Green Burial Cemeteries." Find a comprehensive green burial listing. It is maintained for the US and Canada (by state in the US or by territory or province in Canada). It is the most inclusive list to be found. The Green Council makes the following certified designations: hybrid, natural, or conservation. Also explore Green Burial Council's website (see listing).

Alternative Scattering Sites—States and official municipalities may have a statute referring to the placement of cremains. However, the scattering of cremains is not heavily regulated or followed up on. This is because cremains are sterile and leave no detrimental environmental impact. Generally, it's not a problem for families to scatter on their own land, in gardens, or even unobtrusively on public or private places in nature like the ocean, mountains, creeks, and so on.

There are commercial sites that record in perpetuity the GPS coordinates on private or open lands. Opinion: very expensive!

Better Place Forests—America's First Memorial Forests and Introducing a Natural Alternative to Cemeteries
877-830-8311
hello@betterplaceforests.com
www.BetterPlaceForests.com
The site indicates various trees and geographical sites (some still developing) to choose from for varying costs.

Cremation Institute—Expert Advice on Cremation Ideas, Permits, the Ceremony, and More
www.CremationInstitute.com

Crossroads—Hospice and Palliative Care
Irene Rifkin, Executive Director
888-752–8106
www.CrossroadsHospice.com

Businesses Offering Alternative Disposition of Remains
Celestis Memorial Spaceflights
PO Box 66784
Houston, TX 77266-6784
1-866-866-1186 Toll-free (US and Canada)
1-281-971-4019 International
www.celestis.com
The only company to have successfully conducted memorial spaceflight missions.

Coeio
PO Box 390901
Mountain View, CA
www.coeio.com
"Infinity Burial Suit" for mushroom decomposition.

Cryonics Institute

24355 Sorrentino Court
Clinton Township, MI 48035-3239
586-791-5961
1-866-288-2796 Toll-free (US and Canada)
www.cryonics.org
cihq@aol.com
Freezing bodies in hope of future resurrection.

Eternal Reefs, Inc.

PO Box 3811
Sarasota, FL 34230-3811
1-888-423-7333 Toll-free
1-404-377-9777 Outside US
info@eternalreefs.com
Embed cremains into an undersea concrete reef.

Neptune Memorial Reef

www.nmreef.com/index.html
Largest man-made reef ever conceived, located 3.25 miles east of Key Biscayne,
   Miami, FL, embedding cremains into concrete.

New England Burials at Sea

Captain Brad White
877-897-7700
Boat phone: 617-966-1986
www.NewEnglandBurialsAtSea.com
OceanBurial@aol.com
Offers affordable, individualized, and personal ash-scattering services and full-
   body sea burials all along the East and West Coasts.

Promessa

P. Organic AB
Lyr-Bö 254
SE-474 96 Nösund

Sweden
+46304-20809
www.promessa.se
info@promessa.se
Freeze-drying.

Resomation Ltd
Beechwood St.
Pudsey, UK
LS28 6PT+44 (0) 113 205 7422
resomation.com / about / need-for-change
Alkaline hydrolysis.

Sea Burials
Sydney, Australia
(02) 6495-1511

Summum
707 Genesee Avenue
Salt Lake City, UT 84104
www.summum.org
Mummification.

Trident Society
1620 Tice Valley Blvd., Ste. 100
Walnut Creek, CA 94595
888-307-6001
www.TridentSociety.com
"America's cremation specialists."

Assisted Death—States That Allow It

Also called death with dignity, physician-assisted dying, assisted suicide, compassionate death, aid-in-dying laws.

California (End-of-Life Option Act; 2016)

Colorado (End-of-Life Option Act; 2016)

District of Columbia (Death with Dignity Act; 2017)

Oregon (Death with Dignity Act; 1994/1997)

Vermont (Patient Choice and Control at the End-of-Life Act; 2013)

Internet Resources

Defined and Conversation
    www.deathwithdignity.org/learn/death-with-dignity-acts
Pro and Con Discussion
    wingspanonline.net/?p=2398

Wikipedia Links

Right to Die
    en.wikipedia.org/wiki/Right_to_die
Assisted Suicide
    en.wikipedia.org/wiki/Assisted_suicide
Assisted Suicide in US
    en.wikipedia.org/wiki/Assisted_suicide_in_the_United_States

RESOURCES & DATA FOR HOME FUNERAL GUIDES

A: Items Needed for a Home Funeral

Basic Kit

- Plastic sheets (twin and double)—at least two or more
- Flannel or percale sheets—at least two or more
- Cover blanket(s)
- Washbasin—one or more
- Washcloths—at least half a dozen
- Essential oil natural antibacterial soap and/or fragrance-free natural antibacterial soap—in an easy squirt bottle
- Herbal soap(s)—nonfragrant and naturally fragrant (depends on family's liking)
- Shampoo—dry and wet
- Comb and hairbrush
- Towels—half a dozen or more (used as towels, neck rolls, knee rolls, and more)
- Cotton balls and Q-tips
- Gauze and bandages—adhesive and nonadhesive, different sizes
- Pillows—two or more (used for neck, arms, elbows, knees, and more)
- Tie scarves—many uses (e.g., tying mouth closed when needed)
- Essential oils—a variety for family choices (organic/medicinal grade)
- Cooler for dry ice—ready ice with mitt and brown paper bags. Cooler should hold at least twenty-five pounds

Accessory and Extra Kit

Keep backup items for everything in your basic kit on hand. Other unique or rarely needed items are kept in an extra kit.

- Sheets, pillows, towels, washcloths, cotton balls, and so on
- Scissors
- Tweezers
- Sharp surgical knife or the like (for removing pacemaker when cremation is chosen)
- Two to three gold coins for eyes and/or mouth (Sacajawea or Susan B. Anthony one-dollar coins are perfect)
- Shoestrings—long ones
- Absorbent large gauze pads—more sizes than in basic kit
- Bandages—more sizes than in basic kit
- Extra plastic sheets
- "Chux" (plastic-backed paper underpads)
- Cloth underpads
- Rags—various sizes
- Makeup kit—various foundation hues and simple makeup items like lipsticks, eyeliners, and so on
- Gorilla Glue

Other Handy Items

- Divided trays
- Folding cart with wheels
- Music box and soft meditative instrumental CDs
- Fabrics—altar scarves, table covers, bed/massage table–long fabrics, wall coverings, and more (various colors, lengths, textures)

Other Possible Items

- Cardboard coffin—made-up to offer at a cost
- DIY wood coffin instructions
- DIY shroud-making ideas/instructions

Ritual Kit

Have a ritual kit handy in addition to the basic kit. It supports spontaneous rituals and is essential when planning formal rituals, such as graveside services, memorials, and rememberings.

- Matches and/or lighters (some people are sensitive to the smell of lighters or matches, so discover preferences)
- Candles—beeswax is best; many sizes. Use votive holders and especially wind-protected outdoor holders
- Sacred objects, like small statues or pictures of holy beings, crystals, and unique natural objects
- Mandalas
- Gongs, bells, and rattles (and other instruments)
- Hangings
- Fabric for altar scarves, hangings, and needed cover-ups
- Tables—small lightweight ones are very handy
- Tripods for holding large pictures of beloved ones
- Music—inspirational CDs, instrumentals and songs, and songbooks for group singing
- Prayer books
- Poetry and readings for memorials
- Ceremonial clothing—for self and/or to share with a family or a participant in a service

B: Interview and Intake Process

As a home funeral guide, it is valuable to have a document for interview/consultation. Keep copies in your file and in a travel case. Home funeral training is helpful for learning interviewing and other essential skills.

Information/Data Needed for Interview and Intake Form(s)

- Date of contact and who referred (e.g., person dying/family member /friend)
- Name of dying/deceased person

- Address (and full contact info) for the home funeral
- Personal information of dying/deceased person—include their current circumstances, concerns, and/or status; their date of birth (DOB); their height and approximate weight (this is needed later for the size of the body's container); if they have a pacemaker (if the body will be cremated, the pacemaker will need to be removed); their spirituality and/or religion; if they have an Advanced Care Directive or Power of Attorney (POA); and any other pertinent information
- Contact person(s) and their relationship to dying/deceased person
- Family members—list as many as possible, starting with those nearby
- Friends—persons who will be included in the home funeral (especially important if next of kin/family are not the ones organizing the home funeral)
- Current physician and/or hospice organization—include names and contact information for all medical or hospice personnel involved (e.g., hospice nurses, social workers, home health aides)
- Significant person(s)—e.g., priest, priestess, minister, spiritual guide, and/or community
- Contact information for everyone included on the form

Information Needed for Death Certificate

Have a copy of your state's death certificate (DC) and make blank practice copies. Include primary items on the intake form and have a practice copy of the DC available.

- Place of birth of dying/deceased member
- Their highest level of education and primary occupation
- Their mother's and father's names (mother's maiden name needed) and places of birth

Some information needed for the DC may not be readily known, even by next of kin. Inquiring and researching early is important. Sometimes the dying person does know and can inform. A family member may need to research from the state's database.

Additional Information/Data Needed for Interview and Intake form(s)

- What services does the family want/need?
- What education does the family want/need? (Preparation of body, ritual bath, bedside consult with dying loved one, family session, etc.)
- What final commitment does the family want/choose? (Burial, green burial, cremation)
- Does the family need/want a referral to a mortuary, crematory, and/or cemetery?
- How involved in all phases is each family member/friend?

Be clear with the family/friend group about what services and options you provide. It is helpful to also create a packet providing explanations of a home funeral and terms used. Include laws, statutes, and general protocol for your state, county, and locale. Be sure to inform about your limitations and explain that you are an educator and able to help them understand and do what is legally allowed in your state.

Next of Kin

Next of kin refers to the order of responsibility unless there is an Advanced Care Directive that legally assigns another person. The term generally refers to a person's closest relative. The order is as follows:

- Spouse
- Children (not necessarily in birth order)
- Parents
- Siblings
- Grandchildren
- Grandparents
- Nieces/nephews
- Aunts/uncles
- Great grandchildren
- Great grandparents
- Great nieces/great nephews
- First cousins

When NOT to Do a Home Funeral

This is a vital discussion to have as part of an interview. It is not needed as a written item on the intake form.

- If there is considerable and irreconcilable disagreement in a family or friend group.
- When there are not sufficient persons in a family/friend group to participate in the tasks of a home funeral. This would include, though is not limited to, enough people to bathe, lift, move, and transport a deceased person.
- If a home is inaccessible and does not have enough members to participate, as above.
- When a family burial plot is at too great a distance or across state lines— unless the family chooses to do a home funeral vigil and then make arrangements for transfer. Timing may be critical in this instance.
- When a person has died a great distance away and the family wishes to bring the body home. This may be easy to circumvent across county lines within California (and perhaps within other states). It is important to address these issues from the start and research right away what is possible.
- If the death was a result of an accident or murder or the body is exceptionally disfigured. EXCEPTION: This may be dealt with if the family is willing to acquire coroner permission, if the home funeral guide is experienced enough to educate the family to handle and address body care, and if the family is prepared for such an endeavor. Candid conversation is essential!
- If organ or body donation has been arranged by a deceased person or their family.

These are the primary considerations. There may be others. It is vital for a family to be engaged and ready for a home funeral. It is *not* up to a home funeral guide to take on a home funeral without the family/friends who will participate. *Remember—this is a family-directed event.* A guide and educator is acting as a service to the family. It is essential that a home funeral guide understands their own limitations and is honest about what they are able to educate about and help with.

This book is *not* a course in home funeral education. It is both a narrative of experience and a sketch of what is possible. If you are interested in natural death care, find a training program you resonate with and learn more than what this book can offer.

C: Paperwork and Document Considerations

Know Your State Documents!

If you are not familiar with documents for your state, get copies so you can practice filling them out. It is essential to understand and develop proficiency before educating and assisting a family with the paperwork.

Death Certificate

A death certificate is a legal document establishing the identity of the deceased with information that verifies who they are, their place of birth, education, occupation/vocation, parentage, ethnic origins, and medical/coroner information. It must be recorded with the state through a county office generally called the Office of Vital Records (OVR). Certified copies are obtained at that office. The number of *certified copies* needed varies according to family needs and specific variables, such as number of insurance requests to be filed, social security, and investments owned. Bank accounts generally require only a copy of the certified death certificate. Certified copies are generally returned to the executor. If the family is willing to wait for their requests to be addressed, certified copies may be used multiple times. People with a small estate need only one to three certified copies. If a certified copy is not needed, copies can be made from a certified copy.

Permit for Disposition

This is a document that identifies the deceased and details where and how the "corpse" is to be disposed. This document includes the name of the mortuary, cemetery, or crematorium that will handle the deceased and where the remains will go. There are generally multiple copies generated, which go to the handler. The handler keeps a copy, and a copy is sent back to the issuing county record department. This cross-filing is to verify the legal final handling of the corpse. In California, a copy is available online to download, or you can get copies at the local county records office.

Other Documents

- Advanced Care Directive/Five Wishes—California's documents. Request copies applicable in your state (probably available on the government site for your state). Know and fill out the Advanced Care Directive for yourself!

- Power of Attorney—This document is important when the next of kin is not available or nonexistent.

- Will and Living Trust

- Living Will/Spiritual Will—A document in which one may write what they wish to be known and remembered for, along with bequeathing small items and nonphysical gifts, such as ideas, thoughts, attributes, and skills.

Refer to chapter 10 for more details regarding paperwork considerations. This is a very detailed process that requires familiarity, practice, knowing a state's particularities, and understanding of legal parameters of vital records departments. Visit your county office, get acquainted, and learn what they know about death care at home in your state and how you can help a friend with their paperwork. A professional attitude, yet unofficial capacity, is good to emulate. One does not wish to alert funeral professionals who may misinterpret what we are doing.

Paperwork is *not* something to tackle on your first home funeral unless you research your state's documents and their instructions. Home funeral guide training is strongly suggested.

D: The FTC Rule

Proposed in 1974 to the Federal Trade Commission, approved in 1982, and finally implemented in 1986. Its purpose is to regulate the manner in which services and goods of funeral homes are presented to customers and to establish and protect specific rights to consumers.

Below is an abridged version of the FTC Rule. The rule states that consumers have the right to

- choose *only the items and services they want*; they cannot be forced to buy a "package deal."

- a *printed and itemized price list* from the beginning of making any arrangements.

- obtain *price quotes by phone*; they cannot be required to come into an office to learn those prices.

- see a *price listing of caskets* before being shown a casket catalog or entering the showroom.

Further, the rule prohibits funeral homes from

- *lying about nonexistent laws in order to sell you something*; for example, embalming, or anything you do not need or do not want.

- *refusing their service to you* if you built the casket or purchased one from another source.

- *charging a handling fee if you provided a casket*. Prior to the FTC Rule, funeral homes charged a handling fee if your own casket was brought in. This was obviously to discourage coffins not purchased in-house.[54]

E: Home Funeral Terminology

A **funeral** is a ceremony for celebrating, respecting, sanctifying, or remembering the life of a person who has died. Funerary customs compile a complexity of beliefs and practices from various cultures and religions to remember the dead. The word *funeral* comes from the Latin *funus*, which has a variety of meanings referring to the corpse and funerary rites themselves.

Historical Contexts—Home Funeral

There is a historical context to the words *home funeral*, words now commonly used in the natural death care community. From 1998 to 1999, Jerrigrace Lyons and Janelle Macrae were compiling and coauthoring information for the initial edition that became the Final Passages guidebook. At that time, the Natural Death Care Project was the name they were known by and operated under. Lengthy conversations ensued about how to refer to the entity of which they were writing. They sought a defining name that was both simple and clear. The main idea was that it was *family oriented* and *family based*. It was a funeral, taking place in the context and direction of the family and the home rather

---

54. Slocum and Carlson, *Final Rights*, 98–99.

than a business often referred to as a *funeral home*. The distinction became clear. It was a "flip" of the words from *funeral home* to *home funeral*, with the flip indicating the meaning as well. Thus, "a family-directed home funeral" was it. As others organized to advocate and promote families legally caring for their deceased person in natural ways, other terms were also discussed. Yet the artful word choices of "home funeral" and "family-directed home funeral" say it most clearly. The words caught on and stuck.

Context—"Lying-in-Honor/Lying-in-Grace"

These interchangeable terms, now commonly used by many in the natural death advocacy community, also have an explanation as to their origin and usage.

The common use of these terms also goes back to the initial first edition of the Final Passages guidebook, officially titled, *Final Passages—A Complete Home Funeral Guide*. It is frequently called the "guidebook" for short. These phrases were used there for the first time to the author's knowledge. Perhaps these or similar terms were used by others. They are not copyrighted terms per se and have become common language for those who share this work.

These terms are in contrast to the official use of the words *lying-in-state*, which are commonly used for a "viewing" of military, governmental, aristocratic, or extraordinary figures in an official ceremonial public display.

As stated in the Final Passages guidebook, "Final Passages prefers to use the term lying-in-honor or lying-in-grace to describe someone who is attended by family or friends in a home setting for a more personal and private expression of sorrow and closure."[55]

Other words frequently used are *vigil* and *wake*. These terms work better for some people, yet the terms *lying-in-grace* or *lying-in-honor* resonate best with many home funeral guides. Whichever of these two versions a family resonates with is generally what is adopted for that family observance. Whatever words are used, it is the beauty of honoring someone's body-temple that matters.

---

55. Lyons and Macrae, *Final Passages*, 1.

GLOSSARY

(Adapted for this book by Judith Fenley from a longer edition by Oberon Zell.)

A

Advanced Care Directive: (Also known as *Advance Health Care Directive, Personal Directive, Advance Directive,* or *Advance Decision.*) A legal document in which a person specifies what actions should be taken for their health care if they are no longer able to make decisions for themselves due to illness or other incapacity.

At need: At time of death or soon afterward.

Ashes: Remains of human skeletal fragments after cremation; see *cremains.*

Autopsy: (Greek—"seeing with one's own eyes.") A medical examination of a dead body to determine the cause of death or the character and extent of bodily changes. Also called *obduction.*

B

Bereaved: A person who has suffered the death of someone they loved. Generally considered to be a family member.

Bio Urn: A biodegradable urn designed to convert a person into a tree after death. The urn contains a seed that will grow, transforming death into a return to life through nature.

Burial: Interring a dead body into a grave in the earth; a ceremony at which someone's body is interred; a funeral.

Burial, direct: Generally, no service before the burial. The body is picked up from the hospital, home, or coroner and promptly placed in a coffin/casket (usually a plain pine box) and buried. This may be the mode a home funeral arranges with a business after personal family and friends vigil.

Burial certificate/permit: A legal paper issued by the local government authorizing burial. The permit may authorize removal to a distant point and affirms that the body will be buried at its final destination.

Burial garments: Clothing used to cover a body in preparation for burial.

Burying ground: Also *burial site, cemetery,* or *graveyard;* an area of land set aside for burial of the dead. Sacred burial grounds/sites.

C

Cairn: (Gaelic—"heap of stones.") A pile of stones that marks a spot (such as the location where someone is buried or where a battle took place) or that shows the direction of a trail.

Casket: ("Small box for jewels"; diminutive of "cask.") A six-sided chest made of wood or metal into which the dead human body is placed for burial or cremation. See *coffin.*

Casket veil: A silk or net transparent covering for the casket to keep flies and other insects from the remains.

Cemetery: (Greek—"sleeping place.") A designated place where bodies are buried or entombed, including gravestones, monuments, or other markers to identify the people interred therein. See *burying ground.*

Certificate of Death: See *death certificate.*

Chapel: (Latin—"hooded cloak.") A large room (in a church, a funeral home, or ordained space) in which a farewell service is held.

Coffin: (Greek—"basket.") A rectangular box into which the dead human body is placed for burial or cremation. See *casket.*

Committal service: The final portion of the funeral service at which time the deceased is interred or entombed or the cremains are scattered.

Coroner: (French—"crowner.") A public official whose duty is to investigate causes of unexpected deaths or deaths from contagious diseases or if there was no physician in attendance for a long time prior to death.

Cortege: (Italian—"courtly retinue.") A ceremonial funeral procession.

Corpse: (Latin.) A dead body.

Cremains: The ashes and bone fragments remaining after a cremation.

Cremation authorization: A document generally required by a mortuary or crematorium to be signed by legal next of kin authorizing legally to cremate a body.

Cremation: (Latin—"burn to ashes.") Burning the remains in an oven at super high temperatures (1,400–1,800°F) to reduce them to sterile ashes and bone fragments.

Cremation, direct: The body travels from the home, hospital, or coroner's office straight to the crematorium for immediate cremation. Generally utilized by a mortuary where there is no embalming or service done before the cremation. It is also frequently the avenue a family with a home funeral utilizes when cremation is chosen. The family takes time for vigil and rituals, then arranges and/or transports the body to a crematorium.

Cremation permit: A certificate issued by a local government authorizing cremation of the deceased; also called *Permit for Disposition.*

Cremation vault: A container for an urn when buried on mortuary grounds.

Cremorial: An outdoor space, typically a garden, that is designated for the burial of cremains.

Cot: The stretcherlike carrier used to remove deceased persons from the place of death to a funeral home or to transport them to a home.

D

Death: A permanent cessation of all vital functions without the possibility of resuscitation; the end of physical life.

Death anxiety: A morbid, abnormal, or persistent dread of one's own death or the process of dying.

Deathbed: A place where a person dies or lies during the last few hours before death.

Death certificate: A legal paper signed by the attending physician indicating the cause of death and other vital statistical data pertaining to the deceased, including the intended disposition of the remains.

Death certificate, certified: A legalized copy of the original certificate, issued upon request by the local government for the purpose of substantiating various claims by the family of the deceased, such as insurance and other death benefits.

Death notice: A paragraph in the classified section of a newspaper or on the internet publicizing the death of a person and giving details of the funeral service the survivors wish to have published. See *obituary.*

Death with Dignity Act: Allows terminally ill patients to voluntarily make the decision to end their lives through lethal medication prescribed by a doctor. The law was first enacted in 1997 in Oregon. See *assisted suicide.*

Deceased: Dead; a person who has died (also called *decedent*).

Dirge: (Also called an *elegy, lament, burial hymn, threnody, requiem, funeral march*.) A somber song or lamentation for the dead expressing mourning or grief, especially as part of a funeral rite.

Discorporated: (Latin—"left the body.") Died.

Disinter: (French—"expose.") To remove the remains from the burial place; to dig up / exhume.

Donating a body to science: (Also called *anatomical gifts*.) Donating your body to science after death is a way to eliminate the funeral and burial costs and continue your contributions to society.

Do Not Resuscitate (DNR) order: A medical order written by a doctor instructing health care providers not to do cardiopulmonary resuscitation (CPR) if a patient's breathing stops or if the patient's heart stops beating. A DNR order does not provide instructions for other treatments, such as pain medicine, other medicines, or nutrition.

Doula: (Greek—"female slave.") Also known as a birth companion and postbirth supporter, this is a nonmedical person who assists a woman and her family through childbirth by providing physical assistance and emotional support. An end-of-life doula provides comparable services for the dying. See *psychopomp.*

Dying declaration: The last words of a dying person. Legal testimony that would normally be barred as hearsay yet may be admitted as evidence in certain cases.

E

Elegy: (Greek—"mournful poem.") A sad poem, usually written to praise and express sorrow for someone who is dead. (See *dirge, lament, burial hymn, threnody, requiem, funeral march.*)

Embalm: (French—"preserve with spices.") Replacing the body fluids of a corpse with toxic chemicals (usually pink formaldehyde plus others) and circulating them through the veins and arteries to disinfect, preserve, and restore the corpse to a more lifelike and serene-looking state.

Embalming fluids: Liquid chemicals used in preserving a dead body. Embalming fluid is usually comprised of formaldehyde, which is carcinogenic. Fortunately, there are now several formaldehyde-free embalming fluids, including one made entirely of nontoxic and biodegradable essential oils.

End-of-life care: Health care of patients in the final hours or days of their lives; more broadly, care of all those with a terminal illness that has become advanced, progressive, and incurable.

Endowment care: A trust fund established to provide for the permanent upkeep and care of the cemetery buildings and grounds.

Epitaph: (Greek—"over a tomb.") A short text inscribed on a tombstone in memory of the individual buried there.

Eulogy: (Greek—"good word.") A brief speech that offers praise and celebrates the life of the deceased.

Exhume: (Latin—"out of the earth.") To remove a body from the place where it is buried; to disinter.

F

Flower bearer: An individual who walks before or behind the casket carrying flower tributes sent to the family.

Final rites: The funeral service.

Funeral: (Latin.) A ritual service commemorating the life of the deceased held before burial or cremation with the body present.

Funeral director: A professional who prepares for the burial or disposition of dead human bodies, supervises such burial or disposition, maintains a funeral establishment for such purposes, and counsels with survivors. Also called *mortician, undertaker.*

Funeral home: A business establishment with facilities for the preparation of the dead for burial or cremation, for the viewing of the body, and for funerals; also called *funeral parlor.*

Funerary art: Art produced in connection with burials, including many kinds of tombs and objects specially made for burial to honor the deceased.

G

Grave: An excavation in the earth designated for the burial of human remains.

Grave goods: Personal items, food, and gifts buried with the deceased and intended to accompany them into the afterlife.

Grave liner: A receptacle made of concrete or metal with four sides and a top but no bottom. It is placed over the coffin/casket to protect the remains from the elements and prevent the ground from subsiding as the earth settles. By keeping the surface of the grave level with the ground, it's easier to mow the grass.

Grave marker/memorial: A headstone; a method of identifying the occupant of a particular grave. Permanent grave markers are usually made of metal or stone and display such data as the name of the individual and dates and places of birth and death.

Gravestone: A monument placed above or next to the grave to identify the human remains or cremains buried there.

Graveyard: An area set aside for burial of the dead. See *cemetery.*

Green burial: Burial of the body, without embalming, in a shroud or casket made of biodegradable material to compost and recycle the remains back into the earth.

Green cemetery: A cemetery that allows for the vaultless burial of an unembalmed body, which is shrouded and/or casketed in biodegradable material.

H

Headstone/tombstone: A monument placed above, or next to, the grave to identify the human remains or cremated remains buried there. Also called a *casket coach* or *funeral coach.*

Heir: (Greek—"bereaved.") A person who inherits the property of a deceased person through descent, relationship, will, or legal process.

Home burial: An alternative to disposition in a cemetery. It's allowed by almost all counties, but most require a minimum number of acres and often the filing of a plat map with the planning department.

Home funeral: Care for a decedent and funeral conducted at home by family members. A family can facilitate a home funeral in almost every US state or do it with the assistance of a licensed funeral director.

Hospice: (Latin—"guest house.") A facility, home, or program designed to provide a caring environment for meeting the physical and emotional needs of the terminally ill until death.

I

Inheritance: Property passing at the owner's death to the heir or those entitled to succeed; a legacy.

Inscription: (Latin—"writing.") The writing on a monument in memory of the individual buried there. The inscription usually includes biographical information and the epitaph.

Inter: To bury a dead body in the earth in a grave or tomb.

Inurnment: The placing of cremains in an urn.

Immortal: Not subject to death.

Interment: The act of burying a dead person.

Inhumation: Burial.

K

Keening: (From Gaelic "caoine.") A traditional form of wailing lamentation for the dead. In Scotland and Ireland, it is customary for women to keen at funerals.

L

Last rites: A religious ritual prescribed for those close to death to prepare them for their passage.

Ledger stone: A grave marker that is placed horizontally, flush with the ground to facilitate mowing the grass.

Legacy: A gift of property, especially personal property like money, by will; a bequest; anything handed down from the past by an ancestor or predecessor.

Liner: A nonprotective container used to cover a coffin/casket before burial in the ground.

Lowering device: A mechanism used for lowering the coffin/casket into the grave, having two or more straps that support the coffin/casket over the open grave. Upon release, the straps unwind from a cylinder and slowly lower the coffin/casket into the grave.

Lying-in-state/lying-in-grace: An honored placement following death in which the body is displayed—dressed, made-up, and arranged for viewing by relatives and friends prior to the funeral service.

M

Medical examiner: A government official whose function is to perform autopsies on bodies killed by violence, suicide, accidents, and so on, and to investigate the circumstances of death.

Memento Mori: (Latin—"remember you must die.") A reminder of mortality, especially a human skull.

Memorial donation: A memorial contribution specified to a particular cause or charity, usually in lieu of flowers.

Memorial garden: A cemetery lushly planted with flowers, bushes, and trees among the graves and markers. It could also be a private garden.

Memorial service: A ceremony to remember and honor the life of a person who has died, without the remains being present. "What is remembered lives."

Memorial stone: A stone inscribed with an epitaph or with an attached plaque installed in a cemetery in memory of someone who does not have an actual grave in that cemetery.

Monument: A type of structure created to commemorate a person.

Morbid: (Latin—"deathly.") Relating to unpleasant subjects (such as death).

Mortality: The state or condition of being subject to death; mortal character, nature, or existence. The relative frequency of deaths in a specific population; death rate.

Morgue: A place where the bodies of dead persons are kept temporarily pending identification or release for burial or autopsy.

Moribund: (Latin—"bound to die.") Being in the state of dying; approaching death.

Mort/morte: (Latin.) Death.

Mortal: Subject to death.

Mortician: A person whose job is to prepare dead people for burial and arrange and manage funerals. See *funeral director.*

Mortuary: (Latin—"place of the dead.") A facility specifically designed and constructed for caring for the dead in which bodies are kept until burial; a funeral home.

Mortuary science: The part of the funeral service profession dealing with the proper preparation of the body for final disposition, according to a mortuary institution.

Mourner: One who is present at the funeral out of affection or respect for the deceased.

N

Near-death experience (NDE): A personal experience associated with impending death encompassing multiple possible sensations, including detachment from the body, feelings of levitation, total serenity, security, warmth, the experience of absolute dissolution, and the presence of a bright light.

Necrophobia: (Greek—"fear of death.") The irrational fear of dead things (e.g., corpses) as well as things associated with death (e.g., coffins, tombstones, funerals).

Niche: A hollowed recess in a wall for placing a statue, vase, or urn containing cremains.

O

Obituary: (Latin—"pertaining to death.") A notice of the death of a person placed in a newspaper, magazine, or on the internet, usually including a biographical sketch and photo.

Organ donation: Allowing one's organs or tissues to be removed and transplanted into someone else. Most donated organs and tissues are from people who have died, but a living person can donate some organs, too.

P

Pall: (Latin—"cloak.") Anything that covers, shrouds, or overspreads, especially with darkness or gloom; a cloth, often of velvet, for spreading over a coffin, bier, or tomb; a coffin/casket.

Pallbearers: Individuals whose duty is to carry the coffin/casket when necessary during the funeral service.

Palliative care: (Latin—"under cloak; covert.") Medical care that focuses on mitigating the symptoms of an incurable disease for terminally ill patients and improving quality of life by reducing or eliminating pain, discomfort, anxiety, and/or sleep problems.

Pathologist: A doctor who examines bodies to determine the cause of death.

Pathology: (Greek—"study of emotions.") The study of the essential nature of diseases and especially the structural and functional bodily changes produced by them.

Plot: A specific area of ground in a cemetery owned by a family or individual. A plot usually contains two or more graves.

Postmortem exam: (Greek—"after death.") Autopsy.

Power of Attorney: A written document given by one person or party to another authorizing the latter to act for the former.

Preneed: Paying for burial or cremation service before death.

Private service: This service is by invitation only and may be held at a place of worship, a funeral home, or a family home.

Procession: The vehicular movement of the funeral from the place where the funeral service was conducted to the cemetery. May also apply to a church or home funeral where the mourners follow the casket as it is brought into and taken out of the church or to any intentional designation.

Psychopomp: (Greek—"guide of souls.") A midwife to the dying or end-of-life doula who facilitates the transition of newly deceased souls into the afterlife. A psychopomp may also help at birth to introduce the newborn child's soul into the world.

Purge: (Latin—"cleansing.") A foul discharge from the deceased through the mouth, nose, and ears of matter from the stomach and intestines due to putrefaction caused by ineffectual embalming.

Putrefaction: (Latin—"rotting.") The decomposition of the body upon death, which causes discoloration and the formation of a foul-smelling discharge product (purge).

R

Remains: The deceased human body.

Rememberings: A collection of memories or an event honoring the place of remembering. It is also called a *memorial*. A synonym for memories and/or memorial.

Rigor mortis: (Latin—"stiffness of death.") A temporary rigidity of the muscles of a corpse that happens soon after death.

S

Scattering: The disposal of cremains in a designated area.

Shroud: A covering or dress used to wrap a dead body for burial.

Sky burial: ("Bird-scattered.") A funeral practice in which a human corpse is placed on a mountaintop to decompose while exposed to the elements or to be eaten by scavenging animals, especially carrion birds. It is a specific type of the general practice of excarnation.

Slab: A grave marker, typically made of stone, that is flat and lies flush to the ground.

Suicide: (Latin—"to kill oneself.") Deliberately taking one's own life.

Suicide, physician-assisted: The voluntary termination of one's own life by the administration of a lethal substance with the direct or indirect assistance of a physician. See *Death with Dignity Act.*

Survivors: Immediate family members outliving the deceased.

Sympathy cards: Cards sent to the family to express sympathy.

T

Testament: (Latin—"to bear witness.") See *will.*

Thanatology: (Greek—"study of death.") The scientific study of death investigating the mechanisms and forensic aspects of death, such as bodily changes that accompany death and the postmortem period as well as wider social aspects related to death.

Tomb: A building or chamber above or below the ground in which a dead body is housed.

Tombstone: A monument placed above, or next to, the grave to identify the human remains or cremated remains buried there.

Transit permit: A legal paper issued by the local government authorizing removal of a body to a cemetery for interment. Some cities also require an additional permit if the deceased is to be cremated. May also be called *Permit for Disposition.*

Tumulus: (Latin—"swelling.") An artificial mound of earth, especially over a grave; barrow.

U

Undertaker: Another term for mortician or funeral director.

Urn: A jar or other vessel in which cremains are kept; may be made of metal, ceramics, wood, or stone.

V

Vault: A burial chamber partly or completely underground that encloses a coffin/casket. Also the outside metal or concrete coffin/casket container or grave liner.

Viewing: The portion of the funeral service in which visitors arrive to visit with the deceased. During a visitation, the casket is open so that people in the room can clearly see the body. See *visitation*.

Vigil: (Latin—"watchfulness.") An all-night religious/spiritual service held on the eve or following days of the funeral service or burial. See *wake*.

Vigiling: To be in the process of creating and/or being in a vigil.

Visitation: (Also called a *viewing, wake,* or *calling hours.*) An opportunity for survivors and friends to view the deceased in private, usually in a special room within the funeral home where the body is placed on display in the casket. The viewing often takes place on one or two evenings before the funeral.

W

Wake: A watch kept over the deceased, sometimes lasting the entire night preceding the burial, where everyone remains awake, usually with drinking, storytelling, and festivity.

Wake, living: A wake held for a person who is about to die while they are still alive to enjoy it. Also called a *celebration of life.*

Will: The declaration (testament) of a person's wishes regarding the disposal of their property after death; a revocable legal instrument by which such wishes are expressed.

Will, Living: A composition by a person to bequeath energy, ideals, intangible gifts of insight, values, philosophy, and spiritual insights for posterity to loved ones.

Winding sheet: A large sheet of fabric in which a corpse is wrapped; see *shroud.*

RECOMMENDED READING

Arranged in various subcategories, although many entries could be cross-filed in multiple or alternate categories in this broad topic.

General Death and Dying

De Spelder, Lynne, and Albert Strickland. *The Last Dance.* Mayfield Publishing, 1983.

Didion, John. *The Year of Magical Thinking.* Reprint Edition. Vintage, 2007.

Doughty, Caitlin. *From Here to Eternity: Traveling the World to Find the Good Death.* W. W. Norton & Company, 2017.

Iserson, Kenneth. *Death to Dust: What Happens to Dead Bodies?* Galen Press, 1987.

Jones, Constance. *R.I.P.: The Complete Book of Death and Dying.* HarperCollins/Stonesong Press, 1997.

Lanza, Robert, and Bob Berman. *Biocentrism: How Life and Consciousness are the Keys to Understanding the True Nature of the Universe.* BenBella Books, 2010.

Nuland, Sherwin. *How We Die: Reflections on Life's Final Chapter.* Knopf, 1994.

Rasberry, Sally, and Carole Rae Watanabe. *The Art of Dying.* Celestial Arts, 2001.

Regardie, Israel. *A Garden of Pomegranates.* Llewellyn, 1970.

Taylor, Timothy. *The Buried Soul: How Humans Invented Death.* Fourth Estate, 2002.

Whitaker, Agnes, ed. *All in the End Is Harvest.* Dartman, Longman & Todd, 1984.

Advocacy of Natural Death Care and Home Funerals

Carlson, Lisa. *Caring for the Dead: Your Final Act of Love*. Revised Edition. Upper Access, 1998.

Concern for Dying. *The Living Will and Other Advance Directives: A Legal Guide to Medical Treatment Decisions*. Concern for Dying, 1986.

Doughty, Caitlin. *Smoke Gets in Your Eyes & Other Lessons from the Crematory*. W. W. Norton & Company, 2014.

Harris, Mark. *Grave Matters: A Journey through the Modern Funeral Industry to a Natural Way of Burial*. Reprint Edition. Scribner, 2008.

Kiernan, Stephen P. *Last Rights: Rescuing the End of Life from the Medical System*. St. Martin's Press, 2007.

Lyons, Jerrigrace, and Janelle Macrae. *Final Passages: A Complete Home Funeral Guide*. Final Passages, 2009.

Morgan, Ernest. *Dealing Creatively with Death: A Manual of Death Education and Simple Burial*. Barclay House, 1990.

National Home Funeral Alliance, and Funeral Consumers Alliance. *Restoring Families' Right to Choose: The Call for Funeral Legislation Change in America*, and *What to Do When Home Funeral Rights Are Challenged*. National Home Funeral Alliance, 2015.

Simpson, Michael. *The Facts of Death: A Complete Guide for Being Prepared*. Prentice-Hall, 1979.

Slocum, Joshua, and Lisa Carlson. *Final Rights: Reclaiming the American Way of Death*. Upper Access, 2011.

Starhawk, M. Macha Nightmare, and the Reclaiming Community. *The Pagan Book of Living and Dying*. HarperSanFrancisco, 1997.

Virago, Zenith, Claire Leimbach, and Trypheyna McShane. *The Intimacy of Death & Dying: Simple Guidance to Help You Through*. Inspired Living, 2009.

Webster, Lee. *Changing Landscapes: Exploring the Growth of Ethical, Compassionate, & Environmentally Sustainable Green Funeral Service*. Green Burial Council International, 2017.

———. *Essentials for Practicing Home Funeral Guides*. National Home Funeral Alliance, 2015.

———. *Planning Guide and Workbook for Home Funeral Families.* National Home Funeral Alliance, 2015.

Spiritual Focus, Readings and Rituals

Anderson, Megory. *Sacred Dying: Creating Rituals for Embracing the End of Life.* Revised and Expanded Edition. Marlow & Company, 2003.

Ashcroft-Nowicki, Dolores. *The New Book of the Dead.* Aquarian Press, 1992.

Baldwin, Christina. *Calling the Circle: The First and Future Culture.* Bantam, 1994.

Belanger, Michelle. *Walking the Twilight Path: A Gothic Book of the Dead.* Llewellyn Publications, 2008.

Belk, Donna, and Kateyanne Unullisi. *Home Funeral Ceremonies: A Primer to Honor the Dying and the Dead with Reverence, Light-Heartedness, and Grace.* Sugar Skull Publishing, 2015.

Dardis, Sharon, and Cindy Rogers. *As I Journey On: Meditations for Those Facing Death.* Augsburg Fortress Publishing, 2000.

Day, Christian. *The Witches' Book of the Dead.* Red Wheel/Weiser, 2011.

Evans, Ann Keeler. *Remembering a Life: On the Death of Your Beloved.* Emerald Earth Publishing, 2005.

Fortune, Dion. *Dion Fortune's Book of the Dead.* Red Wheel/Weiser, 2005.

———. *Through the Gates of Death.* Aquarian Press, 1968.

Fremantle, Francesca. *Luminous Emptiness.* Shambala Publications, 2001.

Gold, E. J., and John Lilly. *American Book of the Dead.* Tenth Edition. Gateways Books & Tapes, 2005.

Hickman, Martha W. *Healing After Loss: Daily Meditations for Working Through Grief.* HarperCollins, 1994.

Leary, Timothy, Ralph Metzner, and Richard Alpert. *The Psychedelic Experience: A Manual Based on the Tibetan Book of the Dead.* Citadel Press, 1967.

Levine, Stephen, and Ondrea Levine. *Who Dies? An Investigation of Conscious Living and Conscious Dying.* Knopf Doubleday Publishing Group, 1989.

Madden, Kristin. *Shamanic Guide to Death & Dying.* Spilled Candy Publications, 2005.

Rinpoche, Sogyal. *The Tibetan Book of Living and Dying.* Revised Edition. HarperCollins Publishers, 2012.

Searl, Edward, ed. *Beyond Absence: A Treasury of Poems, Quotations & Readings on Death and Remembrance.* Skinner House Books, 2006.

———. *In Memoriam: A Guide to Modern Funeral and Memorial Services.* Second Edition. Skinner House Books, 2000.

Sunshine, Linda, ed. *Words of Comfort.* Smallwood & Steward, 1996.

Vest, Joe, ed. *The Open Road: Walt Whitman on Death & Dying.* Four Corners Editions, 1996.

York, Sarah. *Remembering Well: Rituals for Celebrating Life & Mourning Death.* Jossey-Bass, 2000.

Zell-Ravenheart, Oberon, and Morning Glory. *Creating Circles & Ceremonies: Rites & Rituals for All Seasons & Reasons.* New Page Books, 2006.

Caregiving, Hospice

Anderson, Megory. *Attending the Dying.* Church Publishing, 2005.

Callanan, Maggie. *Final Journeys: A Practical Guide for Bringing Care and Comfort at the End of Life.* Random House, 2009.

Coberly, Margaret. *Sacred Passage: How to Provide Fearless, Compassionate Care for the Dying.* Shambhala Publications, 2003.

Duda, Deborah. *Coming Home: A Guide to Dying at Home with Dignity.* Aurora Press, 1987.

Kalina, Kathy. *Midwife for Souls: Spiritual Care for the Dying.* Second Edition. Pauline Books & Media, 2007.

Stillwater, Michael, and Gary Malkin. *Graceful Passages: A Companion for Living and Dying.* New World Library, 2003.

Thornton, V. K. *The Survivor's Guide: What You Need to Know & What You Need to Do When Someone Close to You Dies.* Silver Lake Publishing, 2004.

Grief and Mourning

Bonanno, George A. *The Other Side of Sadness.* Basic Books, 2009.

Bush, Ashley Davis. *Transcending Loss: Understanding the Lifelong Impact of Death and How to Make It Meaningful.* Penguin Publishing, 1997.

Finkbeiner, Ann K. *After the Death of a Child: Living with Loss Through the Years.* Johns Hopkins University Press, 1998.

Leech, Peter, and Zeva Singer. *Acknowledgment: Opening to the Grief of Unacceptable Loss.* Wintercreek, 1988.

Leming, Michael R., and George E. Dickinson. *Understanding Dying, Death & Bereavement.* Harcourt Brace College Publishers, 1998.

Lewis, C. S. *A Grief Observed.* HarperOne, 2001.

Poer, Nancy Jewel. *The Tear: A Children's Story of Transformation and Hope When a Loved One Dies.* White Feather Publishing Company, 2011.

Rando, Therese A. *How to Go on Living When Someone You Love Dies.* Random House, 1991.

Romanyshyn, Robert D. *The Soul in Grief: Love, Death and Transformation.* North Atlantic Books, 1999.

Simos, Bertha. *A Time to Grieve: Loss as Universal Human Experience.* Family Service Association, 1979.

Warden, J. Willian. *Grief Counseling and Grief Therapy: A Handbook for the Mental Health Practitioner.* Fourth Edition. Springer Publishing Co., 2009.

York, Sarah. *Remembering Well.* Jossey-Bass, 2000.

Religious Traditions, Doctrines and Philosophy

Goodman, Arnold M. *A Plain Pine Box: A Return to Simple Jewish Funerals and Eternal Traditions.* KTAV Publishing House, 1981.

Kramer, Kenneth. *The Sacred Art of Dying: How the World Religions Understand Death.* Paulist Press, 1998.

Kubler-Ross, Elizabeth. *Death: The Final Stage of Growth.* Simon & Schuster, 1986.

———. *On Death and Dying.* Tavistock Publications, 1970.

———. *Wheel of Life: A Memoir of Living & Dying.* Bantam Books, 1998.

O'Gaea, Ashleen. *In the Service of Life: A Wiccan Perspective on Death.* Citadel Press, 2003.

Wright, Philip, and Carrie West. *Death and the Pagan.* BCM, 2004.

Multicultural Traditions

Ebenstein, Joanna. *Death: A Graveside Companion.* Thames & Hudson, 2017.

Habenstein, Robert W., and William H. Lamers. *Funeral Customs the World Over.* Bulfin Printers, 1960.

Matsunami, Kodo. *International Handbook of Funeral Customs*. Greenwood Press, 1998.

Moss, Robert. *The Dreamer's Book of the Dead*. Destiny, 2005.

Parkes, Colin Murray. *Death and Bereavement Across Cultures*. Routledge, 1997.

Rogak, Lisa. *Death Warmed Over: Funeral Food, Rituals, and Customs from Around the World*. Tenspeed Press, 2004.

Death Psychology and Ethical Issues

Butler, Katy. *Knocking on Heaven's Door: The Path to a Better Way of Death*. Scribner, 2013.

Byock, Ira. *Dying Well*. Penguin Publishing Group, 1998.

Eberle, Scott. *The Final Crossing: Learning to Die in Order to Live*. Lost Borders Press, 2006.

Kastenbaum, Robert. *The Psychology of Death*. Third Edition. Free Association Books, 2000.

Kuhl, David. *What Dying People Want: Practical Wisdom for the End of Life*. Public Affairs, 2003.

Manahan, Nancy, and Becky Bohan. *Living Consciously, Dying Gracefully: A Journey with Cancer and Beyond*. Beaver's Pond Press, 2007.

McGraw, John J. *Brain & Belief: An Exploration of the Human Soul*. Aegis Press, 2004.

Smith, Rodney. *Lessons from the Dying*. Wisdom Publications, 2015.

Historical Perspectives on Death

Barley, Nigel. *Grave Matters: A Lively History of Death Around the World*. Henry Hoh, 1997.

Coleman, Penny. *Corpses, Coffins & Crypts: A History of Burial*. Henry Holt and Company, 1997.

Kerrigan, Michael. *The History of Death*. Lions Press, 2007.

Laderman, Gary. *Rest in Peace: A Cultural History of Death & the Funeral Home in Twentieth-Century America*. Oxford University Press, 2003.

———. *The Sacred Remains: American Attitudes toward Death, 1799–1883*. Yale University, 1996.

Mitford, Jessica. *The American Way of Death.* Simon and Schuster, 1963.

———. *The American Way of Death: Revisited.* Alfred Knopf, 1998.

Puckle, Bertram S. *Funeral Customs: Their Origin and Development.* Omnigraphics, 1990.

Shushan, Gregory. *Conceptions of the Afterlife in Early Civilizations: Universalism, Constructivism & Near-Death Experience.* Continuum, 2009.

Slocum, Joshua, and Lisa Carlson. *Final Rights: Reclaiming the American Way of Death.* Upper Access, 2011.

Temple, Robert. *Netherworld: Discovering the Oracle of the Dead.* Century, 2002.

Turner, Ann Warren. *Houses for the Dead: Burial Customs through the Ages.* David McKay Co., 1976.

Vandenberg, Phillip. *The Mystery of the Oracles.* Translated by George Unwin. MacMillan Publishing, 1979.

Wilkins, Robert. *Death: A History of Man's Obsessions and Fears.* Barnes & Noble, 1996.

BIBLIOGRAPHY

Adler, Margot. *Drawing Down the Moon: Witches, Druids, Goddess Worshipers & Other Pagans in America.* Beacon Press, 1986.

Anderson, Megory. *Sacred Dying: Creating Rituals for Embracing the End of Life.* Avalon Publishing Group, 2001.

Baldwin, Christina. *Calling the Circle: The First and Future Culture.* Bantam Books, 1998.

Campbell, Billy. "Memorial Ecosystems." Accessed January 15, 2020. http://www.memorialecosystems.com/Home/tabid/36/Default.aspx.

Carlson, Lisa. *Caring for the Dead: Your Final Act of Love.* Upper Access, 1998.

Chafer, Charles M. "Memorial Spaceflights." Accessed January 15, 2020. https://www.celestis.com/.

Citelli, Anna, and Raoul Bretzel. "Capsula Mundi." Accessed January 15, 2020. http://www.capsulamundi.it.

Death with Dignity. "Alternative Options to Hasten Death." Accessed January 15, 2020. https://www.deathwithdignity.org/options-to-hasten-death/.

Department of Consumer Affairs: Cemetery and Funeral Bureau. "Consumer Guide to Funeral and Cemetery Purchases." Accessed January 15, 2020. https://cfb.ca.gov/consumer/funeral.shtml.

Doughty, Caitlin. "Ask a Mortician—Is Embalming Dangerous?" Accessed December 20, 2019. https://www.youtube.com/watch?v=p3rIc1qS258&t=10s.

Environmental Protection Agency. "U.S. Environmental Protection Agency." Accessed December 20, 2019. http://www.epa.gov.

Eternal Reefs. "Eternal Reefs." Accessed December, 2019. https://www.eter
nalreefs.com/.

Funeral Consumers Alliance. "Funeral Consumers Alliance." Accessed
December 20, 2019. https://funerals.org/.

Funeral Consumers Alliance of Minnesota. "Alkaline Hydrolysis: Green Cremation." Accessed December 20, 2019. https://fcaofmn.org/alkaline
-hydrolysis-green-cremation.html.

Green Burial Council. "Green Burial Council." Accessed January 15, 2020.
https://www.greenburialcouncil.org.

Hall, Manly P. *Words to the Wise: A Practical Guide to the Esoteric Sciences.* Philosophical Research Society, 1964.

Harris, Mark. *Grave Matters: A Journey through the Modern Funeral Industry to a
Natural Way of Burial.* Scribner, 2007.

John Muir. *A Thousand-Mile Walk to the Gulf: Adventure Memoirs, Travel Sketches
& Wilderness Studies.* The Riverside Press, 1916.

Koyama, Kundō. *Departures,* dir. Yōjirō Takita. Tokyo Broadcasting System, 2008.

Laderman, Gary. *Rest in Peace: A Cultural History of Death and the Funeral Home
in Twentieth-Century America.* Oxford University Press, 2003.

———. *Sacred Remains: American Attitudes toward Death, 1799–1883.* Yale University, 1996.

Lee, Jae Rhim. "Coeio: The Story of a Green Burial Company." Accessed
January 15, 2020. http://coeio.com/.

LeSueur, Meridel. *This with My Last Breath.* Midwest Villages & Voices, 2012.

Lyons, Jerrigrace. "Final Passages." Accessed November 30, 2019.
http://www.finalpassages.org.

Lyons, Jerrigrace, and Janelle Macrae. *Final Passages: A Complete Home Funeral
Guide.* Final Passages Institute, 1999.

Martin, Steve. *Born Standing Up: A Comic's Life.* Scribner, 2007.

Mitford, Jessica. *The American Way of Death.* Simon & Schuster, 1963.

———. *The American Way of Death: Revisited.* Vantage Books, 1998.

Moses, Yolanda. "Why Do We Keep Using the Word 'Caucasian'?" Accessed
January 15, 2020. http://www.sapiens.org/column/race/caucasian-termi
nology-origin.

National Funeral Directors Association. "National Funeral Directors Association." Accessed December 20, 2019. http://www.nfda.org/.

National Home Funeral Alliance. "National Home Funeral Alliance." Accessed January 10, 2020. http://www.homefuneralalliance.org.

National Home Funeral Alliance, and Funeral Consumers Alliance. *Restoring Families' Right to Choose: The Call for Funeral Legislation Change in America.* National Home Funeral Alliance, 2015.

Rumi, Jalal al-Din. *The Essential Rumi.* Translated by Coleman Barks, John Moyne, A. J. Arberry, and Reynold Nicholson. Castle Books, 1997.

Slocum, Joshua, and Lisa Carlson. *Final Rights: Reclaiming the American Way of Death.* Upper Access, 2011.

Spade, Katrina. "Recompose." Accessed January 15, 2020. http://www.recompose.life.

State of California Department of Consumer Affairs. "Consumer Guide to Funeral & Cemetery Purchases." Accessed December 20, 2019. http://www.CFB.CA.gov.

Tolle, Eckhart. *Silence Speaks.* Namaste Publishing and New World Library, 2003.

Van Vuuren, Karen, and Francesca Nicosia. "Dying Wish." Accessed January 2020. http://www.dyingwishmedia.com/faq/.

Virago, Zenith. "Growth through Death." Accessed January 15, 2020. https://vimeo.com/90256161.

———. "Natural Death Care Centre." Accessed December, 2019. http://www.naturaldeathcarecentre.org.

Webster, Lee, and Donna Belk. *Planning Guide and Workbook for Home Funeral Families.* National Home Funeral Alliance, 2015.

Westrate, Elizabeth, dir. *A Family Undertaking.* Icarus Films, 2004.

Wiigh-Mäsak, Susanne. "Ecological Burial." Accessed December 20, 2019. http://www.promessa.se/.

INDEX

A

Accidental death, 93, 119

Advanced Care Directive, xix, xx, 58, 67, 83, 101, 103, 145, 180, 210, 211, 214, 217

Advocate, xx, xxiii, 22, 39, 40, 45, 63, 72–74, 81–84, 86, 111, 136, 175, 180, 181, 190, 193, 195, 196, 216

Altar, 20, 25, 26, 30, 83, 103, 109, 129, 133, 134, 143, 144, 151, 161, 167, 169–171, 208, 209

American way of death, 40–43, 46, 51, 53

Axiom, xxiv, 13, 14

B

Bathing, 134, 135, 164

Bells, 143, 163, 168, 209

Being at peace ritual, 156

Benediction, 131, 144, 164, 169, 170

Bereavement, 5, 32, 146

Book of Shadows, 162

Bureau of Land Management (BLM), 111

Burial, xvii, xx, xxiii, xxv, 17, 22, 30, 41, 43, 44, 47, 53, 54, 71, 93, 104, 107–115, 133, 135, 138, 141–145, 162, 180, 181, 183, 185, 186, 188, 195–197, 199–204, 211, 212, 217–224, 226–228

C

Candle lighting ritual, 168, 169

Candles, 30, 103, 126, 127, 133, 138, 139, 163, 165, 167–169, 209

To Write to the Authors

If you wish to contact the author or would like more information about this book, please write to the author in care of Llewellyn Worldwide Ltd. and we will forward your request. Both the author and the publisher appreciate hearing from you and learning of your enjoyment of this book and how it has helped you. Llewellyn Worldwide Ltd. cannot guarantee that every letter written to the author can be answered, but all will be forwarded. Please write to:

Judith Fenley and Oberon Zell
℅ Llewellyn Worldwide
2143 Wooddale Drive
Woodbury, MN 55125-2989
Please enclose a self-addressed stamped envelope for reply,
or $1.00 to cover costs. If outside the U.S.A., enclose
an international postal reply coupon.

Many of Llewellyn's authors have websites with additional
information and resources. For more information,
please visit our website at http://www.llewellyn.com.